Educating all handicapped children

Educating all handicapped children

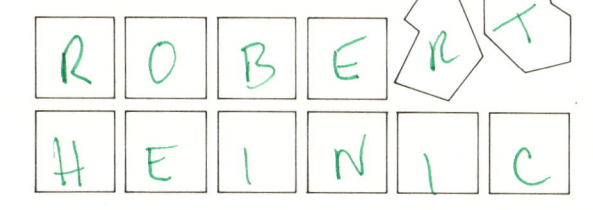

Robert Heinich, Editor
Indiana University

Educational Technology Publications
Englewood Cliffs, New Jersey 07632

Library of Congress Cataloging in Publication Data

Main entry under title:

Educating all handicapped children.

    Includes bibliographies.
    1. Handicapped children--Education--United States--Addresses, essays, lectures. 2. Handicapped children--Education--Law and legislation--United States--Addresses, essays, lectures.
I. Heinich, Robert.
LC4031.E38   371.9'0973   78-12749
ISBN 0-87778-131-1

Printed in the United States of America.

Library of Congress Catalog Card Number: 78-12749.

International Standard Book Number: 0-87778-131-1.

First Printing: January, 1979.

Foreword

The new Education for All Handicapped Children Act places a great deal of responsibility on educational administrators and other authorities to provide a free, appropriate, quality education for all handicapped children. The handicapped child now has to be viewed as the child who happens to have a handicap. This new demand forces administrators to seek new techniques and instructional strategies with a view toward inclusion rather than exclusion.

The conference which served as the base for the papers in this book focused on the reality of mainstreaming and the need for an increased knowledge base about the issues and concerns related to instructional technology in this process. The development of these papers at this time marks a major milestone in achieving the quality educational programming that handicapped learners need and deserve.

In developing the papers for this volume there were two possible approaches. Authors could have isolated and spoken specifically of that portion of the child's education that could be identified as consistent with the theme, or authors could blend that which is technology of instruction with the many other facets of appropriate education. Obviously, the latter approach was chosen; all the authors know that instructional technology must meld with many other services in the educational process if it is to be most beneficial in the teaching-learning process. I believe this manner of treating the subject demonstrates widespread belief that there cannot be an appropriate education for handicapped learners without the integral planning and the use of instructional technology and its products—the media and materials of instruction. Collectively, these papers make a persuasive case for believing that an appropriate education is one which uses the best of educational technologies as part and parcel thereof.

Elwood L. Bland, Chief
Learning Resources Branch
Bureau of Education for the Handicapped
U.S.O.E.

Preface

This series of papers had its origin in a meeting called by Elwood L. Bland, Chief of the Learning Resources Branch, Bureau of Education for the Handicapped.

The purpose of the meeting, held at Annapolis, Maryland, in 1976, was to consider ways of getting into the mainstream of professional communication some of the implications for the use of instructional technology in implementing Public Law 94-142, the Education for All Handicapped Children Act. After considerable discussion, the group decided to commission a series of papers that would provoke discussion of selected key issues among decision-makers in public schools, state departments of education, higher education, and appropriate federal agencies.

The guiding rationale for the series was to take a broad view of instructional technology and look at it in the context of the larger systems in which it functions. As part of their orientation to the project, authors were given the definition of instructional technology made familiar by the Commission on Instructional Technology. In that definition, process and technique are emphasized rather than products. For example, a key section of P.L. 94-142 requires an individualized educational program for each child. Therefore, papers were commissioned to examine newer school and instructional organizational patterns that are based on the concept of individualizing educational programs to determine how those programs could encompass the mainstreamed child.

The first paper, by Burton Blatt, puts P.L. 94-142 in the historical perspective of the Bill of Rights. He cogently argues that the passage of the Education for All Handicapped Children Act is one further extension of the intent of the Congress to include all members of our society in the protection and the freedoms of the Constitution and its subsequent amendments. In this context, it is very possible that the phrase "least restrictive environment" will take its place in history as a guidepost comparable to "separate is inherently unequal," "socially redeeming value," and "due process of law." While obviously not an absolute, the phrase "least restrictive environment" establishes a battleline much more favorable to the parents of handicapped children and those educators and other public servants who have argued for some time that the normal classroom should accommodate a wider range of educational ability. Just how wide a range and under what circumstances will of course be determined over a long period of time.

Clarence Calder considers the problem of curriculum building in classrooms with mainstreamed children. Here there are two classes of problems: one is where the curriculum is a modified version of what the other children may receive, and the second covers those cases where handicapped children may be receiving a different curriculum at certain periods of time. In either case, how that curriculum gets translated into instruction is an extremely important step that, particularly with handicapped children, needs to be outlined at the same time that curricular problems are investigated. In the past we have tended too frequently to treat curriculum and instruction as if they are completely independent activities, but Calder appropriately looks at curriculum-instruction as a continuum. The technology he describes has been successfully used to make the critical transition from curricular goals to instructional specifications. Instructional technology is essential to

Preface

the process he describes. But the way in which it functions within programs so developed will vary considerably as will the media and materials used to implement curricular and instructional decisions.

Without question, special education has done more to develop prescriptive teaching than any other area in education concerned with pedagogical practice. Barbara Bateman takes a look at the interface of prescriptive teaching and individualized instruction, and assesses where we are in relation to bridging the two. A key section of Public Law 94-142 requires an individualized educational program for each child. With that mandate, it would seem appropriate to look at individualized instructional programs for their possible application to the mainstreamed child. If prescriptive teaching and technologies of instruction can be effectively wedded, many of the classroom management problems could be solved more easily. By matching short-term needs assessments to appropriately developed materials, teachers can prescribe instructional sequences with a greater degree of confidence. Of course, in order to be able to do that, there must be available a wide range of materials, appropriately developed, and adequately described, in order to permit the classroom teacher to make those matches. As Bateman points out, the vast majority of materials that we have on the market now were not developed from that perspective. Problems and solutions in getting appropriate materials will be dealt with in later chapters.

I have mentioned that we need to investigate the extent to which what we have learned about individualized instruction in normal classrooms may be extended to the mainstreamed child. Weisgerber, in his chapter, looks at individualized instruction in general. Weisgerber previously has published several volumes on his investigations into individualized instructional programs. He is optimistic about the possibility of extending those techniques to handicapped children.

Many school administrators may want to consider the Individually Guided Education program as a way of reorganizing the total school so that it better fits the needs of handicapped as well as normal children. As Fred Wood describes it, the IGE program operates on the assumption that if educational programs are to be tailored to individuals, then the total resources of the school need to be looked at for more effective and efficient deployment. His position is that the traditional classroom system of school organization is predicated on the assumption that all children in a classroom receive essentially the same instruction. The IGE system permits a much more flexible way of assessing each child in relation to specific subject areas.

As a case study of the application of one such individualized instructional program to mainstreamed children, David Helms analyzes the Individually Prescribed Instruction program developed at the University of Pittsburgh and originally disseminated by the Research for Better Schools. He establishes valuable guiding principles for any school district wishing to use IPI in an adapted form as a part of the standard program in which mainstreamed children happen to be participating. The Individually Prescribed Instruction program is undoubtedly the most thoroughly researched individualized program that we have to date.

As Anna Hyer points out, there is no question that mainstreaming can be hard on both child and teacher. The handicapped child in school now is used to a great deal more attention than he or she is likely to receive in the mainstreamed class, both in terms of instruction and, perhaps even more importantly, in emotional support. The pupil/teacher ratio of regular classes compared to special classes guarantees that. Teachers are going to need a great deal of help in getting prepared to work handicapped children into their classroom routines. Without proper training, teachers are likely to move in one of two opposite directions: (1) they will either spend so much attention on mainstreamed children that the rest of the class will be neglected; or (2) ignore mainstreamed children, keeping them occupied with whatever will suffice, while concentrating all their attention on their normal

Preface

pupils. In their enthusiasm over the passage of P.L. 94-142, its extreme advocates must realize that the long-term advantages to handicapped children in the Act will be best realized by proceeding with deliberate speed.

For those teachers already in service, continuing professional development programs need to be specifically put together to help teachers develop the necessary skills to handle mainstreamed children. Donald Ely discusses the applicability of one of the more successful short-term institute in-service programs to the training of teachers in handling mainstreamed children. The Instructional Development Institute (IDI) has been used with a great deal of success in training teams of school district personnel in instructional development. It would seem that with minor modifications in content, the same institute format could be used as a traveling in-service intensive program of training.

Preservice teacher education will also have to be changed dramatically in order to properly prepare future teachers in managing classrooms with a wider range of child behaviors. Pat Gillespie analyzes the structure of schools and departments of education in our colleges and universities to see how they might better reorganize their activities in order to integrate special education with regular methods classes. She relies on instructional development models to show how this might be done.

P. Kenneth Komoski addresses himself to the problem that Barbara Bateman identified in her chapter on prescriptive teaching. As the head of the Educational Products Information Exchange Institute, Komoski has long been concerned with the problem of improving classroom instruction by getting producers to develop more effective materials through field testing. Producers are reluctant to engage in expensive field testing unless customers indicate that they will buy materials on the basis of field test data. Komoski urges instructional material purchasers to insist on evidence of tryout and revision.

Diane Dormant's paper is concerned with the processes of

teacher selection of instructional materials and the kind of information that teachers need in order to make appropriate selections.

The problem faced by commercial outfits producing for a "thin" market is discussed by Thiagarajan. He makes a persuasive case for how producers can find profit in such a market. Both producers and the Bureau of Education for the Handicapped should be interested in his recommendations.

Closely related to the above is the paper by William H. Allen and Kay E. Goldberg on designing instructional media for educable mentally retarded learners. As many readers know, William H. Allen has a long and productive history in research in educational media, and his and Goldberg's considered analysis of the applicability of that research to the design of materials for the handicapped has produced some very effective and worthwhile guidelines. Producers would do well to give this chapter serious consideration.

Finally, there are two papers dealing with suggestions for research in education of both mildly and severely handicapped. Thomas C. Lovitt addresses the problem of mainstreaming the mildly handicapped. Lovitt chooses to emphasize research in various aspects of the management of the handicapped child in the normal classroom. It would seem to be a wise choice. As mentioned before, the critical problem in P.L. 94-142 is how well classroom teachers will accept handicapped children in their classroom. If Lovitt's suggestions are acted upon by research-funding agencies, teachers could receive a good deal of help from the research suggested.

Alan Hofmeister reinforces Lovitt's concern with field based research that can have direct payoff for practitioners. His emphasis is decidedly on decision- rather than conclusion-oriented research. He argues that the research community needs to shift to research and development models that lead to implementable products, and for evaluation models capable of determining the effectiveness of programs in naturalistic settings. Rather than offering a research agenda, Hofmeister stresses research *approaches* that have higher potential direct benefits for the severely handicapped.

Mention was made before about proceeding with "deliberate speed" in implementing P.L. 94-142. The problems of providing both the least restrictive environment and individualized educational programs are ones that require a good deal of time and patient effort to solve. But, understandably, many are impatient. Certainly, long-suffering parents can hardly be blamed if they assume that P.L. 94-142 has finally provided the kind of institutional attention they have longed for. Exaggerated claims made during the campaign to gain passage of the Act have perhaps given parents unrealistic expectations.

Attention to the needs of physically handicapped but otherwise normal children is, of course, not the main problem. From experience I know that by and large children will pitch in and help physically handicapped children. Teachers also find that adjusting to a physically handicapped child may mean accommodation to modes of response as in testing and written or oral reports but not to the flow of instructional planning and organization. Instructionally, it's business as usual. Not so with a number of other handicaps.

In this series of papers, individualization of instruction is stressed not only because the law mentions individualized educational programs but also because individualizing instruction can help the handicapped child get the training and education needed and at the same time reduce what teachers will consider to be an inordinate drain on their time and efforts. Floating special education teachers, paraprofessionals, volunteers, and student peers may all have to be organized to provide, particularly, the necessary emotional and psychological support needed by such children. Where handicapped children are concerned, individualizing instruction does *not* mean independent study. The handicapped child is going to make us aware of the distinction between individualized instruction and independent study as nothing else has. We may have to abandon the myth that the individual in most frequent contact with the child knows what is best for the child instructionally. Particularly in the case of the handicapped child, the people in most frequent contact should bear the prime responsibility for psychological support, while prescriptions for instruction can be handled by frequent but not constant contact.

We have done little exploration of the effectiveness of remotely controlling instructional contingencies while giving constant psychological and emotional support to the child. Carefully designed, thoroughly tested programmed materials administered under the sympathetic guidance of a paraprofessional or volunteer could help the mainstreamed child considerably without excessive attention from the teacher.

Neither have we explored the possibility of programming for small groups. I am thinking of situations where two or three students go through programmed sequences at the same time, learning with and from (and reinforcing) each other. We need to go further and extend that work to the handicapped and their normal peers.

Unfortunately, teachers may turn in desperation to insufficiently developed materials labeled "appropriate for handicapped children." Bateman, for one, points out how inadequate the vast majority of currently available materials are for use with handicapped children. Komoski, as director of the Educational Products Information Exchange Institute, has been a leading exponent of the movement to force materials producers to show effectiveness of materials by publishing field test data. Hopefully, this movement will start affecting the production of instructional materials. In the meantime, teachers and administrators are referred to the National Information Center on Special Education Materials (NICSEM), at the University of Southern California, for product information.

It seems to me, however, that Komoski should emphasize summative evaluation more than he does and formative evaluation less than he does. Extensive evidence of field tests and revisions may simply mean that a product badly designed to start with has been

Preface

improved. Evidence of field tests resulting in only minor revisions may indicate a product that was well thought through to begin with, but the consumer may wrongly interpret the data to mean a lack of effort on the part of the producer. A producer skillful enough to develop a product in need of little modification should be rewarded, not penalized. Formative evaluation is most useful to the producer, not the consumer.

Field tests of the finished product under typical conditions, conducted by an agency other than the producer, are much more significant to the consumer. After all, the consumer's primary interest is in how well the product works with a reasonable sample of the target audience, and not in the procedures used by the company to develop the product.

This is by no means to be interpreted as demeaning the importance of formative evaluation to the development of instructional materials. What we are talking about here is *what information* is most useful to the *purchaser* of instructional materials.

Field testing is expensive and producers are understandably reluctant to invest in it as long as purchasers show no evidence of interest in such data when they are available. During the early years of programmed instruction, many publishers of programs made field test data available. The Center for Programed Instruction (headed by Komoski) made those data available in a series of yearly indexes. To my knowledge, school purchasers of programmed instruction did not use the available data as part of their selection processes. Publishers soon learned that their sales forces were much more effective than field test results. Publishers and producers will invest in field testing *if* they see the expense justified by increased sales—and the buyers, not the producers, control sales.

The government could help considerably by underwriting the *purchase* of materials that have been field tested adequately. This would mean compiling a list of products that meet stated field test criteria and subsidizing the *purchase* of those products. As products meeting the criteria come on the market, they would be added to the list. Subsidizing the purchaser would be more effective than subsidizing the producer.

Thiagarajan's chapter effectively discusses how producers can be encouraged to get into the market place with materials for the handicapped. The suggestion above would be an added incentive from the point of view of the purchaser.

However, it needs to be pointed out that the nature of field test data will vary according to what extent the product has been designed for "open" or "closed" loop instructional situations. For example, most films are designed to be used in "open" loop situations; that is, in a situation where the final determination of instructional objectives and how those objectives will be achieved will be up to whoever is in charge of instruction. Field test data need to emphasize the *usefulness* of such stimulus materials to various instructional situations. On the other hand, programmed materials are designed as "closed" loop; that is, specifying instructional objectives and leading the learner successfully through the necessary steps to achieve those objectives. The field test data can be much more precise and can predict the degree of success with specified students who have the required entry behaviors.

As Anna Hyer so eloquently states, teachers (and administrators) are going to need all the help they can get. In the final analysis, classroom teachers and their immediate administrators are the keys to the success of mainstreaming.

Robert Heinich
Professor of Education
Indiana University

Authors

1. **Burton Blatt** is Dean, School of Education, Syracuse University, Syracuse, New York.

2. **Clarence R. Calder, Jr.**, is Professor of Education, Department of Elementary Education, School of Education, University of Connecticut, Storrs, Connecticut.

3. **Barbara D. Bateman** is Professor of Education, Department of Special Education, College of Education, University of Oregon, Eugene, Oregon.

4. **Robert A. Weisgerber** is Principal Research Scientist, American Institutes for Research, Palo Alto, California.

5. **Fred H. Wood** is Professor of Education and Head, Division of Curriculum and Instruction, College of Education, The Pennsylvania State University, University Park, Pennsylvania.

6. **David Helms** is with the Research and Development Division, Research for Better Schools, Inc., Philadelphia, Pennsylvania.

7. **Anna L. Hyer** is with the Project on Utilization of Inservice Education R&D Outcomes, National Education Association, Washington, D.C.

8. **Donald P. Ely** is Professor of Education, Area of Instructional Technology, School of Education, Syracuse University, Syracuse, New York.

9. **Patricia H. Gillespie** is Field Associate, Learning Disabilities Assistance Project, Merrimac, Massachusetts.

10. **P. Kenneth Komoski** is Executive Director, Educational Products Information Exchange Institute, New York, New York.

11. **Diane Dormant** is a Training and Instructional Systems Consultant, Bloomington, Indiana.

12. **Sivasailam Thiagarajan** is President, Instructional Alternatives, Bloomington, Indiana.

13. **William H. Allen** is Professor of Education, Department of Instructional Technology, University of Southern California, Los Angeles, California. **Kay E. Goldberg** is with the Department of Special Education, University of Southern California.

14. **Thomas C. Lovitt** is Professor of Education, Child Development and Mental Retardation Center, University of Washington, Seattle, Washington.

15. **Alan M. Hofmeister** is with the Special Education Department, Utah State University, Logan, Utah.

Table of Contents

Foreword by Elwood L. Bland v

Preface by Robert Heinich vii

Authors xvii

1. On the Bill of Rights and Related Matters
   Burton Blatt 3

2. The Curriculum-Instruction Continuum with Respect to Mainstreaming of Handicapped Children
   Clarence R. Calder, Jr. 17

3. Prescriptive Teaching and Individualized Education Programs
   Barbara D. Bateman 39

4. Individualized Learning and the Special Child
   Robert A. Weisgerber 63

5. Implications of Individually Guided Education Pro-

grams for Mainstreaming
Fred H. Wood 85

6. Individually Prescribed Instruction (IPI): Implications for Teaching the Handicapped
David Helms 109

7. The View of P.L. 94-142 from the Classroom
Anna L. Hyer 131

8. Short Term Inservice Programs
Donald P. Ely 155

9. Needed Changes in Preservice Education of Regular Classroom Teachers to Prepare Them to Teach Mainstreamed Children
Patricia H. Gillespie 169

10. How Can the Evaluation of Instructional Materials Help Improve Classroom Instruction Received by Handicapped Learners?
P. Kenneth Komoski 187

11. Teacher Selection of Instructional Materials for Use with Handicapped Learners
Diane Dormant 227

12. How Commercial Producers Can Systematically Develop Effective Instructional Materials for the Handicapped (and Still Make a Profit)
Sivasailam Thiagarajan 241

13. Designing Instructional Media for Educable Mentally Retarded Learners
William H. Allen and Kay E. Goldberg 263

14. Mainstreaming the Mildly Handicapped: Some Research Suggestions
    Thomas C. Lovitt 291

15. What Directions Should Research Take in Developing Educational Programs for the Severely Handicapped?
    Alan M. Hofmeister 331

Educating all handicapped children

1.
On the Bill of Rights and Related Matters

Burton Blatt

The Original Papers
Why the United States? As you know, on July 4, 1776, the Declaration of Independence set down reasons. Entitled by the laws of nature and God, we are a nation equal to other nations. As individuals, we are created equal and we have certain inalienable rights. No foreign government may set aside this country's equality among the family of nations and each individual's equality within the human family. Independence had to be declared when once loyal colonists refused to tolerate a King of Great Britain who would deny us that most valuable of all freedoms, free will. Free will, which even God does not intrude upon, formed the core of the idea we call America. School children *know* all of this, but too few adults do.

Signed on September 17, 1787, and ratified by the States a year later, the Constitution described that more perfect union in terms of justice, common welfare, and liberty. The first ten amendments to the Constitution were enacted on December 15, 1791. Eight of these are known as the Bill of Rights. And for good reason. As the Declaration of Independence proclaimed that all men have the right to life, liberty, and the pursuit of happiness, these and later amendments enlarged and deepened such guarantees. It's all there: the form of our government, the freedoms, due process, equal protection, and equal rights.

But if it's all in the Constitution and its amendments, how did the Founding Fathers explain the treatment of certain "different" people? Why, despite constitutional guarantees, did many people have to fight for their rights? You may not like their answer, but here it is. The idea of equal treatment is based on the premise that people are equally valuable as human beings. Otherwise, such a claim doesn't work. As for a relevant example, in the Virginia Declaration of Rights, which served as the basis of our Bill of Rights, slaves were not considered constituents of society; the principle, "all men are equally free" did not apply to them. The fact of slavery produced the "fact" of inhumanness about that oppressed group. And that fact was "necessary," else how could slavery have been tolerated by a civilized state? How indeed? So the blacks were specifically excluded from enjoyment of supposedly inalienable rights until, of course, the Emancipation Proclamation and the 13th, 14th, and 15th amendments. And as most everyone knows, until enactment of the 19th amendment, women were denied the franchise and even today are denied a great deal more than could ever be articulated in the laws. Obviously, there are other examples that come to mind.

Tradition takes almost forever to die, especially unjust tradition. Therefore, although blacks and women have come a long way, it's only within recent years that they have attained the semblance of true equality. Now we must examine another oppressed group, the so-called handicapped, and redress violations of their inalienable rights; the law is a human instrument that requires constant surveillance and occasional tinkering.

The handicapped have always been a paradox to Americans.

On the Bill of Rights ... 5

And in America. In this Land of Opportunity, they seem unable to seize opportunities. In the Land of the Free, they are enchained. In the Land of Plenty, they are in need. In America the Bountiful, they are treated meanly. For them, the idea of America is little different than the idea of the totalitarian state. But that which was denied blacks and women by statutes, has more often been denied the handicapped by the handshakes and winks of ladies and gentlemen. What was legislated and implemented in the guise of friendship and compassion for the handicapped—sterilization codes, marriage prohibitions, even euthanasia—did not free but further restricted them or denied them their very lives. Especially here, the flight to legalism reflected the weakness rather than the strength of our society and what was not *legislated* was *perpetrated*, in the name of treatment or protection but often with negative consequences. What has been done to those human beings does not make for a pleasant story. What we have done does not make our lives pleasant.

Like the blacks, the severely handicapped especially were not considered to be persons as you and I are persons. Unlike the blacks, the founding laws of our land were silent about them. Unlike the blacks, the handicapped were not considered to be valuable merchandise and, thus, were not a political issue. Times have changed. For whatever reasons—compassion, votes, humanism, dollars—the handicapped are big business today, are political factors not to be taken lightly. My thesis is that, had the original Constitution and Bill of Rights included the handicapped, the new Bill of Rights would be unnecessary. Furthermore, this new Bill of Rights is necessary for exactly the same reasons that the 13th, 14th, 15th, and 19th amendments had become necessary. However, because the Constitution was silent on the handicapped, there is nothing now to amend. So there is Public Law 94-142, the Bill of Rights for Handicapped Children.

I once wrote that, while a person may thrill to the words chiseled on the lintel of the courthouse entrance that a commonwealth must have a government of laws and not of people, it is difficult to live with that belief unshaken. There are times when one has the strong feeling that, while our government may be of laws for people, in the ultimate dimension it must be *of* people *with* laws. There have always been people who worried about governments ruled by laws but not by people. But that's so much theory and, for many years, "all" the handicapped seemed to have had were the laws of the land; theory. There was little in the way of action on their behalf. One purpose to my writing this chapter is to examine the heresy that once there was a lot of theory and little action while today there is much action and little theory.

Education of All Handicapped Children

There should be something called "The Law of Inertia." With seeming inevitability, when action on an important issue is indicated, it is either too early or too late to do anything at the moment. Furthermore, the predominant theme of the day is "business as usual." And nowhere are these two motivations—"inertia" and "business as usual"—observed with more regularity than in government. If forming this nation had been contemplated during our time, the Founding Fathers might have waited so long to declare its independence that it never would have happened; people would have surely become bored with the whole thing. It seems that today we can't get a school bus to go on an agreed route much less create a country—or an educational mandate. Of course, school busing is an important and complex issue. But that's the point; we can't seem to deal with important and complex issues. Maybe technology itself is part of the fault as well as the solution. A computer mistake gets multiplied, its effects influencing the lives of thousands of people. Maybe the telephone is partially to blame; a lie is transmitted all too quickly. Maybe the tube; the mistake is immediately made known to the world (the living room viewer offers almost instantaneous knowledge of what were once the dark secrets of kings and king makers). Maybe as it now seeks to come to our rescue, technology itself must bear some responsibility for the many leaders today who lead so few and for the many advocates in a culture that is characterized by such weak advocacy. Maybe with the magnification of mistakes today, few in government will take responsibility to act. Of course, there is another explanation of the notion that governments change slowly. There's something to the belief that organizations are most successful when they deal vigorously on behalf of individuals but conservatively on issues related to complex systems. Nevertheless, the point remains that governments respond reluctantly to the demand for major systems change, however powerful a case for change may be.

Hence, "everyone's" surprise with the passage of P.L. 94-142. It catches us unprepared, still stunned and still unbelieving. And who's to blame us? Who's to believe that by 1982 the federal government will invest 3.1 billion dollars a year in this program? I don't. But that's my problem more than it need be your reality. So I'll act as if my cynicism is but another of my aberrations. And I'll not appear as if I'm searching for the likely perversions of the legislation. Yet admit it, isn't it a surprise that our government enacted this law and scheduled its full implementation by fiscal year 1978? Didn't most of us merely go through the motions of trying to give support to the bill that eventually became the law? Weren't there only a zealous few who believed in its inevitability? Of course. And who ever believes zealots?

As Goodman noted (1976), the law is a blockbuster. Not only will the handicapped feel its influence, not only will the schools feel its influence, but the entire nation will feel it. Overwhelmingly passed by the Congress, it puts the nation's stamp on the claim that the handicapped child is entitled to a first rate education, thus making the claim for all children. But why did the Congress pass what's believed to be the most significant federal legislation relating to the schools since the enactment of Title I of the Elementary and Secondary Education Act of 1965? And why now?

As reported to the Congress, the situation is alarming. There are reputed to be more than 8,000,000 handicapped children in the United States, but more than half of them do not receive appropriate educational services. A million of these children are excluded or exempted from any public school opportunities, appropriate or otherwise. Because of the unavailability of adequate programs within the public schools, many families are forced to look elsewhere for services, and at their own expense. It seems that teacher training institutions are in better positions than ever before to provide sufficient instruction for regular and special education teachers to serve this group. It seems that now, more than ever before, state and local agencies accept responsibility to provide services to the handicapped, but inadequate resources prevent them from fulfilling such responsibilities. Simply, it was the conclusion of the Congress that it will be in the best interest of our nation if the government would engage more directly and vigorously in educational programs on behalf of the handicapped. The law became the exception to the Law of Inertia.

P.L. 94-142 has been written about to the point of saturation, at least for those who have been on the lookout for it. However, because this will be the first chapter of the book, it may be well to briefly note some of the major elements of the law (Gettings, 1976):

1. A new entitlement formula went into effect in fiscal year 1978. Under it, states will be able to receive amounts equal to the number of handicapped children between ages 3 and 21 receiving special education services multiplied by a specified percentage of the average per pupil expenditure in public schools in the United States. Federal aid will increase from 5% in fiscal year 1978 to 10% in fiscal year 1979. In fiscal year 1982 and in succeeding fiscal years, federal aid will have grown to 40%.

2. To discourage states from including non-handicapped children in the program, the law provides limitations on the numbers who may be counted (to a maximum of 12% of total school age

population between the ages of 5 and 17) and also limits to no more than 2% the percentage of children who may be counted because of specific learning disabilities.

3. To qualify for participation, the state must establish policies for all handicapped children between the ages of 3 and 18 by 1978, and between the ages of 3 and 21 by 1980. Such policies will not apply to children between the ages of 3 to 5 and 18 to 21 where mandatory services are inconsistent with state law or court order.

4. The states will receive up to $300 for each child between the age of 3 and 5 who will receive special education services.

5. The law requires that an individualized educational program must be developed for each handicapped child. First priority must be given to unserved children. The severely handicapped who are not receiving adequate services will be given second priority.

6. To qualify, a state must submit a plan that: guarantees that federal funds will be used in a manner consistent with the law's requirement; includes a program for personnel development; provides free services for children placed by local educational agencies in private schools; guarantees that federal funds will supplement and increase rather than supplant state and local funds; prescribes a program evaluation system; provides for an advisory panel on unmet needs; and specifies procedures for record keeping and accountability. Each participating local education agency must submit a plan similar to the aforementioned.

7. Due process safeguards have been incorporated into the requirement for state and local participation. Federal and state monitoring procedures are included. All participants must include affirmative measures to employ qualified handicapped individuals. Lastly, the legislation requires the Commissioner of Education to conduct whatever studies are necessary to adequately report to the Congress on progress achieved as a result of this legislation.

Obviously, there are and will be problems, some quite serious. For example, while on the one hand many parents are pleased with the "mainstreaming" thrust of the legislation, others worry about the effects of general as contrasted with specialized programming. Teachers too have their concerns. Regular teachers express anxiety about their unpreparedness to assume responsibilities for children with problems unfamiliar to them. Special educators worry about the "least restrictive environment" as another way of saying "removal of intensive specialized services." Both groups of teachers keenly feel the need for major efforts to prepare regular teachers and administrators to assume the new responsibilities demanded of them if the legislation is to work. Of course, institutions that prepare teachers have those concerns magnified in light of their direct responsibilities for preparing teachers. It seems that everyone's worried, but it also seems that everyone thinks this was good legislation and it's a fine thing that it happened at last.

Most of us are uncertain about the consequence of "Child Find." We've had too many experiences where such efforts led less to finding children in need of special services, then "capturing" children in order to receive bounties (reimbursements). Nevertheless, while we worry about the bounty hunters, we're also looking forward to a day when every child in America goes to school, and in an environment that is there to serve rather than to discriminate.

Theory and Practice

In the same manner that the Emancipation Proclamation was not only about black people, this law is not only about handicapped people. I mean that society has it within its capabilities to include the handicapped not only in its regular school programs but everywhere. If we but thought differently about certain things, we would behave differently. It is not that we can't, but we choose not to. And indeed, because we choose not to, we have the seemingly insurmountable problem.

There's another point of view from a different mountain, the idea of those who would enjoin us to simply change ourselves and stop the foolishness of creating legislation and bigger opportunities for people in the business of special education and its derivative occupations. That point of view will not argue against the wisdom that society can change and, thus, the problem could be solved by us merely changing ourselves. However, they do indeed argue that, because there must be laws about something and somebody, there should be such a law as we have before us. They argue that while P.L. 94-142 may not have been necessary had we not made it necessary, the way things are today it's a Godsend, or at least the best we know how to do. Therefore, irrespective of agreement that we would all be better off if we stopped the foolishness around special education, there is also agreement that this law has been long overdue.

We should now turn to the claim that the problem is quite simple. All serious human problems are simple. Simple to avoid and simple to end. For example, ending pollution of the environment is simple to achieve. That kind of problem is not like such complex affairs as finding a cure for cancer or eradicating heart disease. In the former, it seems as if we don't want the problem to go away. In the latter, we can't make the problem go away. Obviously, the situation is different for the individual. The person deals better with his own than with society's problems, be they simple or complex. That's a truism that only the ignorant would argue about.

What needed to be done was done. For the first time since I entered this field years ago, I witnessed the passage of legislation that contained the best thinking in our field, imperfect as it is, and a plan for the most vigorous action. Earlier, I suggested that what is wrong with so much of society, for example the university, is that it's all theory and no action. Others have suggested that what's wrong with society, for example the government, is that it's all action and no theory. Here we have a law based on the best theory available, funded at a higher level than any previous legislation, and which promises to deliver the goods fairly quickly. That's impressive.

The Right Bill for the Right Time

I once said something like, "People should be judged by what's best about them, but governments must be judged by what's worst." If there were such an understanding, the capacity of an individual would be determined less by the averaging of his scores and more by the highest score he received. However, with governments, which in principle should be distrusted, there would be an element of disbelief, of knowing that someone somewhere among the politicians or the bureaucracy is trying to pull the wool over our eyes. Therefore, where governments are concerned, the rule should be that if the behavior is rotten, it's to be expected and incurable. And if the behavior is exemplary, it's an accident or a mirage.

Applying the above law to judgment of our nation's efforts on behalf of so-called handicapped children, we score poorly. The children aren't getting their due. Too many are in inadequate or no classrooms. Too many are growing up without the proper tools they will need to serve society and themselves as well as they might have otherwise.

The early bird catches the worm. But had the worm been late, he wouldn't have been caught. Being early can be good. Being late can be good too. Forget those arguments and recriminations. Today and tomorrow are all that matter now. So what better time than now is there to correct the errors of those who misinterpreted the original Bill of Rights, of those who had unfortunately concluded that the handicapped were to be held exempt from many of the rights and opportunities enjoyed by other citizens? What better time than now is there to proclaim to the world, but most of all to proclaim to ourselves, that each human being counts for something, that merely to be a human being entitles one to a privileged place within society? Probably today more than ever before, we must live as if a decision to deny a person any right enjoyed by others is to be made only after proof is given that the person is a serious threat to the public's good, and only under the most carefully supervised equal protection and due process guarantees, and only after all other means have been exhausted. P.L. 94-142 may become the instrument to correct the errors of the past.

Sure, there will be problems attendant to this legislation. Certainly, there is a definitional issue and, consequently, an epidemiological issue. Are there 8,000,000 handicapped children in the United States? Some say there are more and others say there are less. That's what happens when subjects determined by metaphors are counted. What will be the effects of categorical labeling? Of zero reject? Such questions are not unrelated to ones concerning voting rights for people with severe limitations. Some people do not approve of the extension of the right to vote to severely mentally retarded people, and such sentiment is not merely the voice of prejudiced people venting their meanness. Similarly, there may be problems when the handicapped themselves participate in the development of their educational programs. There may be problems if the demand that evaluation instruments not be racially or culturally discriminating is taken seriously. Will they be intellectually discriminating? Will new norms to be developed from the guidelines be useful in separating children who learn well from those who can't or don't learn well? Undoubtedly, there will be problems arising from the intensification of efforts to locate and identify youngsters with handicaps. If such efforts are weak, we will not do well in locating unserved children. On the other hand, if efforts are strenuous, certain children may be unnecessarily labeled or unnecessarily separated from the mainstream.

What I'm trying to indicate is that there must be a prudent balance between discovery and creation, between what needs to be changed and what should be preserved. And because so little of our society is prudent or balanced today, we should expect problems. We should expect that public involvement in the adoption of policies is a real plus, but such involvement raises the specter of confusion and indecision. Does democracy work in the clinic?

We'll find out. And employment of the handicapped in order to implement the legislation may offer new opportunities, but also problems. Is it better to make a special effort to employ the handicapped or a special effort to employ the best workers? You know the arguments, both ways. And, of course, some current supporters—some of those who led the way to passage of this legislation—may be the same people who will eventually resist implementation. When implementation begins to rock one's own domain, or future, the friend sometimes becomes the foe.

Surely, there will be problems. But there will also be opportunities never before possible. There can be a day when historians and your children's children will look back on this period and say, "That was the time when our ancestors finally learned that, while all humanity is a wonderful and awesome creation, each individual is fragile and dependent. While our people are strong and free, each person needs the protection of the total society. That was the time when our forebears learned that each human being is an irreplaceable link to the past and to the future. Each life is priceless."

That's the message in Public Law 94-142. I pray we take it as seriously as if our very souls depend on it.

References

Gettings, R. M. A summary of selected legislation relating to the handicapped: 1975 (Part I). *Programs for the Handicapped* (U.S. Department of Health, Education, and Welfare), 1976, *6,* 2-15.

Goodman, L. V. A bill of rights for the handicapped. *American Education*, 1976, *12* (6), 6-8.

Author's Note

I'm grateful to Professors Barbara Bateman of the University of Oregon, Herbert Goldstein of Yeshiva University, and Wolf Wolfensberger of Syracuse University for taking their responsibilities as reactors to heart as well as to head. Their observations were extremely helpful as well as gentle. I also want to thank the editors and several "unofficial" reactors, especially Dick Clark, Don Ely, and Andrejs Ozolins of Syracuse University. Their advice made this a better paper.

2.

The Curriculum-Instruction Continuum with Respect to Mainstreaming of Handicapped Children

Clarence R. Calder, Jr.

As a result of legislation and programmatic efforts, many states are attempting to develop instructional programs that can be used to coordinate the education of children with special needs in regular classrooms, and in special education programs. "How do I diagnose the learner's needs?" "What do I do?" and "How do I do it?" are three major questions asked by the classroom teacher faced with the challenge of working with handicapped children in a regular classroom environment.

The major reasons for referring learners for diagnosis and possible placement in one of the many forms of special education programs are learning and/or social/emotional problems. These learners have difficulty learning by ordinary classroom instructional methods. These learning difficulties manifest themselves in the form of a difference between the performance of the learner and that expected by the teacher because of the scope and sequence of the curriculum. The practice usually used to deal with this discrepancy has been to evaluate the learner in order to determine the nature of the problem that makes consistent performance difficult within the scope and sequence of the curriculum.

Until recently, curriculum specialists have given little recognition to individual learning styles and their relationship to how children learn when exposed to any segment of the curriculum at a given time. Science, social studies, English, mathematics, and other areas of the curriculum are most frequently characterized as age-in-grade phenomena. Sixth grade science, fourth grade social studies, eighth grade English, and second grade mathematics are fairly common terms for expressing the relationship of curriculum to age-in-grade placement. However, learners with special needs represent, by definition, discrepancies between developmental status and age-in-grade performance. They have difficulty meeting the demands of the curriculum for one or more reasons. Children with learning disabilities, usually reading and language processing problems, lack one or more of the prerequisite skills for successful participation in the regular school curriculum. Though they may not be able to read adequately, they may be able to obtain the same information through other media. While the learners may be receiving supportive services to assist with the reading difficulty, this assistance does not demonstrate its full impact because the special services are often administered in isolation from the regular curriculum experiences in which the learners participate for the greater part of the day.

The curriculum must be given careful consideration when educators are planning to mainstream learners with special needs. Most of the efforts in special education are intensive and process-based. Special education has made limited use of the comprehensive curriculum programs (Individually Guided Education, Science Curriculum Improvement Study, Individually Prescribed Instruction) developed for general education in the content areas. This chapter will develop an approach that will illustrate how a more effective use of the comprehensive curriculum offerings of general education can be used to enhance the learning and behavioral status of the learner with special needs.

This chapter will also illustrate how alternative learning styles and a diagnostic approach to curriculum development can be used to increase the number of learners with special needs that will move through the regular curriculum with some degree of success. These two interrelated techniques will assist school personnel and parents in the development of a communication system that will enable all those concerned with the progress of an individual to work on the same learning problems during the school day, as well as at home.

The programs suggest ways of limiting age-in-grade phenomena. They place emphasis on the process of learning and use subject matter as a vehicle to reinforce learning. The suggested techniques address the curriculum-instruction continuum with respect to working with learners with special needs in the regular classroom.

The Learner-Curriculum Interaction

Educators have little difficulty in labeling learners (slow, average, gifted) based upon perceived ability to learn subject matter. However, they then find it difficult to develop a curriculum geared to each individual's learning style. Learning style describes *how* an individual learns, not how much or how well he has learned. Learning styles represent an individual's unique operational mode for problem solving, verbal learning, concept formation, and the selection, encoding, and decoding of stimulus information for short and long term memory storage and retrieval.

Gregorc and Ward (1977) found that learners could be classified into one of the following types: Abstract Sequential, Abstract Random, Concrete Sequential, or Concrete Random. Although all learners in their study used all four modes to learn, ninety percent of the individuals interviewed expressed a preference for one or two manners of acquiring information.

When learning styles are considered as an array, opposed to the learner's positioning on only one of the learning continua, a number of questions and issues of a different nature arise with respect to instruction and curriculum development. These issues and questions will have a direct impact on the formulation of curriculum decisions related to such mainstreaming issues as: least restrictive environment; individualization of learning; design and evaluation processes; and elimination of definitional labels.

Hunt (1971) found that although ability and learning style are correlated, learning style can be distinguished from ability for learners of junior high school age and above. This point is important when planning a curriculum for learners with special needs. This difference requires emphasis because of the tendency of teachers to think of learners only in terms of ability. This points to the important issues of how to provide classroom teachers with a non-content oriented, non-judgmental denominator through which each learner may achieve curricular goals.

The learning styles approach to learning has been substantiated by the research of: Ohnmacht (1966); Scatterly (1976); and Sunshine and DiVesta (1976). Significant correlations between learning style and learning abilities have been found in research by Sanders *et al.* (1975) and Simon and Ward (1975).

Alternative Learning Styles in Action

The conventional approach to solving a learning problem is to present the task to the learner at a slower rate, use a different book, or to provide the learner with some tutorial help. Many remedial and tutorial programs use the same instructional techniques that caused the original learning problem. I would like to introduce an approach that uses the content areas of the curriculum as a vehicle for the individual to experience the "how to learn" dimension of the learning process. A curriculum that is sensitive to an individual's learning style and can make substitutions in the instructional technique causing the original problem is essential to learners with special needs.

Moffett (1968) suggests a curriculum that moves with the learner along two dimensions of increasing abstraction. On the first dimension, the distance between speaker and audience widens (egocentric speech to public statement), while the second dimension provides for the learner to move into participating in what is happening, to reporting, to generalizing, and finally to theorizing. The key notion of Moffett's theory is that aside from art, music, and physical education, the only subject of the school is language, since all other subjects are learned in and through language. According to his views, reading, writing, speaking, and listening should be taught through content. I would agree, but would not exclude art, music, physical education, home economics, or industrial arts from contributing to the development of the learner's reading, writing, speaking, and listening skills. Coffey (1976), Calder (1967), and Calder and Zalatino (1970) provide research that illustrates how these skills can be enhanced through the subject areas of music, art, and industrial arts.

Stotsky (1975) in her article "Sentence-Combining as a Curricular Activity: Its Effect on Written Language Development and Reading Comprehension" also indicates how the content areas can be used to enhance the learner's process skills. She goes on to indicate that sentence-combining writing exercises may have not only illuminated a new method for helping learners develop greater structural understanding of mature reading material, but also suggested the possible intellectual benefit of writing itself.

Direct experiences, role playing, concrete materials, visual materials, and symbolic representations of verbal abstractions are examples of instructional techniques or learning styles that could enhance an individual's learning process. In developing an educational plan for any learner with special needs, careful consideration should be given to alternative learning styles and using the content areas of the curriculum as a vehicle to developing the processes of learning. The learner should be provided an opportunity to learn a concept through verbal abstraction or through the manipulation of concrete materials, real objects, or any combination of these experiences. It is important that these learning processes be planned and organized to allow achievement of the desired learner outcomes.

Grouping of learners creates some serious problems. Once a group is established, no matter what criteria are used, differentiation of instruction is still apt to lead to varying degrees or different timing of the same task. For example, Reading Group I might be on page 45 of the 4th grade reader; Group II might be just starting the same book; and Group III might be in the last half of the 3rd grade reader. Two or three skill-deficient learners are lagging behind and have been referred to the resource teacher who might be using more of the same abstract stimuli that have already given them trouble.

In the suggested program three or four learners might be reading and evaluating a script for a puppet show; three learners might be viewing a captioned social studies filmstrip; two or three learners might be working on vowel principles as they make a chart using science words; and another group might be playing an environmental education game that requires the reader to select the main idea of a paragraph. All these learners and others could be working simultaneously in a variety of learning styles that meet their individual needs.

This paper will suggest a diagnostic approach to curriculum development that will enable both the resource teacher and the regular classroom teacher to use both the content areas and individual learning styles to improve reading, writing, listening, and speaking skills. Herber (1970) contended that skills taught in reading classes are applicable to content materials, but learners must adapt the skill to meet the peculiarities of each subject they study. He articulated a need for a "... whole new strategy in teaching reading through content areas, a strategy that uses what we know about the direct teaching of reading but adapts that knowledge to fit the structure and responsibilities ... in each content area." Vacca (1974) substantiates this concept when he indicates that teaching reading in the content areas requires guidance on the part of the content teacher in the development of both concepts (content) and skills (process). Basic reading skills should be incorporated into the instructional strategies of subject matter teachers without interfering with the content being taught.

A review of Title I programs across the country shows that they have not succeeded in developing reading programs that use the content areas for reinforcing reading skills. These compensatory reading programs usually take place in isolation from the regular classroom conducted by Title I teachers and/or paraprofessionals and outside the content areas of the curriculum. Classroom teachers are seldom informed about the nature of the supportive services being provided the learner in the compensatory program. The content areas of the curriculum are usually not tapped into these programs to develop concepts (content) and skills (process). However, the 1976 Federal Regulations for Title I programs require the development of an educational plan for each learner. These plans could assist in opening the lines of communications between classroom teachers and Title I teachers, paraprofessionals, and parents.

Mainstreaming programs that make use of a resource teacher should make every effort not to educate the learner in isolation from what is happening in the curriculum of the regular classroom. Both the classroom teacher and resource teacher need to develop instructional and learning strategies that use the content areas of the regular classroom curriculum for learners with special needs. This cooperation will increase the total commitment to eliminating the learner's diagnosed learning or behavioral problem.

Decision-Making Model

The decision-making process for the teacher and learner is presented in Figure 2.1, taken from Calder and Antan (1970).

Figure 2.1. Decision-Making Model

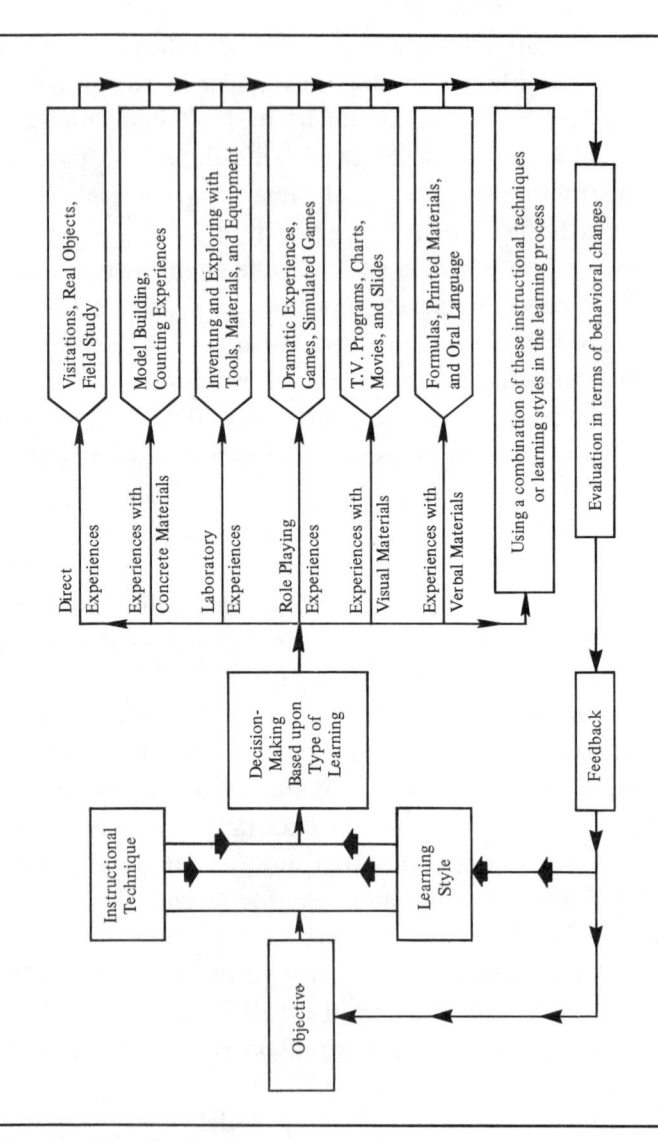

From *Techniques and Activities to Stimulate Verbal Learning*, by Clarence Calder and E. Antan (New York: Macmillan, 1970). Used with permission. Copyright © 1970 The Macmillan Company.

Rationale. Many learners are classified as nonverbal, nonreaders, culturally or educationally deprived individuals who are lost to the productive process and to society because they do not learn in the present curriculum of our schools. The curriculum has been designed for learners who have no special needs. The curriculum meets the needs of most learners to some extent because they manifest most of the necessary prerequisites for full participation at all levels of education.

By definition, every learner with special needs has a problem, usually one ascribed to learning and/or behavioral factors. It is important to point out that learners are seldom referred because they don't know social studies, but rather because they have difficulty *learning* social studies. The curriculum escapes unscathed and the learner is designated as a learning problem. The major problem for the child with special needs in the regular classroom is that the learner is confronted with a curriculum that has been developed to exclude him or her. The decision-making model presents a graphic illustration of one approach that can be used to attack the problem.

Using the Decision-Making Model

To use the model, the teacher must first consider the learner. Consideration should be given to the learner's developmental stage, intellectual and emotional development, and the learning task to be performed. The teacher must make the following decisions: what to teach (objective), how to present the material (instructional technique), and how the learner learns (learning style). A determination needs to be made with regard to what extent the desired change in behavior has taken place (evaluation). The components of the decision-making model are interrelated and interdependent.

Type and complexity of the learning task should be determined with the help of valid diagnostic instruments. Diagnostic tests are useful in determining the strengths and weaknesses of the learner in language skills, reading, mathematics, and other basic skill areas. Informal tests, conferences, and observations can also be used to diagnose the learner's needs.

Principles to Guide Decision-Making

Consideration should be given to the following principles when selecting any learning task:

1. The learner should possess the basic readiness skills needed to ensure some degree of success in the new task.
2. The learner should be made aware of the value and meaning of the new task.
3. The task should be analyzed to determine the difficulties that may be encountered because of any special needs of the learner.
4. The task should begin with familiar experiences and skills and progress to new experiences and skills.
5. The task should be presented in a manner that will provide the learner with a degree of success and satisfaction.
6. The task should be planned and a procedure developed for presenting it to the learner. When possible the plan should be initiated and executed by the learner.
7. The task should include options that meet the learner's learning style.
8. The task should have flexibility and provide for differentiated assignments in order to meet the individual needs of the learner.
9. The task should be planned to provide the learner with reinforced repetition and practice to ensure retention.
10. The task should provide for constant performance evaluation by the learner, teacher, paraprofessional, or peer tutor.
11. The assignment of a new task should be the result of

continuous evaluation of the learner's performance on the present task.

The operation of the decision-making model requires a break with tradition because, instead of looking only at what has been learned, we also look at the how of learning. Curriculum developers and researchers often refer to "learning how to learn" as the strategies and skills needed to learn a new task. The content areas tend to make up the curriculum and place a greater emphasis on the "what is learned" rather than on the "how to learn." Curriculum itself does not develop the how of learning nor does it foster the training of individual learning styles. Labouvie, Liwin, and Urberg (1975) refer to the necessity for the "how to learn" curriculum: "If we hope to eventually exploit the individual differences in the optimization of instruction, we must first establish a sound theoretical base vis-a-vis basic cognitive processes, abilities, and external variables affecting them."

This theory is supported by the research of Barret (1975) and Sanders *et al.* (1975). They found that the "how to learn" strategies and skills of a learner can be modified through training.

What is being suggested in the decision-making model is a redirection of efforts toward the development of a curriculum that allows for the analysis of learning tasks to establish guidelines for the selection of an individual's instructional or learning style needed for achievement and success.

Decision-making requires a careful analysis of the various instructional techniques and learning styles that can be used to facilitate each learning act. Selection should be made on the basis of how effective the learning style is in obtaining the desired behavior change in the learner. The instructional techniques and learning style presented in the model should be understood by the teacher in relationship to the learner and the task to be learned. It is important to remember that these learning modes are usually used by all learners, but that a majority of individuals express a definite preference for one or two manners of acquiring information.

The evaluation component has a two-pronged thrust, one concerned with the actual acquisition of the skill, while the second is concerned with what strategy was used to learn the skill. If the evaluation indicates that the learner has fallen short of mastery or some lesser standard of achievement, one or all of the components of the model may require adjustment. The feedback loop indicates how the obtained information is returned to the various components.

Learner's Record Sheet

A learner's record sheet should be used by the teacher to keep a record of each child's learning style as well as success in learning a skill. The record sheet should be set up to enable the teacher to assess learning difficulties and diagnose possible solutions. Column 1 of the record sheet contains the objective or objectives based on a diagnosis of the learner's special needs in a specific skill area. These are the long and short term goals found on a learner's educational plan. Column 2 should label the various content areas in the curriculum where this skill could be developed. Several columns then indicate the instructional techniques and/or learning style used to bring about a change in the learner's behavior. A final column 11 is for brief evaluation comments.

The learner's record sheet represents a diagnostic and evaluative approach that requires no complicated statistics to find out what alternative instructional techniques and learning styles are the most effective with each learner. A combination of learning styles and instructional techniques may be used before a plus is obtained for a particular task. As the record grows, the teacher develops an inventory of what the learner has learned and how the task was learned.

Diagnostic Approach to Curriculum Development (DACD)

The Diagnostic Approach to Curriculum Development is a strategy for assisting classroom teachers to better meet the special needs of a learner. DACD is a programmatic effort that uses data collected from formal and informal diagnostic tests to establish the curriculum for each learner. It is a program for working with learners with special needs in the regular classroom through special education services. The following is a brief description of major components of the DACD program.

Desired Learner Outcomes. The DACD program is developed around Desired Learner Outcomes (DLO), which are a form of behavioral objectives that are content-free and age-free. Each objective is written in a way that makes it possible to apply it to social studies, language arts, and/or science. It can apply to four-year-olds as well as to twelve-year-olds, and it is adaptable to cultural and experiential differences among learners.

DLO's are written with two main components; the first is the "standard" and the second is the "learner response." They are categorized into Developmental Aural Skills, Developmental Visual Skills, and Social/Emotional Development as illustrated in Table 2.1.

TABLE 2.1

A SAMPLE DLO FROM THE DEVELOPMENTAL AURAL SKILLS, DEVELOPMENTAL VISUAL SKILLS, AND SOCIAL/EMOTIONAL DEVELOPMENT AREAS

Developmental Area	Standard	Learner Response
Aural Skills	a sentence	write the word(s) named by the instructor
Visual Skills	specific disassembled object	assemble the object
Social/Emotional	an opportunity to work independently to construct an object(s) as indicated in the directions provided.	works independently to construct an object(s) as indicated in the directions provided.

Developmental Behaviors. The following list of Developmental Behaviors defines the classification of behavior statements known as Desired Learner Outcomes. By concentrating on these behavioral components, it is possible to create situations in which the performance of the learner with special needs is easily observed and assessed. It is also possible to vary the task levels at which different learners are working while developing a common learning outcome.

Developmental Aural Skills	Developmental Visual Skills	Social/Emotional Development
Aural Discrimination	Visual Discrimination	Construction
Aural Recognition	Visual Sequencing	Mapping
Aural Sequential/Memory	Visual Copying	Imagery
Aural Concept Manipulation	Visual Memory	Competitive Games
Oral Production	Visual Figure-Ground	Non-Competitive Games
Aural Graphic Symbolization	Visual Association	Gross-Fine Motor
	Visual Classification	Body Image
	Visual Closure	
	Visual Graphic Symbolization	

Introduction to Diagnostic/Instructional System. The DACD program attempts to close the gap between the diagnostic identification of the status of the learner and the selection of instructional alternatives that follow from the diagnostic information.

An effective diagnostic/instruction system that will meet the needs of learners with learning and behavioral disorders should, minimally, consist of (1) a communication component, (2) an assessment component, and (3) an instructional component. In the following, we will discuss the communication and assessment components, since instructional considerations are treated in other chapters in this volume.

The Communication Component. The communication system should provide a reliable linkage between the diagnostic/assessment component and the instructional component. It needs to show the user how instruction can cut across age levels and content areas. The component, to be effective, must provide the user with a means of getting from the diagnosis to the instruction and for making diagnosis more directly related to referral cases. The communication system needs to be simple, direct, and flexible.

In the program under discussion, the Behavior Resource Guide (Cawley *et al.*, 1974) is the communication link in the system. The Behavior Resource Guide (BRG) consists of four sections. The first is a set of charts that provides the user with intercorrelation between certain DLO's and selected psychoeducational tests. This section of the BRG allows the user to identify tests or sub-tests from major psychoeducational tests that can be used to measure a specific behavioral process.

The Test to DLO correlation is used to identify specific items that can be used to assess a behavior when there is a definitive referral. This section allows the user who has obtained certain information from a psychoeducational test to identify the Desired Learner Outcomes which were measured by the test. The second section of the Behavior Resource Guide provides the user with information that shows which of the items on a particular psychoeducational test measure a specific behavior. This procedure is a reversal of that performed in the DLO to Test section. The purpose of this section is to use the test information that may be in a learner's folder to identify the behavior measured by the test.

The third section is a set of charts that provides the user with an intercorrelation between the DLO used in section one and approximately one thousand commercially produced instructional materials. The DLO to Materials section enables the user who had identified a learner's behavior in need of modification to select instructional materials that can be used to assist in bringing about the desired learner outcome.

In the Resource Guide the 266 DLO's are correlated with approximately one thousand commercially prepared instructional programs or components of these programs.

The fourth section allows the user to go from Materials to DLO's. Instructional materials are listed along with Desired Learner Outcomes (DLO's) that can be appropriately used to bring about the desired behavioral change.

The Behavior Resource Guide is an open system and items can be added at any time. It is the core of the communication system and illustrates how diagnostic information can be used to plan instruction.

Assessment Component. An important component of the Diagnostic Approach to Curriculum Development is assessment. This component should have the capability of providing information that has instructional relevance. Because the special needs of atypical learners are expressed in terms of learning and behavioral problems, assessment should provide information concerning these needs.

Formal and informal diagnostic testing is used in this program to make an assessment of the learner's strengths and weaknesses. For example, if the learner was given the *Gates-McKillop Reading Diagnostic Test* and had difficulty with sections (1) Oral Reading, (2) Words: Flash, (3) Words: Untimed, and (4) Phrases, but not difficulty with (6) Giving Letter Sounds and (7) Naming Capital Letters, how is this information used to develop an educational plan for the learner? This question is difficult to answer if we examine the present curriculum of many of our schools. Are these areas of difficulty related only to reading or are they the responsibility of the total curriculum and should be reinforced as the learner moves through science, social studies, language arts, art, music, and physical education?

The Behavior Resource Guide can be used to assist in the development of the learner's educational plan, one that cuts across the total school curriculum. It should be remembered that the BRG is the link between the educational diagnosis and instruction. Sections 1, 2, 3, 4, 6, and 7 of the *Gates-McKillop Reading Diagnostic Test* are correlated in the BRG with Visual Graphic Sym-

The Curriculum-Instruction Continuum

bolization, one of the Developmental Visual Skill Areas. Table 2.2 illustrates the specific Desired Learner Outcomes which the sections of the *Gates-McKillop Reading Diagnostic Test* are measuring.

TABLE 2.2

AN EXAMPLE OF THE SPECIFIC DLO'S THAT THE DIFFERENT SUBTESTS OF THE *GATES-MCKILLOP READING DIAGNOSTIC TEST* ARE MEASURING

Gates-McKillop Reading Diagnostic Test		Desired Learner Outcomes Found in the BRG
Test Section	**Standard**	**Learner Response**
1. Oral Reading	a paragraph(s)	read the paragraph orally
2. Words: Flash	monosyllabic and polysyllabic words	orally state the words
3. Words: Untimed	monosyllabic and polysyllabic words	orally state the words
4. Phrases	a set of sentences	orally state the sentence (or phrase)
6. Giving Letter Sounds	a set of letters or numerals	name the letters or numerals
7. Naming Capital Letters	single letters and letter combinations	produce a sound that can be represented by the letters

The Diagnostic Approach to Curriculum Development is not without its problems. One major difficulty is that of test bias. We frequently find the learner's behavior to be a function of what we ask. Therefore, the selection of tests or other means of assessing a learner represents a probable bias in the diagnostic process. Careful consideration needs to be given to the selection of any diagnostic tool that is going to be used to describe a learner, and equal care is needed to use this diagnostic information to plan the learner's instructional program. This problem of selection bias permeates both observational systems and the test-dominated systems.

Another difficulty encountered in a diagnostic program is masking bias. This results when the assessment of behavior and the determination of strengths and weaknesses are masked by the presence of content. For example, if the learner is requested to state orally a set of words (e.g., Gates-McKillop Reading-Words: Untimed) and fails, what type of assessment does one make?

1. "I gave George a set of words. He could not orally state these words."

or

2. "I gave George a set of words. He cannot orally state words."

or

3. "George is low in one of the abilities constituting intelligence. He is slow."

The tendency to extrapolate definitions and concepts or classes of behavior from samples of behavior has more value when one of the major purposes of testing is to classify and/or label a learner for purposes of placement. However, P.L. 94-142 has changed the emphasis to one that requires the development of an educational plan for the learner, a plan that needs to have utility for both the regular classroom teacher and special education teacher. The diagnostic information collected should be more specific about the behavioral characteristics of the task. The learner with special needs is defined as having learning and/or behavioral problems and educators must be able to view the learner independently of content as well as within content.

The two levels of the Behavior Skills Inventory (BSI) developed by Cawley *et al.* (1974) are criterion-referenced tests with items directly linked to curricula plus additional diagnostic activities. The BSI is an attempt to develop a diagnostic tool that allows the assessment of the learner's behavioral problem independently of content as well as within content. The BSI as an inventory is similar to the everyday behavior of the diagnostically oriented teacher in that content and behavior are dealt with simultaneously and/or independently. The reliability demonstrated in assessing behavior in the different content areas should be reasonable support for the fact that the special needs of the learner can be realized during the total day and across the curriculum. Programming for learners with special needs can take place in a number of settings: a self-contained classroom where the classroom teacher is responsible for teaching the different subjects; a combination of the resource center and the regular classroom; a team arrangement where several teachers share in the management of the entire instructional program; and a departmental program where a learner has a different teacher for each subject. However, the success of the DACD depends upon the teachers having an understanding of how they can diagnose the special needs of the learner and bring about the desired learner outcome using the various content areas of the curriculum.

This component of the program depends upon the diagnostic skills and competencies of the special educator being interrelated with the curriculum skills and competencies of the general educator. This matching of resources extends to both the skill and competency level of the professional personnel who work with learners with special needs and to the interrelating of behaviors and curricula with commercial and teacher-prepared instructional materials.

Developing Behaviorally Based Instruction. The third component, as noted above, is instruction itself. While this chapter does not describe the instructional aspects of the DACD model, the reader is reminded that the instructional activities planned for learners should cut across the content of the curriculum and be interrelated with the Desired Learner Outcomes in the BRG described above.

Conclusion

In view of what we now know can be accomplished when working with learners with special needs, we cannot continue to require the learner to adjust to existing curriculum patterns and instructional practices. We must take a serious look at these learners and provide them with the least restrictive environment in which to learn. The DACD program described briefly in this chapter is one means of approaching a solution to the problems of children with special needs.

References

Allen, V. L., Devin-Sheehan, L., and Feldman, R. S. "Research on Children Tutoring Children: A Critical Review," *Review of Educational Research*, 1976, Vol. 46, 3, pp. 355-385.

Barret, B. B. "Training and Transfer in Combinatorial Problem Solving: The Development of Formal Reasoning During Early Adolescence," *Developmental Psychology*, 1975, Vol. 11, 5, pp. 567-74.

Calder, C. R. "Self-Directed Reading Materials," *The Reading Teacher*, Vol. 21, 3, 1967.

Calder, C. R., and Zalatino, S. "Children's Ability to Follow Directions," *The Reading Teacher*, Vol. 24, 3, 1970.

Calder, C., and Antan, E. *Techniques and Activities to Stimulate Verbal Learning,* New York, Macmillan, 1970.

Coffey, J. "Reading Via Rock'n Roll," *Tallahassee Democrat*, Thursday, November 23, 1976.

Cawley, J., Calder, C., Mann, P., McClung, R., Ramanauskas, S., and Suiter, P. *Behavior Resource Guide*, Tulsa, Oklahoma, Educational Progress, 1974.

Cawley, J., Calder, C., Mann, P., McClung, R., Ramanauskas, S., and Suiter, P. *Behavior Skills Inventory*, Tulsa, Oklahoma, Educational Progress, 1974.

Durrell, D. D. "Patterns in Pupil-Team Learning," Boston University, *Unpublished Paper*, 1964.

Gregorc, A., and Ward, H. "Individual Redefined—Implications for Learning and Teaching," *National Association of Secondary School Principals,* 1977.

Herber, H.L. *Teaching Reading in Content Areas,* Englewood Cliffs, New Jersey: Prentice-Hall, 1970.

Hunt. D. E. *Matching Models in Education: The Coordination of Teaching Methods with Student Characteristics,* Toronto, Ontario Institute for Studies in Education, 1971.

Labouvie, V. G., Liwin, J. R., and Urberg, K. A. "The Relationship Between Cognitive Abilities and Learning—A Second Look," *Journal of Educational Research,* 1975, Vol. 67, 4, pp. 558-569.

Moffett, J. *Teaching the Universe of Discourse,* Boston, Houghton Mifflin, 1968.

Ohnmacht, F. W. "Effects of Field Independence on Reversal and Non-Reversal Shifts in Concept Formation," *Perceptual and Motor Skills,* 1966, Vol. 22, pp. 491-497.

Sanders, J.A., Sterns, H. L., Smith, M., and Sanders, R. E. "Modification of Concept Identification Performance in Older Adults," *Developmental Psychology,* 1975, pp. 824-829.

Scatterly, D.J. "Cognitive Style, Spatial Ability, and School Achievement," *Journal of Educational Psychology,* 1976, Vol. 68, pp. 36-42.

Simon, A., and Ward, L. O. "The Relation Between the Ability to Derive Concepts from Various Visual Figures and Chronological Age in Primary School Children," *Journal of Genetic Psychology,* 1975, Vol. 26, pp. 27-40.

Stotsky, S. "Sentence-Combining as a Curricular Activity: Its Effect on Written Language Development and Reading Comprehension," *Research in the Teaching of English,* 1975, Vol. 9, 1, Sp. pp. 30-71.

Sunshine, P. M., and Di Vesta, F. "Effects of Density and Format on Letter Discrimination by Beginning Readers with Different Learning Styles," *Journal of Educational Psychology,* 1976, Vol. 68, 1, pp. 15-19.

Vacca, R. "Content Area Reading: A Functional Concept," *Michigan Reading Journal*, Spring 1974, pp. 31-32.

Author's Note

The author wishes to express his appreciation to the following for their helpful comments on an earlier draft of this paper: Robert H. Anderson, Dean, College of Education, Texas Tech University, Lubbock, Texas, and William Goldman, Professor, Department of Special Education, Fitchburg State College, Fitchburg, Massachusetts.

3.
Prescriptive Teaching and Individualized Education Programs

Barbara D. Bateman

Once upon a time, a special educator opined that Special Education began with Adam and Eve, whose information processing deficits interfered with following directions. As a result of these deficits, a remedial token economy was established and to this day bread is contingent upon effort expended.

Adam was also orthopedically impaired, suffering as he did the loss of a rib. Historians still debate the effect of the resulting stigma on him; some say he compensated and others claim he may have overcompensated for his deficiency. Recent revisionists have even claimed he developed associated delusions of grandeur and may therefore be properly regarded as the first to be placed in the emotionally disturbed category.

Whether or not this view of the beginning of special education is historically accurate, it is clear that from its inception, whenever and wherever it was, special education has been, or should have been, attempting to plan and implement individualized educational programs (IEP's) appropriate to the unique needs of each handicapped child. Now, P.L. 94-142 provides the opportunity and the mandate for all professionals who indeed have developed such expertise to share it widely. The purpose of this chapter is to explore the relationship between prescriptive teaching and the IEP required by P.L. 94-142.

Individualized Education Programs

Special educators have long had education programs. The new requirement of P.L. 94-142 is that they must now be individualized. Our first inquiry must therefore be as to the nature of individualization. The term "individualized education" wears a halo but too often it communicates imprecisely, if at all. It may mean one child is placed in reading Book 7 while another is in Book 5 or 9; or that a volunteer tutor provides a half-hour of one-to-one instruction each day; or that each student may contract for an hour a day of ceramics, firefighting, or primitive painting. Or perhaps it means that in an ungraded primary school some children may spend four years when most spend three, or that some students study "new math" while others learn "traditional arithmetic," or that some learn to read by phonics while others learn whole words. "Individualization" may mean learner selection of objectives. In short, the term is used without precision.

"Individualization" of instruction may refer to *what* is taught, *how, when*, and conceivably, *where* and by *whom* it is taught.

What. Simply, the issue is whether some children need to be taught different things than other children. When we look at the range of mental, physical, and social abilities and disabilities present in children it is clear some have unique needs. A less simple issue is whether the educational agencies should and can teach to *all* the needs of all the children. Historically, schools were established to teach academics. The later expansion of goals to include driver training, sex education, vocational training, karate, film-making, and so on, has not been universally applauded, but it has occurred.

Now P.L. 94-142 has mandated that the *what* of instruction shall be individualized to the unique special educational needs of all handicapped children. A New York appellate court has held the state may be required to pay tuition for a physically handicapped child to attend summer camp. (*In the matter of Richard G.*, N.Y.Sup.Ct., App.Div., 2nd Dept., May 17, 1976) Another New York court ordered reimbursement under state education law for maintaining a retarded child in an institution not approved as an educational institution and said that a mentally retarded child must be taught "how to hold a spoon, feed herself, dress herself, toilet training ..." (*In the matter of Tracy Ann Cox*, No. H4721-75, N.Y. Family Ct., Queens County, April 8, 1976)

Some compromise is, of course, required between teaching everything and teaching only traditional academics. Where this line is to be drawn for handicapped and non-handicapped alike remains to be determined.

How. No dictum in all of education and special education is more widely heard than, "No one method is best for all children." If current professional educators were to take a vow in order to ply their trade, surely one line would be "I will never advocate all children be taught the same way." The underpinning of this creed is the belief that there are known (or at least knowable) interactions between measurable characteristics of children and certain defined (or at least definable) educational methodologies or *how's* of teaching and managing. These presumed aptitude, trait, or achievement-treatment interactions will be discussed later. For now suffice it to note that little consensus presently exists as to the precise nature of those interactions.

When. While there is little consensus as to how to match child and methodology, there is near total agreement that children learn at different rates and that, therefore, the *when* of introducing new learning experiences must be varied appropriately. Practice is far from perfect, but we are nonetheless more expert in monitoring rate of acquisition and assessing mastery than we are in many other areas of potential individualization.

Where. Placement decisions have received unprecedented attention recently. The access to education cases and the concept of least restrictive environment (apparently borrowed with relatively little critical evaluation from right to treatment litigation) in P.L. 94-142 have burgeoned in many directions—"mainstreaming" being one of the most visible. Few claim an empirical base for the proposition that the *where* of instruction necessarily has a substantial positive effect on academic achievement. Rather, the belief is that placement with non-handicapped to the maximum extent possible is a civil right, consistent with democratic and constitutional principles. Therefore, the considerations that will govern the *where* of instruction in the foreseeable future may not be primarily academic. Many educators believe that segregated education for the handicapped cannot possibly constitute appropriate preparation for life outside school with the non-handicapped. The persuasiveness of this argument depends on how large or exclusive a role one believes the school plays in "life preparation." Among the recognized, but not yet solved, problems posed by the new placement considerations are the reluctance of regular educators to take on those mainstreaming responsibilities for which they feel inadequately prepared and the possible power of teachers' unions to negotiate limitations on placement possibilities for handicapped children.

Who. Perhaps because of administrative difficulties, relatively few claims have been made that major efforts should be made to match children and teachers. State licensing procedures provide, in theory and with debatable success, assurance of all teachers' qualifications. Under P.L. 94-142 the team conducting evaluations and developing IEP's must meet these state standards, and the IEP must list the individuals responsible for implementing the educational programs.

What Is an Individualized Education Program?

Under P.L. 94-142, individualized education is formalized by the IEP—a written document developed in a planning conference by the teacher(s), parent(s), a representative of the local education agency qualified in school administration, supervision, or special education, and when appropriate, the child. It must be written within 30 days after determining the child is eligible for special education or within 30 attendance days from the beginning of school for a child already known to be eligible.

The IEP must include (a) child's present levels of educational performance, (b) annual goals which describe expected behaviors, (c) short term instructional objectives, (d) services to be provided (including special instructional media and materials and type of physical education program), (e) description of extent to which the child will be able to participate in regular education programs, (f) the projected date for initiation and anticipated duration of services, and (g) appropriate objective criteria, evaluating procedures, and schedules (at least annually) for determining whether the instructional objectives are being achieved.

The IEP is not intended as a legally binding contract. The education agency must provide the services determined in the IEP but may not be held accountable if the goals or objectives are not reached. Much potential confusion and litigation as to the meaning of free appropriate public education has apparently been avoided by defining "appropriate" education as the provision of the services delineated in the IEP. It is also important to note that parents are entitled to participate in developing the IEP.

Relationships Between Prescriptive Teaching and Individualized Education Programs

If prescriptive teaching is broadly conceptualized as the total process of individually planning, implementing, and evaluating the educational program for one child, then the process of developing the IEP would be one important step subsumed within prescriptive teaching. On the other hand, if prescriptive teaching is viewed narrowly as (a) specific acts of teaching a given child to perform a specific skill in a way, (b) different from how another child with similar entering skills would be taught, and (c) derived from personalogical variables unique to the first child as determined by psychoeducational evaluation, then prescriptive teaching must be distinguished from the IEP which does not address teaching methodology or its derivation. Concepts such as prescriptive teaching are subject to a range of definitions and usages, when swept into the popular domain. It seems appropriate for our purposes to use Peter's (1965) now classic definition of prescriptive teaching:

> ... a method of utilizing diagnostic information for the modification of educational programs ... by determining the educational relevance of the child's disability, and devising teaching procedures to yield desirable changes in the child's academic program, emotional condition, and social adjustment (p. 1).

Peter's three-dimensional model for translating diagnostic findings into a teaching prescription includes (1) situational and (2) problem variables which determine the modifications necessary in the (3) school variables. The school variables, in order of ease of modifiability, are consistent approach, teaching methods, specific objectives, ancillary services, placement personnel, subject matter, instructional materials, special equipment, school plant, and auxiliary agencies.

A most fundamental and important similarity between prescriptive teaching and the IEP is that they both reject the old syllogism:
>Beth is a trainably mentally retarded child.
>X is the placement, curriculum, program for TMR children.
>Therefore, Beth will receive X.

and accept a new one:
>Beth needs to learn to dress herself.
>X person and program can teach dressing skills. Therefore, Beth will receive X.

Prescriptive Teaching and Individualized Education Programs 45

Taken together, P.L. 94-142 procedures for determining eligibility *and* for completing the IEP require attention to all of Peter's prescriptive teaching variables *except* the two educational variables most readily adapted (in his view)—consistent approach and teaching methods. Thus, the most striking difference between prescriptive teaching and the IEP is that prescriptive teaching contains the major missing pieces not seen in the IEP. The critical gaps in the IEP occur between the specification of behavioral objectives and annual review. In the otherwise non-specified teaching process, the IEP requires only a listing of media and materials to be employed. Table 3.1 compares the IEP with a description of the process of prescriptive teaching which is my own expansion and extrapolation of Peter's "consistent approach and teaching methods."

TABLE 3.1

A COMPARISON OF ELEMENTS IN PRESCRIPTIVE TEACHING AND A P.L. 94-142 IEP

Prescriptive Teaching	IEP
Assessment of Child's Present Level	yes
Specification of Goals	yes
Specification of Objectives	yes
Specification of Teaching Tasks Inherent in Objectives	no
a. specify how mastery will be demonstrated	no
1. specify response requirements	no
a. teach necessary responses	no
b. specify antecedent events—what teacher will do	no
c. specify required child responses	no
1. find or develop materials and media to provide teaching format and child response practice	yes
d. specify correction procedures	no
e. specify consequent events	no
f. specify evaluation procedures for each task	no
Specification of Daily or Near Daily Evaluation of Child Mastery Objectives	annually only
Modify Tasks as Necessary	no

Of course, the IEP may, and should, contain all the elements listed as characteristic of prescriptive teaching. This discussion focuses on what the IEP is required to contain. Many districts, overwhelmed by paperwork and/or too few adequately trained personnel, may realistically limit IEP's to these required minimums. Even at this minimum level, it must be noted that the required measurable objectives specification will be a giant step forward for some special education programs and it is the *sine qua non* for further progress.

In special education the law has readily required that handicapped children be granted access to public education and to regular classrooms, but it has been most reluctant to address the quality of what transpires within those classrooms. P.L. 94-142 illustrates this vividly in that while education agencies will be responsible for delivering the services listed in the IEP, they may not be held accountable if the child fails to progress or to achieve the annual goals. The administrative skeleton of education is mandated in great detail—the evaluation procedures, needs, goals, objectives, dates, services, review, due process protections, and so on. But the law is conspicuously silent as to learner outcomes and the *teaching* procedures to be used. The rules specifically disavow any requirement that the teaching be effective. Thus, both the method and the quality of teaching handicapped children are still left largely to professional discretion; and many believe that is precisely as it should be.

Why does the IEP fail to require any specification as to methods to be employed in achieving the annual goals or the instructional objectives? Those of us not privy to the facts can merely speculate. One probable factor is the historic reluctance of law-makers to intrude too specifically into other professional domains. However, if this were the sole explanation, would we not expect to see a requirement such as "teaching methods employed must be acceptable to the professional community and be demonstrably and reasonably likely to result in the achievement of the specified

Prescriptive Teaching and Individualized Education Programs 47

objectives"? Was the professional community itself reluctant to be charged with demonstrating a rational basis for the selection of methodology individualized to each child's characteristics? If not, perhaps it should have been. Surely this is the great chasm in our expertise. Or is it? An interesting bridge, traversed by increasing numbers, has been built across the chasm—that of precise monitoring of pupil progress. An instructional objective, complete with mastery criteria, is formulated and any reasonable method implemented. If that method is shown by daily rate data or other careful, regular observation to be moving the learner toward success at an acceptable pace, it is continued. If not, some other method is selected and its efficacy monitored, and so on. These evaluation systems themselves properly make no claim to predicting comparative success of methodologies prior to implementation. Their proponents do urge compilation of data across children to that ultimate end, however, and such efforts have been undertaken.

This monitoring approach allows either for the possibility that different children do learn better by different methods or, alternatively, that there is a best method for achieving any particular objective, given specified entry behaviors. The proposition that different methods are appropriate to teach the same skills or concepts to different children is known as aptitude-treatment interaction (also as trait-treatment interaction, and achievement-treatment interaction) and is of importance in special education where it has had, until recently, uncritical acceptance.

Aptitude-Treatment Interaction. A thorough review of the research pursuing a match between learner characteristics and teaching methods is far beyond the scope of this chapter. A few generalizations are in order, however. Most of us, as individuals if not as professionals, "feel" that somehow individual learning styles do differ from each other and for each of us certain teaching methods are more effective than others. However, results of research exploring these interactions have been mixed at best, and dismal in the views of some (e.g., Bracht, 1970). Some of the areas where hopes have been strongest have been especially disappointing—e.g., our inability across many investigations to match learners' sensory modality preferences with methods of teaching reading (Haring and Bateman, 1977). Some of the scattered studies which have found significant interactions (see Berliner and Cahen, 1973, for a review) suggest a promising hypothesis not inconsistent with common sense—namely, that the farther the learner is from mastery as to the objective being taught, the more efficacious are deductive, highly structured, rule-oriented methods; and, conversely, the nearer the learner is to independent performance, the more appropriate it becomes to use discovery, inductive, or self-selected methods (Haring and Bateman, 1977; Rosenshine, 1976; Tobias, 1976).

The search for meaningful aptitude-treatment interactions seems likely to continue and hopefully will do so with increasing success as the models and hypotheses directing the research become more sophisticated (Salomon, 1972).

To the extent that handicapped children tend to be, by definition, further than others from mastery in their areas of greatest need, it follows that highly structured deductive methods will frequently be the most successful.

Developing the Individualized Education Program

P.L. 94-142 promises a free, appropriate public education to handicapped children. The free and public education aspects are protected by such adversarial safeguards as notice to parents, due process hearings, the least restrictive environment mandate, nondiscriminatory testing, rights of appeal, and so on. The "appropriate" element is not itself adversarial, as are the protections above, but will be achieved through the cooperative development of the IEP. In this section we shall assume all procedural matters are conducted with appropriate parental involvement and are in full compliance with P.L. 94-142 and we shall focus on the content of the IEP.

Zeller (1976) has proposed a possible IEP process probably consistent with P.L. 94-142 and certainly with sound educational practice: (1) child referred to special education; (2) acquire diagnostic data; (3) determine eligibility; (4) establish goals and objectives; (5) define service needs; (6) select tentative placement; (7) provide design for specific programming strategies; (8) confirm or revise placement; and (9) review IEP at least annually. The National Association of State Directors of Special Education (NASDSE) (1976) has prepared a flow chart depicting this basic process. Both the Zeller and NASDSE models, among others, elaborate on the minimum requirements of P.L. 94-142 in that they recognize the need for what might be called a two-stage IEP. The first stage is the "total service" plan as required by law; the second is a more specific "individual implementation" plan which expands on the instructional objectives merely listed in the first stage. This individual implementation plan (Zeller's "programming strategies") goes beyond the letter of the law and represents the true heart of prescriptive teaching. Early experience in some states suggests that this two-stage IEP is not only educationally sound and necessary, but also it is a practical protection for parents concerned that a district's paper commitment to services to be delivered in the total services plan might outstrip actual implementation.[1]

Evaluation and Assessment. In the sequence of events from identification of a handicapped child as eligible for an IEP to the successful implementation of that IEP, the first area of concern is the relationship between the evaluation data on the child and the planning of the IEP.

Evaluation is implicitly used in two slightly different senses in P.L. 94-142: (a) to determine if a child is handicapped as defined by the law, and (b) to assess current levels of educational performance for the IEP. Prior to development of the IEP, the child must have been determined to be handicapped and in need of special education and related services. This determination must employ instruments which are (a) validated, (b) recommended for the purposes used, and (c) are culturally and racially non-discriminatory.[2] The evaluation must include data on (a) physical condition, (b) sociocultural background, and (c) adaptive behavior in home and school. Questions beyond the scope of this discussion have been raised as to appropriateness of the definitions of categories of handicapping conditions used in P.L. 94-142, *viz.*, learning disabilities (e.g., Lloyd, Sabatino, Miller, and Miller, 1977), and as to the present existence of tests which meet the conditions above and which meet the intent of educationally relevant assessment (Nazzaro, 1976).

This section will be concerned primarily with the second phase of evaluation when it has already been determined that the child is handicapped under the terms of P.L. 94-142 and is entitled to an IEP.[3] Evaluation information gathered in determining eligibility under P.L. 94-142 may or may not be helpful in developing the IEP. For instance, in determining that a child has a specific learning disability, standardized academic achievement tests will be used in most cases. Those same data clearly would be useful in describing the current level of academic performance in the IEP. However, other eligibility data, such as that used to exclude economic disadvantage as the primary cause of the severe academic discrepancy, would be of little use. Similarly, some data used to establish that a child has epilepsy and is thus "health impaired" might have little use in the IEP, but behavioral data on frequency of seizures might be of the utmost importance if, for instance, one of the goals is to reduce the frequency of seizures.

One other preliminary observation is that the IEP apparently requires an assessment of *each* child's current educational performance including academic, social, vocational and prevocational, psychomotor, and self-help. Perhaps this requirement will be modified in the rules and/or in practice to read "as appropriate" or "where unique educational needs are believed to exist." We assume it is appropriate to determine whether unique special educa-

Prescriptive Teaching and Individualized Education Programs 51

tional needs exist in any of these areas or others (e.g., language) and deal only with those unique needs.

Once unique needs have been established, the IEP must be developed to show how those needs will be met by the local education agency. Our task is to explore this development of the IEP. Zeller's first six steps comprise the development of the mandated IEP or total services plan. Beyond technical compliance with all proper procedures, a process seeming to necessitate checklists of procedures to be observed at every date, the first substantive, professional concern after determination of eligibility is to establish current levels of performance and prioritize goals. The data must be geared toward two questions: (1) What does the child *most* need to be taught, and (2) Where or at what level do we begin instruction? Two contrasting and artificially exaggerated views of evaluation are the "test centered" and the "child centered" processes. Many diagnosticians, of course, employ a combination. In the "test centered" approach, a battery of tests is selected, usually based on availability and familiarity to the evaluation personnel. From that repertoire of tests, those "appropriate" (often by age) for the child in question are administered. The child's weak areas as shown on the tests are examined and if packaged materials are available which purport to improve the deficient skills, they are recommended. The child's strengths are often described and a recommendation made that the teacher employ these strong areas.

The "child centered" approach often begins with observing the child and asking parents, teachers, and the child, when appropriate, what seems to be priority concerns. If the areas of expressive language and motor coordination loom large, the intensive or formal evaluation would begin there and include criterion-referenced tests, observation under a planned variety of conditions, and so on.

Parents' perceptions and values as to the proper areas of instructional emphases and desirable annual goals are potentially very valuable and should weigh heavily in the formulation of goals. Since behavioral technology and methodology have become widely accepted, the problem has lessened, but some school personnel dealing newly with severely handicapped children will still have to guard carefully against professionals or parents underestimating the progress children make when well taught. All participants in the IEP process should become familiar with the accomplishments of young and severely handicapped children in exemplary behavioral programs. Parents must be informed, e.g., of the academic accomplishments of preschool Down's Syndrome youngsters. This is not to say academic goals would necessarily have top priority for all children, but that the proper prioritizing of goals cannot be done without knowledge as to what is possible and reasonable.

The importance of prioritizing goals cannot be overstated. A proper prioritization will begin with an objective diagnosis of the child's needs and will also take into account parental wishes and the logic of future instructional sequences and options. Teaching attending behaviors or teaching a child to read will, e.g., greatly increase the ease and feasibility of teaching many other things later.

Short Term Objectives. P.L. 94-142 requires the IEP include "measurable intermediate steps between the present level of educational performance and the annual goals." The short term objectives should themselves contain the objective evaluation criteria procedures and schedules required by P.L. 94-142. The more precisely the goals and objectives are stated, the more valuable the IEP will be to child and teacher.

Educational and Related Services. The IEP must include educational and related services. The proposed rules indicate the district *must* deliver these services but may not be held accountable if the child fails to progress. The needed services must be listed without regard to availability and must be delivered, even for second priority handicapped children (those presently receiving basic education but less than a full service program).

The scope of the IEP is broader in its inclusion of related services than all but the most comprehensive notions of prescriptive teaching. The prepared rules state that the related services to be provided are those necessary to enable the child to benefit from special education. It remains to be seen how, if at all, this falls short of total services. The rules are also clear in placing ultimate responsibility for the provision of these services on the state educational agency, even though within many states other agencies may have had the responsibility in the past and may still actually provide the services.

Materials and Media in the IEP. Teaching, whether clearly specified, as in what we have called prescriptive teaching, or loosely, as in an IEP, almost always uses materials and media—a point urged strongly by those who sought inclusion of them in the IEP. If materials and media were understood to mean only those special instructional aids required by handicapped children such as braille writers, wheelchair ramps, electric typewriters for some orthopedically impaired children, etc., there would be no question as to the appropriateness of listing them. If materials and media were understood to mean only those which have been empirically demonstrated to teach successfully what they purport to teach under the conditions (e.g., given specified learner entry behaviors) they purport to teach it, again, no issues would be raised. However, current interpretations of the requirement range from those which list "shaping procedures" and "manipulative toys" as materials and media to others which specify pages in commercial workbooks. A major difficulty with the latter approach to specifying particular "packages" or commercial materials is that as few as one percent of all instructional materials have been revised to reflect the results of using them with children (Axelrod, 1976). Few instructional materials have a solid data base for claiming to be effective at all, let alone that they will work with a particular handicapped child. The few that do tend to be those (a) developed by task analysis, (b) revised on the basis of child performance, and (c) widely tested on low or potentially low performing children.

Prominent among the small number of demonstrably successful materials meeting these criteria are the DISTAR programs (see Carnine, 1977), whose development addressed every element of prescriptive teaching listed in Table 3.1. DISTAR programs are also consistent with the hypothesis advanced earlier that potentially low performing children benefit most from highly structured deductive teaching methods.

The concern many feel about the IEP's focus on materials and media is that the door is open to easy abuses such as (1) listing available "packages" and then employing objectives which fit the packages, rather than the child; (2) using whatever packages are available or favored without regard to demonstrated efficacy or critical evaluation of the materials; and (3) using materials that fail to produce the intended outcome and continuing with them because they are included in the IEP.

If the IEP is developed in the recommended two-stage process, then the second stage could list materials or *types* of materials or procedures that have already been found to be effective in moving that child toward the objective. However, to make a specific commitment to a particular package in the first stage, prior to establishing its effectiveness with either large numbers or the child in question, is less appealing.

The specification of successful materials and media prior to placement and prior to prolonged diagnostic teaching presumes a predictive ability few if any of us have and can hardly operate to the child's advantage. It would seem appropriate that the first stage IEP concentrate heavily on prioritizing annual goals and specifying needed services; and that the second stage program implementers determine as quickly and efficiently as possible which available materials and media are *in fact* successful with that child. Then they can be listed.

The IEP must not be treated so lightly that the developers feel free to "just list anything—we'll change it later," nor must it be cast in bronze. When possible, the IEP might list materials and media illustrative of those to be used or might even list those to be tried first with a notation that others will be employed if those listed do not result in satisfactory progress.

Major potential benefits from listing materials and media are that more and better efficacy data could become available to the field and *that*, in turn, could encourage practitioners to become more demanding that such data be provided when commercial materials are published.

Physical Education. Every IEP must list the type of physical education program in which the child will participate. Physical education, as defined in the rules, includes special physical education, adapted physical education, and motor development. Unless a child has highly specific or unusual physical education needs, it may be sufficient to indicate which of those three types of programs will be used. If the needs are unique or if the prioritized goals include physical education, then more detail would be expected.

Other IEP Requirements. The IEP must also include (a) dates all educational and related services will begin and length of period they will be given, (b) a description of the extent to which child will participate in regular education programs, (c) justification for type of placement child will have, and (d) a list of the individuals responsible for implementing the IEP.

Summary and Conclusions

This discussion has focused on the IEP as it may be cooperatively developed by parents and professionals knowledgeable about the child and special education services. The IEP should be a cooperative undertaking and will be fully beneficial only to the extent it is so developed, implemented, and evaluated. P.L. 94-142 also contains potentially non-cooperative, i.e., adversarial, procedures and safeguards which are fully as important as the cooperative program planning. They are there to insure the program will be developed and implemented. Those responsible for IEP's must be equally concerned with procedures and substance. Our narrow focus has excluded even such closely related matters as the least restrictive principle in selecting the placement as specified in the IEP. Those implementing P.L. 94-142 may not so arbitrarily narrow their focus.

IEP's will help some children. They are a large step in the right direction. They fail, however, to address constructively the issue of how to improve teaching itself. Let us listen to a teacher:

> I know precisely what John's problem is. In oral reading he repeats known words and phrases which precede unknown words; he guesses from context at any word longer than four letters, and randomly guesses at when, where, these, they, then, and with. He does not say the appropriate short vowel sounds when shown vowels in isolation nor does he write the appropriate vowel when its sound is given, and overall he reads third grade materials at an average rate of 27 wpm, with nine errors.
>
> Furthermore, I know precisely how to monitor his progress. His charts show no substantial change over the last seven interventions I've tried—he's been in programs A, B, and X; he's been tutored by a mom, a peer, and a high school TA; and he's been in remedial reading for the past seven years.
>
> What I don't know is how to teach him not to guess, how to straighten out when, where, they, then, these, and with; how to teach short vowels so they stick, or how to break the repetition habit.
>
> The IEP requires me to list objectives based on assessment; to list what I'll try next, and to evaluate progress at least once a year. I can do that, but it doesn't meet John's need or mine. I need something better than trial and error to guide my teaching tactics. I want to know what will work with John and how to do it.

In sum, given the present state of the teaching world and our present understanding of IEP's, these observations are offered:

1. The inclusion of measurable objectives in the IEP will be an essential and appropriate step forward for those who have not previously used objectives.
2. The failure of the IEP to require specification of the teach-

Prescriptive Teaching and Individualized Education Programs 57

ing process reflects the failure of the field to agree on how this should be done.

Some believe that children are so different, one from another, that the best we can do is *try*, almost in trial and error fashion, a tactic or material or lesson and carefully monitor its effectiveness for that child. Others assert that we can identify and assess certain personalogical variables such as modality preference or learning style, and thereby predict and implement a successful "matched" treatment. Another group recognizes that while children do learn at different rates and that effective reinforcers must be systematically identified for each child, that *the nature or content of the task or concept* to be learned is the primary consideration in determining how it ought to be taught. The evidence showing the efficacy of certain educational materials, such as DISTAR, derived from task and concept analysis, is impressive by any standard and dazzling by usual educational efficacy standards. The monitoring approach also produces consistently successful teaching. No approach can at the present time be recommended more strongly than a combination of beginning with task-analytically-derived materials and monitoring the child's progress carefully.

3. Many traditional assessment tests do not readily yield teaching implications. Those that do, are task specific and/or criterion-referenced, and useful for IEP program planning.
4. The IEP's required listing of media and materials suggests the state of the art of materials development is further along than some perceive. The possible abuses of this listing must be guarded against and an effort made to use the potential data source of the listing to expand our knowledge of which materials do and do not accomplish their objectives.
5. P.L. 94-142 mandates administrative procedures and record keeping in great detail. It does not require or guarantee improvement of teaching itself. We are accountable only

for going through motions; we are not yet legislatively or judicially accountable for successful teaching.

Recommendations

1. If IEP's are to be maximally successful in improving educational outcomes for handicapped children, one of the greatest needs is for increased professional competence in developing and implementing programmed teaching sequences based on task and concept analysis. Few educators have yet learned how to analyze tasks and concepts so they (1) can be taught accurately, easily, and with maximum utility, (2) do not conflict with later learning, and (3) can be modified later to encompass exceptions or extensions. Presently we must rely on those educational materials and programs that have been based on task and concept analysis and have a data base of demonstrated efficacy with difficult to teach children. We must also rapidly develop a large cadre of persons competent in these analyses and in programming teaching sequences. High funding priority must be given to this personnel training.

2. Minimum criteria should be established and promulgated for demonstrated materials' efficacy. A blue-ribbon list of materials meeting these criteria should be widely disseminated and continuously updated. Practitioners should be urged to give priority consideration to materials from the list.

3. Procedures should be established for mandatory disclosure of efficacy data, if any, on all educational materials when they are published or disseminated.

4. States should be encouraged to develop data systems for retrieval and dissemination of information on the objectives taught under IEP's and the efficacy of procedures and materials used.

5. Practitioners should be encouraged to use only those materials and procedures in implementing IEP's which they can support as (1) reasonably likely to succeed, and (2) more likely to succeed than others equally available and feasible.

6. Full recognition should be given to the fact that until more teachers are better trained in how to teach skills and concepts and how to manage behavior, appropriate education will remain a promise of the future. Teacher training programs which demonstrate competency in teaching teachers to improve child performance must be supported and all others modified or eliminated. When all else is said and done, the skill of the teacher is the most important variable over which we have control in the teaching-learning process. Without expert teaching, IEP's will not substantially improve the quality of education for handicapped children and true prescriptive teaching will be impossible.

Notes

1. The parents' right to challenge district conduct after the IEP is approved and before the required annual review is less clear than is their right to participate fully in the development of the IEP. Thus, it may be to their advantage to give final approval of the IEP when actual implementation of the specifics is underway.
2. Although P.L. 94-142 is silent as to sexist tests, other applicable legislation and litigation also prevent their use with handicapped children.
3. Many educators have wondered if a law mandates an IEP only for handicapped children who need special education and related services might it not violate the equal protection rights of non-handicapped children? Certainly from an educational view all children ideally should be entitled to an IEP, but the 14th Amendment Equal Protection clause arguably does not prevent the state from discriminating between handicapped and non-handicapped in this fashion since there may be a rational basis for so doing. It should be noted that while P.L. 94-142 defines handicapped as needing special education *and* related services,

probably the *and* must be construed as *and/or* in order to be consistent with the intent of the statute as a whole.

Otherwise a handicapped child who needed only special education but no physical therapy, special transportation, etc., might be deemed ineligible. Similarly, a child who needed only physical therapy could conceivably be excluded.

References

Axelrod, H. Instructional materials selection and evaluation. *Enlightenment*, 1976, *1*, 31-34.

Berliner, D. C., and Cahen, L. S. Trait-treatment interaction and learning. In F. Kerlinger (Ed.), *Review of research in education (Vol. 1)*. Itasca, Ill.: Peacock, 1973.

Bracht, G. H. Experimental factors related to aptitude-treatment interactions. *Review of Educational Research*, 1970, *40*, 627-645.

Carnine, D. Direct instruction. In N. Haring and B. Bateman, *Teaching the learning disabled child*. Englewood Cliffs, N.J.: Prentice-Hall, Inc., 1977.

Haring, H., and Bateman, B. *Teaching the learning disabled child*. Englewood Cliffs, N.J.: Prentice-Hall, Inc., 1977.

Lloyd, J., Sabatino, D., Miller, T., and Miller, S. Proposed federal guidelines: Some open questions. *Journal of Learning Disabilities*, 1977, *10*, 69-71.

National Association of State Directors of Special Education. *Functions of the placement committee in special education: A resource manual*, 1976.

Nazzaro, J. Comprehensive assessment for educational planning. In F. Weintraub, A. Abeson, J. Ballard, and M. LaVor (Eds.), *Public policy and the education of exceptional children*. Reston, Virginia: Council for Exceptional Children, 1976.

Peter, L. *Prescriptive teaching*. New York: McGraw-Hill, 1965.

Ridberg, E., Parke, R., and Hetherington, E. Modification of impulsive and reflective cognitive styles through observation of film-mediated models. *Developmental Psychology*, 1971, *5*, 369-377.

Rosenshine, B. Classroom instruction. In N. L. Gage (Ed.), *Psychology of teaching; the 77th yearbook of the National Society for the Study of Education*. Chicago: National Society for the Study of Education, 1976.

Salomon, G. Heuristic models for the generation of aptitude-treatment interaction hypotheses. *Review of Educational Research*, 1972, *42*, 327-343.

Tobias, S. Achievement-treatment interactions. *Review of Educational Research,* 1976, *46,* 61-74.

Zeller, R. W. Perspectives in the individualized education program of P.L. 94-142. Working Paper No. 24. Eugene, Ore.: Northwest Special Education Learning Resources System, University of Oregon, 1976.

Author's Note

The author wishes to express her appreciation to the following for their helpful comments on an earlier draft of this paper: Jack Cawley, Educational Psychology, University of Connecticut, Storrs, Connecticut, and Robert Weisgerber, American Institutes for Research, Palo Alto, California.

4.
Individualized Learning and the Special Child

Robert A. Weisgerber

Background

Formalized, compulsory schooling evolved as an *administrative* arrangement intended to assure furtherance of our cultural and socioeconomic system through the education of each new generation. That formalized education would focus on the "average" student was pretty much a "given" throughout the first two-thirds of this century. Interestingly enough, individualization as an innovative practice in the schools can be traced back to the 1920's, although for those who could afford it one-to-one tutorial assistance has always been an alternative form of education.

Led by B. F. Skinner in the late 1950's, educators began to experiment with self-paced, small-step instruction. While some dramatic breakthroughs were accomplished, this "promising" area failed to sustain itself. O. K. Moore's work with very young slow learners and educable retardates, in which they happily and effectively learned to read and write in a special autotelic* "respon-

---

Autotelic is defined as an activity engaged in for its own sake, largely due to its intrinsic qualities rather than as a result of outside influence.

sive" environment, was an exciting breakthrough during the early 1960's (Moore, 1968).

In the 1960's, the American Institutes for Research (AIR) undertook a landmark longitudinal study called Project TALENT (Flanagan, 1970), involving some 400,000 high school students. It revealed that, as graduates, these citizens frequently found their formal schooling to be of little relevance to their needs and to their later lives. It seemed evident to Flanagan, as it had to other educational innovators (Goodlad and Anderson, 1963; Glaser, 1966), that learning should be centered on individual differences, not on the biases of teachers, administrators, or tradition. Respectively, their pioneering work led to PLAN*, IGE, IPI, and other systematic approaches to individualization.

Operational Definition, Concepts, and Models

Galileo once said, "You cannot teach a man anything; you can only help him to find it within himself." It is common knowledge that a student who sees no purpose to what he is "being taught," or who cannot grasp it due to its complexity, or who is simply bored with the pace of instruction, will not really *learn* the material being presented even though he may receive passing grades. In a position paper for the ERIC Clearinghouse on Media and Technology, Weisgerber (1972), offered a detailed discussion and definition of individualization that is *learner centered*. Generally, the definition states that the student should be involved in an active rather than passive way in shaping his or her own education. In other words, *individualized education should be responsive to the person as a human being with unique values, concerns, potentials, and problems*, real or imagined. It follows that a student in a truly individualized learning environment is generally aware that education has been *personalized* to meet his or her needs and that it facilitates *independent* progress. This definition applies equally to mainstreamed handicapped students as well as to their non-handicapped classmates.

Having stated the ideal, it is useful to keep in mind that nothing in the definition requires that educational planning and instruction be completely different for every student, but simply that it should differ as a function of the learner's (not the instructor's) needs. Nor does the definition imply that a preschooler or a developmentally disabled student must consciously participate beyond his or her capacity to do so, though it does suggest that such involvement may be a long-term possibility. Subsequent discussion will show how growth of personal responsibility can be incorporated in an instructional strategy.

At this point, it seems appropriate to acknowledge that, on balance, special educators have typically been more attuned to individualizing their instructional methods, trying to respond to learners' strengths and weaknesses, than have regular educators. The terminology used in this chapter (and in the papers and concepts cited in it) are largely that of regular education, and it is there where individualization for the mainstreamed handicapped will be most difficult, yet needed. That is, as handicapped students move toward "less restricted environments," it is generally implied that the new environment is less artificially structured and more within the variations associated with typical educational practice. As the environment becomes less prestructured, in a protective sense, it is absolutely essential that handicapped children learn how to cope with the situation and with teachers and students who are not always sensitive to their needs.

Key Concepts

Three closely related concepts underlie individualized education as it has developed in the last ten years. The first is the concept of individual differences, the second is individual potential, and the third is mastery learning. These concepts apply equally to handicapped and non-handicapped, and are essential to keep in mind when the mainstreaming of handicapped students is being discussed.

Individual differences make us all unique beings, differing along a number of dimensions: intellectual, social, attitudinal, physical, emotional, perceptual, and so on. Individual differences imply variance along continuums of ability, interests, and developed skills. In other words, each of us has strengths and weaknesses that we bring to the educational enterprise. One of the more thorough discussions of individual differences can be found in the collaborative volume *Individuality in Learning* (Messick and Associates, 1976), which covers cognitive styles, sex differences, environmental influences, and cultural impact.

Individual potential, a term appearing frequently in special education literature, simply means that each person, each individually differing student, can reach a level of performance commensurate with his or her unique makeup. Moreover, it assumes that a person's potential is not determined by his or her present state, but is able to be raised and that environmental influences (including the nature of special or regular instruction) can act to inhibit or expand that potential. Love (1972) has characterized mainstreaming in ecological terms. Weisgerber (1974) graphically illustrated the ecological relationships of the regular classroom environment and the special class environment in terms of human influences on the handicapped child (see Figure 4.1).

The third concept imbedded in individualized education is *mastery learning*. Bloom's (1968) eloquent arguments against normative grading, and later for formative and summative evaluation of student achievement (Bloom, Hastings, and Madaus, 1971), have importance for identifying a student's present level of development along a growth continuum, and for monitoring change. What is interesting, and something to be careful about, is how the mastery continuum is designed. Is it, as Gagné (1965) stated, a scale of learning hierarchies, with increasing levels of sophistication required of the learner as he or she moves from rote to problem solving skills? Or is it rather a structural way of looking at curriculum content, a kind of incremental teaching that led nearly all of us to

Figure 4.1

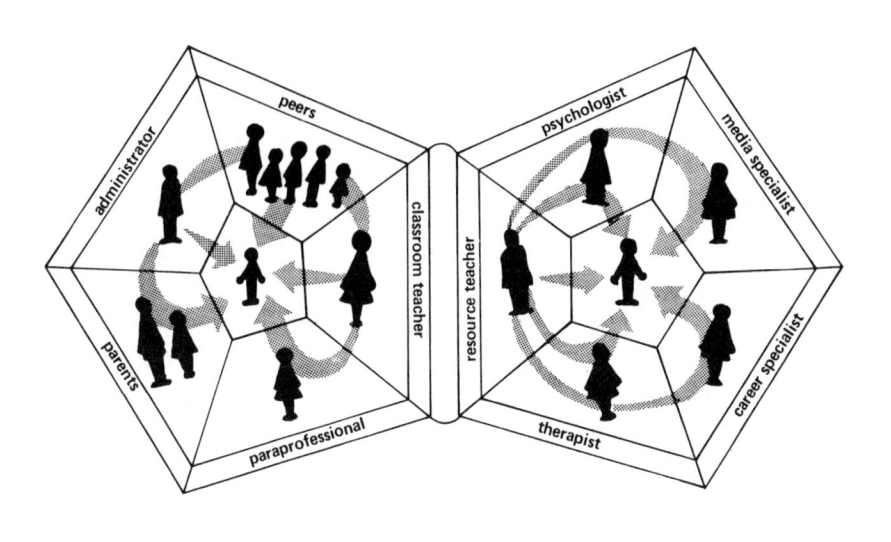

Ecological model of regular and specialist instructional teams serving the handicapped child.

learn the alphabet in isolation before we learned the alphabet imbedded in words? In either event, mastery learning says the learner should be able to demonstrate what he or she knows or can do.

Models Describing Student Growth

One of the most widely cited models within special education is one aligned with the "least restrictive environment" approach; it presumes that the reaching of individual potential can be enhanced by movement *up or down* the cascade model of alternative educational environments, as proposed by Deno (National Advisory Council on Education Professions Development, 1976). Unfortunately, the cascade model is essentially administrative in its distinctions, and stresses the locus of instruction, the constituency of students, and implicitly the presumed special training thought to be essential. What would be more helpful is a recasting of the cascade model in terms that acknowledge the degree of independence and self-sufficiency of the student and describe appropriate developmental growth stages. (Such growth could be social as well as academic.) A rather simple example was used by Weisgerber (1975) to describe how AIR's instructional materials for teaching blind students to read inkprint with an Optacon guided the student toward greater self-sufficiency in three stages: Tutorial Guidance, Self-Paced Practice Under Supervision, and finally Self-Selection of Subject Matter and Self-Monitoring.

An alternative model, offered by Woog and Berkell (1975), displays various levels of individualization, with greater degrees of choice behavior being possible as one moves upward from traditional instruction through variable pacing, aptitude-treatment-interaction, contract learning, and independent study; at one end, pace, strategy, and objectives are chosen by the teacher, while at the other end these are selected solely by the student.

Significance of the Key Concepts in Terms of P.L. 94-142

The requirements of P.L. 94-142 *outline* the elements that must be present in the written program but fall short of being helpful to the teacher in the field who must ultimately implement them. Indeed, local authorities and state officials are also largely "in the dark" as to how to proceed. Rightly or wrongly, there is concern in the field about the use of a mathematical formula to determine eligibility, at least in its present form and based on its apparent assumptions about test interpretability.

The regulations are not explicit about the way performance is to be assessed (which areas of individual difference are to be included), the degree of specificity that is appropriate for the planning of goals and objectives (reflecting the individual's potential in relation to a particular learning environment, learning materials, or

Individualized Learning and the Special Child

instructional support team), nor the distinctions between the criteria to be used for different kinds of evaluation purposes (mastery expressed in personal growth terms versus mastery as academic accomplishments).

It can be conceded rather quickly that the legislation cannot (and probably should not) go into detail in these matters. However, it is critical that *guidelines* for the implementation of P.L. 94-142 eventually address them fully or, as has already been implied by government officials, less stringent requirements for documentation be imposed.

In formulating its guidelines to the field, the Office of Education should itself be guided by processes that have been shown to be feasible at the local level, and are already in use in varying degrees. Some supported research projects and demonstration projects have contributed a great deal to our understanding of "what works." Simply put, these processes are (1) *profiling* the student's potential and present status, (2) *matching* the profile to appropriate learning experiences, (3) *adapting* the instructional approach, environment, and materials as necessary, and (4) *evaluating* outcome performance as well as the processes involved in shaping that performance. (*Evaluating* is not discussed here.)

Profiling the Student's Potential and Present Status

Individualization is not something done *to* students but something done *with* students. Accordingly, the assessment of potential and present status involves more than administration of a battery of tests. True, testing serves an important function in determining the student's existing competencies, be they in academic areas, processing areas, or motor skills areas. And, testing can be objectively administered and interpreted to reveal the magnitude of differences among individuals to be served. However, in order to focus individualization on *learning* rather than instruction, it is important that (within the student's capacity to do so) an accounting be made of the *student's* self-appraisal, including his or her concerns, preferences, and expectations.

Implicitly, a profile for the student will reveal strengths and weaknesses across the various areas being assessed. *Both* can be important since weaknesses translate into objectives for change, and strengths provide clues for approaching instruction in positive, productive ways.

Matching the Profile to Appropriate Learning Experiences

The selection of learning experiences that are likely to be effective for the individual should be less a matter of intuition and insight than a matter of heuristic determination. Careful documentation of trial instructional procedures (consisting of short instructional segments or modules) should be carried out so that there is a clear understanding (by the instructor and the student) of what works for the student. This documentation should be maintained as a readily accessible progress record, leading to better successive estimations of what *will* work, not just what *has* worked.

Fortunately, individualization does not mean that every experience must be unique to a particular student. (Even in group-paced, lecture situations a large share of the students may be served quite adequately.) As a practical consequence, the level of documentation for "what works" should be centered on instructional chunks, that is, on the types of modules and patterns of activities that have been carried out successfully.

Adapting the Instructional Approach, Environment, and Materials

Familiarity with the student's current testing and past performance (information supplied from records or instructors) will suggest *environmental* settings in which the student responds favorably. What may not be evident, and should be established, is whether the setting was strictly controlled (e.g., a positive reinforcement token economy) or general in nature (e.g., the typical, "regular" classroom).

Individualized Learning and the Special Child

The *approach* to instruction that is most suitable for a particular student should reflect that student's expressed preferences as well as its demonstrated effectiveness. For some students this may mean a preference for demonstrations and role modeling; others may prefer teaming with classmates; still others may prefer opportunities for independent study. Caution should be exercised in concluding, from these expressed preferences, that any one approach should be relied on. The lessons of student boredom in programmed instruction give testimony to the fallacy of a single method; and, in any event, students need help in *learning how to learn* even when they are in educational situations not especially designed for them.

The choice of *instructional media and materials* is, quite naturally, another crucial area requiring planning, awareness of previous effects when auditory, pictorial, or print materials were used, and awareness of any sensory limitations that the special student may have. See, for example, the thorough discussion by Northcott (1973) of the challenges confronted by mainstreaming of deaf students.

The adaptations of the instructional approach, environment, or materials to suit the needs of the handicapped student can often be accomplished in a fairly straightforward way, and surprisingly few are needed. The exercise of common sense judgment on the teacher's part can minimize problem areas; for example, the avoidance of meaningless phrases to the blind person, such as, "This part fits in here."

On the other hand, some adaptations (necessitated by some kinds of handicapping conditions) may be quite beyond the resourcefulness or means of the regular teacher. In such circumstances, close collaboration with media specialists, special education teachers, or other resource persons, together with adequate budgetary supplements, are clearly justified.

Large-Scale Systems of Individualization

The individualization of learning has been the subject of considerable discussion in educational circles since about 1970, when a number of systems-oriented approaches were introduced at the national level. Most of these systems are still in use, with an increasing number of participating schools and an aggregate of students numbering into the hundreds of thousands. There is much that can be learned from these systematic efforts that is applicable to the handicapped, even though the systems themselves were not originally designed with the special-needs student in mind.

Computer-Assisted Instruction

In the CAI model, the body of information (course content) is defined in advance, in much the same way as programmed instruction during the 1960's had been, but the capacity of the computer allows a considerably enlarged range of branching opportunities and remediation loops. Probably the two best known CAI systems having relevance for the handicapped are PLATO, a result of Bitzer's work at the University of Illinois (Bitzer, Lyman, and Easley, 1966), and the CAI system developed by Suppes at Stanford University (Suppes, 1965).

Aspects of the PLATO project which bear special mention, because of their potential significance for the handicapped, include:

- the linkage of the computer to multimedia display options, which has ramifications for those students with sensory handicaps; and
- the flexibility of the PLATO system to be adapted to a wide range of subject areas, including a number of college level courses, which has ramifications for more mature handicapped students.

The CAI work of Suppes at Stanford University has been largely focused on the concept of "drill-and-practice." This research, summarized by Jamison, Suppes, and Wells (1974), emphasized in-

struction in mathematics and beginning reading. Some significant aspects of this approach are:
- Drill-and-practice instruction has been viewed as supplemental to regular instruction, on the order of ten to thirty minutes per student per week, with greater exposure resulting in greater gains in performance.
- It has been tried with handicapped persons (312 deaf students) with positive results.
- Remote terminals have been widely placed in schools around the country, and even tried in homes.

Computer-Managed Instruction

A fundamental difference between computer-assisted instruction and computer-managed instruction is that the latter avoids the time/access restrictions of the former. The CMI student does not interact *directly* with the computer either as a source of information or as a tutor. Rather, the computer is used as a support system in conjunction with particular instructional materials, and monitors progress toward specific instructional objectives. CMI has been used by the United States Navy to cut training costs markedly by reducing training time an average of 42%, using well designed programs of individualization (Polcyn, 1976).

One educational CMI system that is in wide use across the country is PLAN* (Program for Learning in Accordance with Needs) (Flanagan, 1972; Weisgerber and Rahmlow, 1971). In PLAN*, the computer is used to score and log student performance and to match the selection of Teaching-Learning Units (TLU's) to the student's abilities and career aspirations. Originally developed by AIR on behalf of Westinghouse Learning Corporation (WLC), and marketed by WLC for about eight years, the system has gone through a number of changes, the most recent of which allows the school district the options of (1) sharing the central computer through remote terminals, (2) utilizing a mini-computer at the local level to process both business affairs and PLAN* data, or (3) incorporating TLU's, objectives, or other PLAN* components into the curriculum without any requirement for computer management.

Currently, the PLAN* directory lists some 119 schools using the system in the states of Illinois, Iowa, New York, Montana, Florida, Indiana, Colorado, Georgia, Michigan, Kansas, California, Minnesota, Missouri, Louisiana, Maine, Pennsylvania, Arizona, Nebraska, and Washington, D.C. PLAN* has been used with increasing frequency for disadvantaged students and inner-city populations in Brooklyn, Oakland, Washington, D.C., Los Angeles, and New Orleans. In interesting contrast, it is also being used to good effect in a 56-student, "one-room country school" in Wyoming.

Research. PLAN* has been most heavily researched in Illinois, where faculty at Northern Illinois University conducted several studies in the Aurora Public Schools. As reported in Westinghouse newsletters, the researchers found that (1) PLAN* students showed greater gains than those in traditional classrooms, (2) black and Latin children seemed to be closing the gap between themselves and majority youngsters, and (3) PLAN* students' self-esteem had radically improved.

Dr. Elda Wilson, Director of Special Education at Bradley University, studied teacher attitudes in 15 PLAN* schools in 6 states. She found that among the 234 teachers responding to her 100-item Teacher Attitude Scale, 85% thought PLAN* should be continued the next year. 79% thought students had a better learning experience than they had previously, 73% preferred teaching in PLAN*, and 73% felt PLAN* students developed a better self-concept.

PLAN Curriculum and Materials.* The curriculum spans language arts, reading, mathematics, science, and social studies. It ranges in level from kindergarten through high school. In addition, some schools have added their own objectives in Spanish, art, physical education, industrial arts, and home economics; and the computer management system helps them to keep track of their own objectives as well as the regular PLAN* curriculum. A feature of PLAN* is that students not only receive assignments of an individualized nature but also ones calling for interaction with peers and others.

The basic complement of materials involves Teaching-Learning Units used in conjunction with standard texts and supplemented with audio cassettes, instructional guides (giving supplemental information about content to the student), activity sheets, teacher directions, TLU tests, and placement/achievement tests. Training orientation manuals and computer manuals are provided, and training workshops are conducted periodically for teachers and administrators. Costs for the system vary considerably, depending on the amount of instructional materials supplied locally, the extent of the PLAN* curriculum that is chosen for use, and the amount of computer utilization that is elected. However, Westinghouse Learning Corporation maintains that "many schools have been able to have PLAN* without spending any more money per student than they do for more traditional classrooms" (Westinghouse Learning Corporation, 1976).

Other Major Systems

Four other approaches that have been widely adopted are IPI (Individually Prescribed Instruction), IGE (Individually Guided Education), ATS (Audio-Tutorial System), and PSI (Personalized System of Instruction). Briefly, the key features of these systems are:
- (IPI) A carefully graduated, highly sequenced curriculum in which the student must demonstrate mastery at each level (fully discussed in Chapter 6).
- (IGE) A multi-unit way of reorganizing the regular school to afford greater opportunity for one-to-one teaching in combination with small-group and large-group instruction (fully discussed in Chapter 5).
- (ATS) Widely copied at the college level, this is a system

for independent study (developed by Samuel Postlethwait at Purdue University) utilizing audiotape directions, workbooks, and still and motion visual materials.
- (PSI) This is a college-oriented system also referred to as the Keller plan and involves a heavy use of proctors (i.e., informed teacher substitutes) to allow greater instructor contact with students, and the opportunity to repeatedly "challenge" a unit of study without fear of failure until mastery is demonstrated.

The above partial listing of individualization efforts reveals considerable diversity in approach, but all share a common intent ... making it possible for the regular classroom teacher to focus attention on individuals to a greater extent than is possible in the traditional classroom.

This is a laudatory aim but not one that is without risk nor guaranteed to produce positive results. In a recent large-scale, longitudinal study of school programs, some of which involved individualization, the American Institutes for Research (1976) found no clearcut evidence to show that innovations were consistently correlated with higher achievement as measured by standardized tests. Setting aside any discussions of the appropriateness of norm-referenced standardized tests as used in the Coles/Chalupsky study, as opposed to the use of criterion-referenced tests or even the assessment of other personal/social outcomes, it is evident that changes in educational practices are *not* likely to lead to tangible, demonstrable benefits unless:

(1) sufficient planning takes place prior to program start-up;
(2) requirements for extra time and effort and for administrative commitment are squarely met when the program is first implemented; and
(3) evaluative expectations about these new programs are set at reasonable levels, taking into account the "shakedown" problems that participants often encounter (Weisgerber, 1976).

Some Factors of Special Interest

In considering the potential of individualization for handicapped persons, who no doubt will increasingly be placed in education environments that are "least restrictive" as mandated in P.L. 94-142, this writer has freely drawn upon his own training and background in instructional media and technology, upon his involvement in the development of PLAN*, and upon recent research he has conducted with a view to improving various living skills and educational opportunities for the handicapped. Within that framework, the following factors seem to be of considerable importance, and should not be ignored during any BEH program planning that focuses on individualization.

1. *Attitudes* and misconceptions *about* the handicapped and *by* the handicapped can override, and interfere with, and even prevent effective individualization. Just as teachers can kill student initiative through condescension, handicapped students can kill teacher enthusiasm by bitter reactions to unintentional goofs.

2. *Teacher training* in the techniques of individualization is absolutely critical, since the students cannot be expected to believe in something if it frustrates and confuses the teacher. Clearly, if teacher competency cannot be demonstrated, the handicapped student can hardly count on having his or her needs met.

3. *Team planning* by the special educator and regular educator(s) should be frequent and a matter of routine, not simply in response to problems that arise. Furthermore, it takes teamwork to assure that the plan is carried out; the roles of paraprofessionals and peer tutoring should not be overlooked.

4. *Instructional development* is a new movement, spearheaded by educational technologists, that has been used with good results. Based on an analysis of content, instructional resources, and goals, and used in such special areas as medical and dental studies, it merits attention as a way to specify how and when the various media should be incorporated into individualized programs (see Gagné and Briggs, 1974; Kemp, 1977).

5. *The availability of technological aids and devices* to augment the handicapped person's performance can be an important contributor to independence in and out of school. As an example, a blind reader trained to use the Optacon could use the regular PLAN* TLU's, but brailling them all would constitute a formidable local burden.

6. To facilitate individualized services, new *cost models* should be developed in lieu of the excess-cost-by-category blanket arrangement that is currently used. New models should give local districts more discretion in the degree to which they provide resource people, materials, or even specialized training (such as in the use of new electronic environmental sensors), if these can be shown to meet individual educational needs. In other words, schools should have the same flexibility and options for equipping and training students that are available through rehabilitation counselors after graduation.

7. *Learning styles* represent one of the most intriguing educational concepts introduced in recent years. Variously referred to by the terms Aptitude-Treatment Interaction, Trait-Treatment Interaction, Ability-Treatment Interaction, and Achievement-Treatment Interaction, ATI has attracted the interest and study of a number of scholars and prominent researchers, including Cronbach and Snow (1969) on individual difference in learning ability as a function of instructional variables, Snow (1970) on relationships between media and aptitudes, Salomon (1972) on heuristic models for testing alternative instructional methods, and Tobias (1976) on prior achievement as a basis for prescribing alternative treatments. The complexity of issues raised in this research defies summary here and, unfortunately, the findings of these researchers lack consistency. Nevertheless, ATI is an area in which a learner's characteristics are thought to have a bearing on the appropriateness of particular instructional approaches and thus has obvious theoretical implications for the handicapped, and for individualization in general. It will bear watching in the future, particularly

if it can prove to be useful for cognitive mapping, and consequent program planning.

8. *New physiological and behavioral research*, equally intriguing, and less well known to regular educators, is research on the differential functioning of the left and right hemispheres of the brain. Sperry (1975) and Grady (1976) have related this work to education and argue that emphasis on verbal instruction favors the left hemisphere, where speech is controlled. Grady states:

> The left hemisphere, characterized by linear, logical, and verbal operations, is dominant. Education's three R's—reading, writing, and arithmetic—all are types of learning associated with the left hemisphere. However, the right hemisphere, characterized by intuitive, holistic, and nonverbal operations, is also important.

Assimilative, analyzing, and problem-solving skills are more associated with holistic thinking than they are with linear thinking and are more in demand when a learner is in a self-guided and self-monitored situation. Conjecturally, this line of reasoning could help explain why some students are unable to adjust to individualized learning while others (presumably right hemisphere types) embrace it readily.

Suggested Avenues for Research and Development

Turning to practical, "next-step" areas of promise, a number of projects seem worthy of federal support in order to fully explore the potential of individualization for the handicapped and to devise guidelines or identify models for its effective implementation. Some promising R&D topics would include:

Exploratory Studies

- A project to *establish reliable, workable procedures* for (a) the "profiling" of different handicapped students, (b) "matching" those students to relevant course content, (c) "adapting" the instructional variables as appropriate, and (d) "evaluating" the process and the resulting perfor-

mance in a standard way that will be credible and acceptable to the majority of special educators. These workable procedures should then be broadly disseminated by means of newly developed guidebooks in each of the four areas.
- A project aimed at *sensitizing* regular teachers, regular students, administrators, counselors, and even parents to handicapped students' actual concerns and needs (not stereotyped ones), and simultaneously helping them to discover these students' hidden potential, which is often surprising.
- A project to *explore the potential of the ombudsman* (client advocate) in local school districts or at county levels in order to assure individual, personalized services for handicapped students. Such a person would function not so much as a legal arbiter but rather as a spokesperson or counsel to assist the individual, the school, the parents, and others to work cooperatively toward mutual goals.
- A project aimed at increasing the *flexible use of human resources*, both school staff and concerned others. Differential staffing, which accompanies some forms of individualization, has shown that different people have different skills, and expensive professionals are not always most appropriate for a task at hand.

Evaluative Studies
- A series of projects to *identify "exemplary" programs* in which P.L. 94-142 appears to have been carried out cost-effectively while increasing the scope of services to handicapped students. To be exemplary, student benefits within the school district should be *clearly* documented. This procedure is more likely to produce true "demonstration projects" (worthy of support) than the present BEH/legislative mandated categorical programs.
- A project to *identify and describe non-traditional* education and training *approaches* that appear to meet handi-

capped students' needs for independent living skills and vocational viability. Dignity doesn't come from being educated and "smart" ... it comes from being able to apply what you've learned in useful ways. There are probably many more educational programs for the handicapped that emphasize the former than the latter.
- A project to *review* the structure and function of the BEH funded network of *materials centers* to determine the extent to which they have (or can) support individualized programs for handicapped students in accordance with P.L. 94-142. In this respect, individualization would seem to portend a need for effective interface between educators in the field and a national information system.
- A project for *improving the liaison and coordination within various departments of the federal government* (and at state levels as well) concerning their efforts to serve the handicapped. Few of the federal programs which offer training appear to function cooperatively and few exhibit any depth of understanding about individualization techniques.

References

American Institutes for Research. *Impact of educational innovation on student performance: Project methods and findings for three cohorts, Project LONGSTEP final report: Volume I, Executive Summary.* Palo Alto, Calif.: Author, 1976.

Bitzer, D. L., Lyman, E. R., and Easley, J. A., Jr. The uses of PLATO, a computer controlled teaching system. *Audiovisual Instruction*, January 1966.

Bloom, B. S. Learning for mastery. *Evaluation Comment* (Center for the Study of Evaluation of Instructional Programs, University of California at Los Angeles), May 1968, *1*(2).

Bloom, B. S., Hastings, J. T., and Madaus, G. F. *Handbook on formative and summative evaluation of student learning.* New York: McGraw-Hill Book Company, 1971.

Cronbach, L. J., and Snow, R. E. *Individual differences in learning ability as a function of instructional variables.* Stanford, Calif.: Stanford University, 1969.

Flanagan, J.C. The goals of Project PLAN. *Education,* February-March 1970, *90*(3), 191-206.

Flanagan, J. C. The PLAN System as an Application of Educational Technology. *Educational Technology,* 1972, *12*(9), 17-21.

Florida State Department of Education. *Individualizing instruction for competency-based education.* Author, July 1975.

Gagné, R.M. *The conditions of learning.* New York: Holt, Rinehart, and Winston, Inc., 1965.

Gagné, R.M., and Briggs, L.J. *Principles of instructional design.* New York: Holt, Rinehart, and Winston, Inc., 1974.

Glaser, R. Psychological bases for instructional design. *AV Communication Review,* 1966, *14*, 433-449.

Goodlad, J. I., and Anderson, R. H. *Nongraded elementary school.* New York: Harcourt, Brace, and World, Inc., 1963.

Grady, M. P. Students need media for a balanced brain. *Audiovisual Instruction,* November 1976, *21*(9), 46-48.

Jamison, D., Suppes, P., and Wells, S. The effectiveness of alternative instructional media: A survey. *Review of Educational Research,* Winter 1974, *44*(1), 1-67.

Kemp, J. E. *Instructional design, A plan for unit and course development* (Second Edition). Belmont, Calif.: Fearon Publishers, Inc., 1977.

Love, H. D. *Educating exceptional children in regular classrooms.* Springfield, Illinois: Charles C. Thomas Publishers, 1972.

Messick, S., and Associates. *Individuality in learning.* San Francisco, Calif.: Jossey-Bass, Inc., 1976.

Moore, O. K. Autotelic responsive environments and exceptional children. In R. A. Weisgerber (Ed.), *Instructional process and media innovation.* Chicago, Illinois: Rand McNally, 1968.

National Advisory Council on Education Professions Development. *Mainstreaming: Helping teachers meet the challenge.* Washington, D.C.: Author, 1976.

Northcott, W.H. (Ed.) *The hearing impaired child in a regular classroom: Preschool, elementary, and secondary years.* Washington, D.C. The Alexander Graham Bell Association for the Deaf, Inc., 1973.

Polcyn, K. A. The U.S. Navy computer managed instruction (CMI) satellite demonstration. *Educational Technology,* December 1976, *16*(12), 21-25.

Salomon, G. Heuristic models for the generation of aptitude-treatment interaction hypotheses. *Review of Educational Research,* Summer 1972, *42*(3), 289-326.

Snow, R.E. Research on media and aptitudes. In G. Salomon and R.E. Snow (Eds.), *Commentaries on research in instructional media: An examination of conceptual schemes. Viewpoints.* Bulletin of the Indiana University School of Education, 1970, *46*(5), 63-91.

Sperry, R. Left-brain, right-brain. *Saturday Review,* August 9, 1975, 30-33.

Suppes, P. *Computer-assisted instruction in the schools: Potentialities, problems, prospects.* Technical Report No. 81. Stanford, Calif.: Institute for Mathematical Studies in the Social Sciences, Stanford University, October 1965.

Tobias, S. Achievement treatment interactions. *Review of Educational Research,* Winter 1976, *46*(1), 61-74.

Weisgerber, R. A. *Trends, issues, and activities in individualized learning.* Stanford, Calif.: ERIC Clearinghouse on Media and Technology, 1972.

Weisgerber, R. A. Individualizing for the handicapped child in the regular classroom. *Educational Technology,* November 1974, *14*(11), 33-35.

Weisgerber, R. A. Planning for the individualization of learning with blind students. *Education of Visually Handicapped*, December 1975, 7(4), 112-115.

Weisgerber, R. A. Individualized learning. In S. E. Goodman (Ed.), *Handbook on contemporary education*. New York: R. R. Bowker Company, 1976.

Weisgerber, R. A., and Rahmlow, H. F. The process of learning in PLAN. In R. A. Weisgerber (Ed.), *Developmental efforts in individualized learning*. Itasca, Illinois: F. E. Peacock Publishers, Inc., 1971.

Westinghouse Learning Corporation. *PLAN*: An individualized learning system*. Iowa City, Iowa: Author, 1976.

Woog, P., and Berkell, D. A conceptual model of individualization. *Educational Technology*, September 1975, *15*(9), 33-35.

Author's Note

The author wishes to express his appreciation to the following for their helpful comments on an earlier draft of this chapter: Barbara Bateman, College of Education, University of Oregon, Eugene, Oregon, and Margaret C. Wang, Learning Research and Development Center, University of Pittsburgh, Pittsburgh, Pennsylvania.

5.
Implications of Individually Guided Education Programs for Mainstreaming

Fred H. Wood

No one model can be used by all schools to mainstream all handicapped children. There are, however, some essential characteristics that should be present in models adopted to fulfill the intent of P.L. 94-142. This chapter will identify some of those characteristics and then describe one model, Individually Guided Education (IGE)—a model that might be used to mainstream mildly and moderately handicapped children into the regular classroom for instruction. The reader is reminded that this is only one aspect of mainstreaming and, while the model under consideration holds considerable promise for some children, it is not appropriate for the more severely handicapped.

Essential Characteristics of a Mainstreaming Model

The essential characteristics for models that might be adopted to mainstream can be classified into three categories. The first, Program Characteristics, includes organization of staff, instruction, curriculum, parent involvement, and student involvement. The second, Staff Development Characteristics, is concerned with model adoption, in-service strategies, support systems, and ongoing improvement. The third, Outcome Characteristics, deals with the desired effects of the model on students, teachers, and parents.

The specific characteristics identified under each category are based upon an analysis of the literature on mainstreaming and individualization. These characteristics are not considered inclusive but, in the judgment of this writer, are crucial for an effective mainstreaming model. Those that are mandated or implied by P.L. 94-142 are asterisked.

Model Characteristics

Since there is a need for increased communication and cooperative planning and teaching among classroom teachers and special education staff in working with mainstreamed students, the program should include:

* teaming arrangements that facilitate communication, planning, and teaching where the classroom teacher and specialist work together to educate handicapped students assigned to them;
* role specialization in the areas of diagnosis, planning, implementation, and assessment to allow for maximum use of the special talents and skills of both the classroom teacher and specialist;
— multi-aged grouping and other organizational techniques which allow teams of regular classroom and special education teachers to get to know and plan instruction for the same students over two or more years;
* teaming by regular and special education teachers to monitor progress of the handicapped students assigned to them; and
— teaming by regular and special education teachers to schedule students, space, time, curriculum, materials, and staff.

Implications of Individually Guided Education Programs 87

Since students—both handicapped and non-handicapped—who will be attending the school/classes that adopt a mainstreaming model will represent a wide range of abilities, needs, interests, learning styles, strengths, achievements, handicaps, and learning disabilities, the model should include:
* a wide range of options in the amount of time one spends in the regular classroom, special resource room, and special classes for the handicapped;
* a systematic diagnostic planning process for developing individualized learning programs for each child which includes long range goals, short term objectives, and appropriate learning experiences based upon data indicating the child's current level of achievement and development;
* a systematic management of a wide range of learning opportunities which vary the medium of instruction, degree of structure and direction given students, instructional mode (large group, small group, independent study, peer-peer, etc.), type of reinforcer, people, and setting;
— the use of community resources in the learning program; and
* continuous assessment of students' progress and adjustment of their learning program based upon those data.

Since parents of handicapped and non-handicapped students will have a wide range of feelings and questions about their child's involvement in the mainstreaming model and the nature of the program at their child's school, the model should provide for:
* open two-way communications between parents and the school staff;
* increased positive participation of parents in the school program;
* shared responsibilities of parents and teachers for decisions about the nature of the child's learning program;
* involvement of parents and students in identifying the child's goals, objectives, and learning program in assessing

the child's educational progress and in other important decisions affecting the child.

Since handicapped and non-handicapped students have had limited contact with each other and both have a need to respect and understand each other and to become more responsible and independent, the model should provide:
- an opportunity for students to develop, understand, and value the differences and similarities that exist among all humans; and
- an opportunity for students to develop independence, self-confidence, and a positive view of themselves.

Staff Development Characteristics

Due to the limited time (1978-1980) available to implement a model to mainstream handicapped students and the varied experiences regular classroom and special education teachers have had with handicapped children and individualized instruction, the model should include:
- a systematic process for involving the school staff in the decision to adopt the model;
- systematic in-service strategies and support materials that will facilitate efficient and effective development of skills, understandings, and attitudes necessary to operationalize the model;
- local personnel trained to facilitate the in-service and systematic change; and
- in-service through actual staff work with handicapped students who are in the regular classroom.

Since the extent to which the handicapped will be mainstreamed in the regular classroom depends heavily upon the degree to which the staff in the adopting school refines their initial implementation of the model, the model should include:
- procedures for continuous assessment of staff and program

Implications of Individually Guided Education Programs 89

operations and development of plans and in-service to improve current practice;
— formal and informal means of obtaining and using feedback to improve professional performance; and
* a school-wide committee to monitor and promote progress toward the implementation of a model.

Outcome Characteristics

Since the selection of a model will be made to achieve certain ends, the implementation of the model should have a positive effect on:
— staff attitudes toward individualization, the model itself, and the educational climate in their school;
— student achievement so that it is as good as or better than prior to adoption of the model during the first two years of implementation;
* student—handicapped and non-handicapped—attitudes
* toward school, themselves, and their ability to operate in a self-directed, independent manner; and
— parent attitudes toward the school, staff, program, and their child.

The staff development process that supports the model should develop:
* staff commitment to individualize instruction and continuous professional and program improvement;
* the skills and understanding for regular and special teachers necessary to individualize instruction and implement the model; and
* the ability to carry out the legal responsibilities described in P.L. 94-142.

The Model: Organizational Characteristics

There are a growing number of models designed to facilitate mainstreaming of the handicapped. Nyquist (1975) has identified a variety of such models, ranging from accommodation of handicapped students in the protected settings of the special school or classroom with only limited opportunities to participate in the non-academic phase of the regular program, to accommodation of handicapped students in all phases of the regular program. These models reflect Deno's (1970) view of mainstreaming as a commitment to appropriately move handicapped children from special schools and full-time special classes to part-time special classes, to regular classes with supplementary instructional services, and then to full participation in the regular classroom. Embedded in this view of mainstreaming is the position that *all* handicapped children would not and should not be placed in the regular classroom.

However, the focus of this chapter is on selecting a model to accommodate the greatest number of handicapped students in the regular learning environment. The Madison Plan, (Blum, 1971), the Stevens Point Program, (Adams, 1972), the Houston Plan (Meisgeier, 1976), the Norfolk Plan (Newton and Stevenson, 1976), the Maryland Continuum Design (Mopsik and Hession, 1976), and the Prescriptive Education Program (Frankel, 1976) all reflect this view of mainstreaming. Each has been adopted by a limited number of schools committed to moving handicapped children into the regular program. All contain some, but not all, of the essential model characteristics noted earlier.

There is, however, one model which has been adopted by over 3,000 elementary and secondary schools to individualize instruction that does appear to respond to virtually all the essential model characteristics. This model is Individually Guided Education (IGE) and has been used by several schools to mainstream the handicapped into the regular classroom. It is a model which allows maximum involvement of the mildly and moderately handicapped in the regular learning environment with or without supplementary assistance.

The IGE Model

The IGE Model was developed by the Wisconsin Research and Development Center. This model brings a number of innovative practices typically used in isolation into a total system designed to facilitate individualized and personalized instruction in elementary and secondary schools. It provides various degrees of structure and choice for students based upon diagnostic data about the learner's needs, interests, skills, learning style, academic ability, and learning strengths and disabilities. It also takes into account both parent and student desires and concerns.

IGE has two major thrusts, individualization and continuous improvement. Individualization refers to organizing and operating in a school so that the program is adapted to the child. Options are designed and made available in the instructional program and students are systematically placed with learning options that match their needs. The second thrust, continuous improvement, relates to organizing the school and operating in a manner that promotes change and improvement of staff performance and the instructional program.

The major components of the IGE Model include (1) team teaching and multi-age grouping, (2) teacher-advisor, (3) individualized curriculum, (4) systematic planning process, (5) parent-home-school involvement, and (6) continuous improvement. The first five components respond directly to the organizational characteristics, while the sixth is related to staff development.

These components are implemented in a manner that is congruent with 35 process outcomes or goals (IGE Outcomes) which define the parameters of this model. While these Outcomes are implemented in each IGE school, the specific ways they are operationalized is determined by the school staff. The IGE Outcomes are reported in the Appendix of this chapter.

Team Teaching and Multi-Age Grouping

The Model calls for the school to be organized into smaller units or teaching teams. The teams in elementary schools usually include 3 or 4 teachers and from 60 to 110 students and in secondary schools 5 or 6 teachers and 120 to 180 students. Each team is comprised of students from two or more age-grade groups, teachers who represent a cross section of the staff, aides, a team leader, and other adults who might become involved in instruction.

The teaching staff is assigned so that each team has a wide range of skills and expertise at its disposal. Role specialization is practiced to make use of the special competencies of each staff member.

These teams make every effort to create small, very personal mini-schools within the school where teachers and students work and learn together over two or three years. The students and teachers get to know each other well and develop warm, close, positive relationships that make individualization possible. Individualization is facilitated because of the teachers' in-depth knowledge of such things as student needs, interests, skills, and learning styles and the trust that develops between students and adults. The teaming and time factors are both critical in creating this knowledge and trust.

Individualization is also supported in the model by having the teaching team conduct as much of the students' instruction as possible. This enables the teachers who know the most about the students to plan, implement, and assess their instructional program.

Another important facilitator of individualization is the fact that the team has control of its instructional time, space, material, staff, and students. Thus, additional time can be scheduled for team members to plan or to work with individuals or small groups of students. This also enables the teams to select appropriate instructional materials, rather than being confined to an approved textbook. Lack of these kinds of control has been a block to many teachers trying to individualize.

Each team is provided a space within the school so they and their students have a home base when they are not involved in instruction. This is a spot where each student and each teacher has some personal turf. Student lockers and teachers' offices are usually in this space or just adjacent to it.

Implications for Mainstreaming. The uses of teaming and multi-aged grouping as described here have several implications for mainstreaming. For example, the membership of each instructional team could include a teacher trained in special education. This staffing arrangement provides the regular classroom teachers with immediate access to the expertise they need to teach the handicapped children assigned to them.

In planning instruction, the special teacher can work with other team members to diagnose student needs, identify and develop appropriate learning experiences and materials, and teach handicapped students in their team. The special teacher is also available to share this same expertise when planning and conducting instruction for non-handicapped children. This strengthens the program available to all children.

Where the regular classroom teachers are able to handle instruction for the handicapped, they are scheduled to teach them in groups with the non-handicapped. When students need the special education teacher, the team reschedules that teacher and the students who need special instruction into a resource class. Even here one might find non-handicapped students, if they had the same instructional needs as the handicapped. In other words, the team can create their own "resource room" within their teaching space using their own staff.

The assignment of a special education teacher to teams also increases communication between special and regular teachers, first, because they interact daily as they plan and teach all the students assigned to them. Second, communication is improved because the regular teachers have someone who can help them determine when students need the special services of a separate class or specialist such as the school psychologist or speech therapist. Third, communication is improved because the team members have someone they work with and trust who has the expertise to bring in and make effective use of other special education staff.

The use of multi-aged grouping also facilitates mainstreaming because it allows two or more years for the team to work with the same handicapped children. Since it usually takes an extended time to get to know students well enough to build appropriate learning programs for them, the longer time in the same team enables the regular teachers to accrue the advantages currently enjoyed by the special education teachers. Thus, it is easier to have continuity of learning from year to year and to provide appropriate learning programs. Also, the relationships and security that build when students are with familiar adults over the several years are important to both the handicapped and non-handicapped child.

The Teacher-Advisor

Today, most teachers are encouraged to act as advisors when students need them. In the IGE school, teachers are not only encouraged to do this, they are *expected* to. The role of teacher-advisor is a key component of the IGE model and includes program planning, progress reporting, and human development.

The teacher-advisor concept is structured into the educational experience of every student throughout his or her school career. Meetings are routinely scheduled by the team; daily in the elementary and, at least, weekly in the secondary schools. This assures regular interaction between advisees as well as between advisees and advisor. Some students require more time and attention than others; all students require some time.

Program Planning. More than any other member of the school staff, the advisor is responsible for coordinating the planning of learning programs for each advisee in the manner which best accommodates his or her needs, interests, and abilities. Advisors collect diagnostic data on each advisee and share those data when the teaching team plans the learning program for their students. During the planning process, the advisors make sure each of their advisees' needs are—to the extent possible—taken into account in the learning options the team develops.

Once the learning program is planned by the team, the advisor, with parents, assists advisees in developing personalized programs which take advantage of the available opportunities. If mistakes are made in the options selected for a student, the advisor is empowered to make an immediate change after consultation with the parents and the child.

Though the teachers on the team assume responsibility for specific details of the instructional program, the advisor insures that overall balance, control, and structure are present in each advisee's program. The advisor also makes sure that the student's long-term program will meet all district and state requirements. Adequate program planning assumes that the advisor will collect and record each advisee's abilities, interests, and goals, as well as a complete record of accomplishments, past test results, need for direction, learning skills and disabilities, teacher comments, and other diagnostic data.

Progress Reporting. At a minimum of twice a year, the advisor convenes a parent/student/advisor meeting for each advisee. These conferences provide an opportunity for students to report their progress to their parents; parents to make suggestions and comments about their child's learning program; and all three parties to talk about matters of mutual concern and to shape the student's program for the next several months.

The advisor's role in the reporting procedure is one of assisting the students to prepare for the conference and supporting them while they make their reports. The advisor insures that the students note accomplishments since the last conference, mention present objectives and activities, and describe plans for future objectives and learning activities. The degree to which students take the lead in this conference is dependent on their maturity and readiness for such a responsibility.

The advisor, in the secondary schools, is also able to keep both the student and parents informed about the total number of credits earned, the number now being pursued, and those yet to be met. Each conference is an opportunity to compare the student's learning program against his or her overall, long-range goals and allows a dialogue between parents, students, and advisor that does not exist in most traditional situations.

Human Development. A school that emphasizes success for all students makes the basic assumption that all students can succeed, that there is something inherently *right* about every student, and that every student has potential. As the third area of their responsibility, advisors must transmit this sense of confidence to their advisees. Through regular weekly meetings with small groups of advisees, advisors help their advisees recognize their own potential, to clarify their worth as individuals, to examine their beliefs and values, to set personal short and long-range goals, and to develop an understanding of and ability to interact with others.

With the current emphasis on humanizing the curriculum, the IGE Model makes it much less likely that a student will complete any school year without having a meaningful relationship or engage in honest communication with teachers and students. The human development activities encourage students to develop the maturity, the excitement, and the self-confidence that is possible when one knows that someone cares.

Monitoring Student Success. Finally, the advisors monitor their advisees' successes and growth toward long- and short-range goals. It is the advisors' responsibility to determine whether the program developed for each of their advisees is being implemented and if that program is producing the desired results. This responsibility shapes their activities as they conduct program planning, progress reporting, and human development activities.

Implications for Mainstreaming. When handicapped children are mainstreamed in an IGE school, they would also be assigned a teacher-advisor. Mildly handicapped students who do not require the attention of a specialist are assigned to a regular classroom teacher. Those who are moderately handicapped but who are still able to learn in the regular classroom are assigned to the special educator on the team. Placement with an appropriate advisor is most important and is done through careful planning by the entire team. Other specialists are involved in this decision when deemed necessary by the specialist on the team.

This advisement system has several positive implications for mainstreaming as defined by P.L. 94-142. It responds directly to the requirement to involve parents in developing their child's goals and program. Parents of handicapped children now have a person who keeps them informed of their child's progress and who involves them in any changes in placement or program. They know that even though their child is in the regular classroom, there is someone monitoring his or her progress and making sure he or she is receiving an appropriate education. Someone is there whom they can contact when they have concerns about what is happening to their child.

The fears that have been expressed by some parents about their child not getting enough attention when the handicapped are mainstreamed can be dealt with in a personal, direct way through their child's teacher-advisor. The advisor will also be able to communicate the personal and social value of mainstreaming for the non-handicapped to the parents on a regular basis.

In the human development sessions, both handicapped and non-handicapped have an opportunity to develop a mutual understanding of each other. It is in these sessions that the handicapped will develop the skills and support they need to cope and interact with their non-handicapped peers. Here, also, is one place where the non-handicapped will learn empathy, concern, and respect for others and identify things they have in common with all their peers.

The progress reporting sessions provide the handicapped with positive feedback about their growth. These sessions also provide parents with an opportunity to see how their child is progressing toward independence and self-reliance in an environment which includes non-handicapped children. Such conferences are an ideal time for parents to examine their child's records and to provide the advisor with additional information helpful in individualizing and personalizing their child's learning program.

Individualized Curriculum

The IGE curriculum includes three ways of organizing the learning process. They are, Short Courses/Units, Contracted Learning, and Out-of-School Study. These categories are intended to be descriptive rather than limiting. That is, short courses/units might very well include some community study; out-of-school study might draw on the resources of short courses/units; and contracted learning units might very well involve a significant amount of time outside the school.

Short Courses/Units. Short Courses (or Units) are pre-planned programs, running for two to nine weeks, and are directed at the achievement of a specific set of behavioral objectives. These courses are taught to a number of students scheduled to meet at specific times. Some emphasize a single discipline, others are interdisciplinary in nature.

The sequence for short courses or units is flexible; all students need not take the same ones. Each student, based upon his or her diagnosed strengths and weaknesses, will be advised to take the short courses he or she needs.

Prerequisites are kept at a minimum, especially in the secondary schools. These offerings are designed so that students can, if they desire, combine short courses into groupings which would be comparable to the present block structure of most curricula. Other students may opt not to follow the present structure.

Short Courses/Units ideally: (a) allow students to select some learning objectives and activities that accommodate their individual needs and goals, (b) use pretesting as a basis for determining sophistication and abstractness of content, teaching methods, and emphasis, (c) provide for teacher evaluation based on observation, work sampling, paper and pencil tests, and student self-evaluation, and (d) allow students to proceed through their learning program at a pace commensurate with their abilities and interests.

Contracted Learning. As the school implements IGE, the instruction moves from an emphasis on short courses to small group and paired learning contracts. Between 5% and 55% of the instruction for each student may be completed through contracts. The degree to which students are involved in this kind of learning depends upon their learning style, learning skills, and cooperative decision-making on the part of the advisor, parent, and student.

Contracts are planned by the student, advisor, and teacher and are conducted with parental consent. The contract is given structure by a written statement which indicates (a) the objectives to be achieved, (b) learning experiences, (c) materials to be used, (d) the teacher's role, (e) where the learning is to take place, and (f) the length of time to be devoted to meeting the objectives.

The contract allows a student to take a short course in a basically self-directed fashion, operating under the general direction of a teacher or advisor. Such units would also allow the school to create special courses or units for individual or small groups of students. It is a type of unit designed specifically to get at objectives in the curriculum that the student, the advisor, and/or parents feel are important for him or her in reaching his or her overall goals and satisfying individual needs.

Out-of-School Study. Out-of-school study, in the strictest sense, is a special kind of contracted learning. These experiences involve both learning in the classroom with a teacher and a work and educational experience in the local community with adults in various governmental and social agencies, businesses, and schools.

Most out-of-school learning is directed by a contract that includes instructional objectives, defined learning experiences, backup materials, in-school learning sessions, observation and work in the community, and time to meet with the teacher supervising the out-of-school program. The teacher is responsible for helping the student clarify and understand what he or she is experiencing. The student is evaluated against the cooperatively developed objectives.

Options to Personalize the Curriculum. In addition to these three alternative ways of structuring the curriculum, the IGE Model provides for options within Short Courses, Contracted Learning, and Out-of-School Study. These options include adjusting the objective, media, mode, learning experience, evaluation, and learning environment based upon diagnostic student data. The matching of students to the appropriate options within a particular short course or contract is the key to individualization as described by the IGE Outcomes.

Implications for Mainstreaming. The learning alternatives of the IGE Model are essential to mainstreaming the handicapped. This view of instructional options suggests that more than the placement of a student in a short course or resource room within the team is important. Once the child is placed, the teacher must adjust such things as the objective, instructional materials, learning experiences, amount of structure and direction, and assessment procedures to the individual child.

These kinds of adjustments allow students of diverse abilities and interests to learn together. It is more likely that handicapped and non-handicapped children will be able to learn in the regular classroom under these conditions.

The use of contracted small group learning also allows grouping of students for special instructional needs within the classroom. This, coupled with the availability of the special education teacher, enables the team to handle more of the handicapped child's program within the regular classroom. This kind of contract also permits teachers to group students with common needs to work on an objective(s) with much less consideration as to whether or not the students are handicapped.

Out-of-School Study can be employed by both the handicapped and non-handicapped to achieve a number of important goals. For the handicapped child, this learning option provides an opportunity to prepare for the world of work and to cope with living in the adult society. It is also an alternative means of learning through real concrete experiences, rather than through reading and other more abstract instructional strategies.

Systematic Planning Process

Since sound planning is crucial to successful development of an individualized program, the IGE Model includes a systematic planning cycle. This cycle involves teachers in the following sequence of activities:

* setting overall goals for their students' learning;
* diagnosing student needs, interests, learning styles, basic skills, goals, and learning strengths and handicaps;
* planning instruction to provide appropriate learning options for their students based upon these diagnostic data;
* scheduling students into appropriate learning experiences and settings;
* implementing instructional plans; and
* assessing the effects of instruction.

These activities are repeated at several levels as the learning program is developed and refined. First, at the team level, where the broad offerings for students are identified and tentative decisions are made about specific options—objectives, media, mode, etc.—within short courses/units, contracted learning, and out-of-school study. The next sequence of planning occurs once students are scheduled. Here the teachers diagnose students assigned to their offerings, and further adjust the objectives and learning experiences to accommodate individual differences. The next level occurs as the planned program is in progress and teachers and advisors discover other adjustments that are needed to meet the needs of the students assigned to them.

Since the team has control over scheduling its time, space, materials, staff, and students, they can be more flexible than in most schools. This flexibility allows teachers to make the program modifications implied by the IGE Planning Cycle and required to have an individualized program. This control over scheduling of resources also allows the teachers to use all the learning opportunities available in their school, including those not provided by the team.

Throughout the IGE planning process, students are involved—to the extent possible—in the decisions shaping their learning program. Their involvement in goal and objective setting, selection and development of learning experiences, and self-assessment depends on their maturity and readiness for such responsibilities. The IGE Model places a major emphasis on developing students who can take on these responsibilities and eventually become dependable, independent learners.

Implications for Mainstreaming. Since mainstreaming requires cooperative planning among regular classroom teachers and specialists, it is essential that the planning process they use be systematic and continuous. The IGE Planning Cycle is both systematic and continuous and provides an efficient means of building and refining individualized programs for students with a wide range of educational needs, interests, and abilities.

A review of the IGE Outcomes related to this component also reveals that all of the requirements of P.L. 94-142 for building individualized programs for each handicapped child can be accommodated in this planning process. These legal requirements include a statement of the student's present level of performance; a statement of annual goals and short term instructional objectives; specific education services to be provided the child; and a time when the proposed program is to be implemented and assessed.

References

Adams, C. A program for mainstreaming at Stevens Point, Wisconsin, *Bureau Memorandum,* 1972, 6(3), 9-11.

Beldon Associates. *Individually Guided Education Program: National evaluation study, 1972-73.* Unpublished Research Report. Beldon Associates, Dallas, Texas, 1973.

Blum, E.R. The Madison Plan as an alternative to special class placement: An interview with Frank Hewett. *Education and Training of the Mentally Retarded,* 1971, 6(1), 29-42.

Boardman, C.R., and Hudson, C.C. *Development of a cost analysis model which schools may use to determine budget needs for implementing Individually Guided Education (IGE).* Unpublished Research Report. University of Nebraska, Lincoln, 1973.

Deno, E. Strategies for improvement of educational opportunities for handicapped children. In M.C. Reynolds and M.D. Davis (Eds.), *Exceptional children in regular classrooms.* Minneapolis: University of Minnesota, July 1970.

Frankel, H.M. Portland Public Schools' prescriptive education program. In Philip H. Mann (Ed.), *Mainstreaming special education.* Reston, Virginia: Council for Exceptional Children, 1976.

Goodman, L.V. A Bill of Rights for the handicapped, *American Education,* July 1976.

Hackett, J., and McKelligin, G. *Individually Guided Education in multiunit organization.* Unpublished Research Report. Janesville, Wisconsin, 1973.

Kelley, E.A. Implementation of the IGE Model: Impact on teachers, *Phi Delta Kappan,* 1974, 55, 570.

Kelley, E.A., Wood, F.H., and Jockel R. *Teacher perceptions of school climate and the implementation of Individually Guided Education (IGE).* Unpublished Research Report. University of Nebraska, Lincoln, 1973.

Lazich, G.S. *The effects of the Wisconsin design for reading skills developed in K-3, Nile Michigan, 1971-73.* Unpublished Research Report. Niles Public Schools, Niles, Michigan, 1974.

Mayfield, I.R. *A comparative study: Two methods of teaching mathematics—conventional and individualized.* Unpublished Research Report. Jackson, Mississippi, 1973.

Meisgeier, C. Mainstreaming in a system context. In P.H. Mann (Ed.), *Shared responsibility for handicapped students: Advising and programming.* Miami, Florida: Bannyan Books, Inc., 1976.

Mopsik, S.I., and Hession, L.A. The Maryland design for a continuum of special education sources. In P.H. Mann (Ed.), *Mainstreaming special education,* Council for Exceptional Children, 1976.

Newton, E.R., and Stevenson, C.A. Mainstreaming in the Norfolk Public School System. In P.H. Mann (Ed.), *Shared responsibility for handicapped students: Advising and programming.* Miami, Florida: Bannyan Books, 1976.

Nyquist, E.B. *Mainstreaming: Idea and actuality.* State Education Department, Albany, N.Y., 1975.

Paden, J.S. *Study of the possible effects of early stages of implementing IGE upon standardized achievement scores.* /I/D/E/A/ Staff Memorandum, Dayton, Ohio, 1973.

Williams, M.H., and Godwin, C.M. *Children's attitudes and implementation of Individually Guided Education (IGE).* Unpublished Research Report. University of Nebraska, Lincoln, 1973.

Wood, F.H. Attitudes toward a personalized, individualized high school program. *NASSP Bulletin,* 1976, *60,* 21-25.

Wood, F.H., and Brunworth, G.C. *Assessment of growth in student self-direction.* Unpublished Research Report. Penn State University, 1975.

Author's Note

The author wishes to express his appreciation to the following for their helpful comments on an earlier draft of this chapter: Barbara Bateman, College of Education, University of Oregon, Eugene, Oregon; Philip Cartwright, Professor of Special Education, The Pennsylvania State University, University Park, Pennsylvania; and Peter Fanning, Director, Special Education, Colorado State Department of Education, Denver, Colorado.

APPENDIX
IGE Outcomes

1. All staff members examine their own goals and the goals of any new program before they decide to adopt the program.
2. The school district approves the school staff's decision to adopt a new program before it is implemented.
3. The school is organized into teams or learning communities ... and each team has students, teachers, aides, and a team leader.
4. Each teaching team contains a diverse staff.
5. The teaching team members have effective working relationships ... they respond to one another's needs, show trust in each other's motives and abilities, and use techniques of open communication.
6. Each team includes approximately equal numbers of two or more student age groups.
7. Each student identifies with a specific teacher he or she views as a warm, supportive person who is concerned with enhancing the student's self-concept and sharing accountability for the student's learning program.
8. Individual teachers as well as teams of teachers develop and implement personalized in-service programs.

9. Each teaching team cultivates open communications with parents and with the community.
10. Teaching team members have sufficient time for group meetings.
11. Teaching team members select the broad educational goals for their team.
12. Teaching team members use role specialization and division of labor as they plan, implement, and assess their activities.
13. Each student's learning program is based on specific learning objectives.
14. Learning programs include a variety of learning activities ... and the learning activities include the use of different media by various sizes of student groups.
15. The student and teacher consider these factors when selecting the student's learning activities: peer relationships ... achievement ... learning styles ... interest in subject areas ... and self-concept.
16. Students select learning activities from their own team's offerings, except when unique learning needs can only be met by other teachers in other settings.
17. Teaching team members make those decisions that affect their team's arrangements of time, facilities, materials, staff, and students.
18. The staff and students use people and places in the local community as resources to broaden the learning options available to students.
19. Students are increasingly responsible for assessing their own progress and achievement ... and they work with the teachers in a variety of ways to measure how well their learning has taken place.
20. Students work individually, with other students, with staff members, and with their parents as they plan and evaluate their progress toward educational goals.
21. Teachers and students work together to systematically gath-

Implications of Individually Guided Education Programs

er, record, and apply useful information about each student's interests, abilities, and achievement as they plan personalized learning programs.
22. The steering committee formulates school-wide policies and operational procedures and resolves problems involving two or more teams.
23. The steering committee coordinates school-wide in-service programs for the total staff.
24. The school has joined a cooperating group of schools that assist each other in implementing new programs and identifying and solving problems by interchanging personnel.
25. The school works with the cooperating group of schools to stimulate and share solutions to educational problems and to have an outside source of new ideas.
26. Teaching team members analyze and improve the ways they work together as a functioning group.
27. Teaching team members constructively critique the learning program plans for individual students and for the team.
28. The steering committee members analyze and improve the processes they use in working as a group.
29. Students know the objectives of the learning activities in which they are engaged.
30. Students accept increasing responsibility for selecting their learning objectives.
31. Students accept increasing responsibility for selecting and developing learning activities for specific learning objectives.
32. Students accept increasing responsibility for their total learning programs.
33. The steering committee ensures the continuity of educational goals and learning objectives throughout the school ... and keeps them consistent with the broad goals of the school system.
34. Students take an active part in making decisions on school-wide activities and policies.

35. Teaching team members use formal and informal methods of observing and constructively critiquing one another's performance in the learning environment.

6.
Individually Prescribed Instruction (IPI): Implications for Teaching the Handicapped

David Helms

Given the facts of normal human variability, psychologists and educators have argued persistently that student learning should be more efficient when instruction is adapted to individual student differences. With the increase in the range of variability that will distinguish learners, as the handicapped move more into the educational mainstream, it seems predictable that the need for attending to students, individually, will become a more insistent demand upon teachers than it has been previously. Thus, implementation of P.L. 94-142 will heighten the need for a technology of individualized instruction, not only to sustain or enhance the efficiency of learning of handicapped and non-handicapped students as they are instructed together, but, at a more fundamental level, to simply assist the teacher in attending in a reasonable and equitable manner to the multiplicity of diverse and compelling instructional needs of all students.

The law does, in fact, require that handicapped children be provided individualized education programs and that these programs be a matter of written record. However, because special educators have been long-time advocates of individualized education programs and because the definition of such *programs*, as it appears in the law, does not specify individualized *instruction*, per se, it would be difficult to argue conclusively that the law has mandated individualized instruction for the handicapped as a logical consequence of the greater heterogeneity introduced into many classrooms.

The chief distinction between individualized education *programs*, as defined by the law, and individualized *instruction* seems to be the greater frequency of diagnosis, prescription, and evaluation in individualized instruction. And, although individualized education programs only require evaluation "on at least an annual basis," the law's requirement of short-term instructional objectives and its implicit preference for more frequent evaluations of students' individual achievement of these objectives could make individualized education programs and individualized instruction very close kin, indeed.

It is interesting to note in this connection that among the skills that the National Advisory Council on Education Professions Development (1976) has predicted teachers will need, as the handicapped are more and more educated with the non-handicapped, are those for individualizing instruction. The set of skills listed by the Council appears below.

 (a) Teachers should understand how a handicap affects a child's ability to learn in the classroom.

 (b) Building on this understanding, teachers need to become competent in recognition of handicaps and prescription of learning experiences. They will need to be able to identify specific conditions and prescribe appropriate instructional experiences. The level of sophistication in this area need not be high, as expert advice and support

should be available through one of many possible delivery models.
- (c) In conjunction with diagnosis and prescription of learning experiences, regular classroom teachers will need skills in the individualization of instruction. The variance posed by handicapped children necessitates at least some degree of individualization, requiring a familiarity with resources and instructional materials for handicapped children.
- (d) Teachers will need a better understanding of the emotions of handicapped children. Not only must they be able to empathize with the handicapped, but also they must be able to focus a part of the education experience on the child's emotional development.
- (e) Teachers need to develop a conceptual and practical understanding of the process of mainstreaming. Integral to this is the development of a new understanding of the role of the special education teacher as a consultant and resource person. Perhaps most importantly, teachers will need to develop competence and self-confidence in dealing with handicapped children based upon skills developed through experience, additional in-service training, and use of support services.
- (f) Finally, teachers will need to be able to apply this collective understanding in their interactions with parents of the handicapped and with non-handicapped.

The skills listed by the Council, including those for individualizing instruction, are predicated entirely upon projected needs of teachers in attending to handicapped students as they become more numerous in regular educational environments. The Council does not emphasize the proportional decrease in teacher attention to non-handicapped children that likely will result from the disproportionate needs of the handicapped. Yet, this decrease can be anticipated with some certainty.

Here, then, are the multiple opportunities for, and challenges to, instructional technology, i.e., providing teachers with a strategy and materials that will aid them: (1) in attending to the instructional needs of learners, individually, in a classroom characterized by an expanded range of learner differences; (2) in attending to the variety of special needs of handicapped children in regular classroom settings; and (3) in maintaining or improving the quality of instruction offered to all students under the aforementioned circumstances. It is this writer's belief that Individually Prescribed Instruction (IPI), or similar instructional systems that are specifically designed to assist teachers in matching students with instruction according to their individually determined needs, can take us a long way toward meeting the opportunities and challenges of educating the handicapped *and* non-handicapped.

Against this background and expectation, this chapter is devoted to: (1) a brief discussion of the IPI experience, and (2) the identification of some implications for the implementation of the Education for All Handicapped Children Act that may be gleaned from among those perspectives on IPI. Before proceeding, however, several disclaimers are in order. First, let it be noted that the writer is reporting his own observations gained from experience with Research for Better Schools' (RBS) program development and dissemination work. He is not speaking for RBS or the Learning Research and Development Center (LRDC) of the University of Pittsburgh, the creator of IPI. Second, the writer does not purport to have special qualifications for educating the handicapped nor did the curriculum and instruction work of RBS give particular attention to the special needs of the handicapped during the period of time under discussion in this paper. Finally, it should be understood that the continual references to specifics of the IPI program are only intended as experienced-based examples to illustrate or further explicate individualization needs or possibilities. There is no intention to promote the adoption of this specific product. Indeed, a basic notion that guided the preparation of this chapter holds that, while the technology represented by IPI should be very relevant to mainstream education, specific applications of that technology with handicapped students very likely would benefit from adaptations determined by careful studies of the technology in use.

Description of the IPI Program

Individually Prescribed Instruction was initially conceived and developed in the middle 1960's by LRDC and the Oakleaf Elementary School located in suburban Pittsburgh. The center and the school engaged in the Oakleaf Project in order to redesign the school's curricular and instructional materials and to facilitate teachers' attempts to adapt instruction to meet the different learning needs of students. RBS, a Philadelphia-based educational laboratory, entered the scene in 1966 when the IPI products were ready for wide-scale testing and demonstration.

During its subsequent long association with LRDC, RBS became increasingly responsible for IPI program dissemination/implementation activities, training of school administrators and teachers for individualization of instruction, evaluation of program implementation and effects, and data-based program revisions. The following discussions are based largely upon the writer's participation in these actions and his association with and study of the work of the LRDC. Two publications in particular, Lindvall and Bolvin (1967) and Lindvall and Cox (1970), have also influenced much of the description of IPI that is presented here.

The use of "program" in connection with IPI is done deliberately and requires clarification. IPI is more than a set of instructional materials; it is a way of thinking about and carrying out instruction based upon a body of psychological theory and research. At the heart of this approach to instruction is the assumption that learning is a function of the appropriateness of the match of students with instruction, relative to their learning needs as they have been determined for each learner, individually.

Figure 6.1

The Behavioral Science Basis of IPI

Behavioral Components	IPI Elements
(a) analysis of the competence, state of knowledge and skill, to be achieved	(a) continuum of behaviorally specified content objectives
(b) description of the initial state with which the learner begins	(b) criterion-referenced, Curriculum Placement Tests and Unit Diagnostic Pretests
(c) conditions that can be implemented to bring about change from the initial state of the learner to the state described as the competence	(c) provisions for instructional options including self-instructional booklets correlated with the objectives
(d) assessment procedures for determining the immediate and long-range outcomes of the conditions that are put into effect to facilitate change from the initial state of competence to further development	(d) criterion-referenced Curriculum Embedded Tests (short run) and Unit Diagnostic Posttests (long run)

Overview of the Program. Working from this orientation, IPI was shaped to conform with certain behavioral science concepts of instruction explained by Glaser in 1965. (These were updated by Glaser in 1975.) The essential components of this approach as Glaser explained, are listed at the left of Figure 6.1, and the corresponding elements of IPI that are intended to accommodate those concerns in the classroom are juxtapositioned on the right.

Even a minimally satisfactory presentation of the IPI program requires more attention to the elements listed in Figure 6.2, and this attention will be given shortly. However, an emerging overall

Individually Prescribed Instruction (IPI) 115

Figure 6.2

IPI Operational Plan

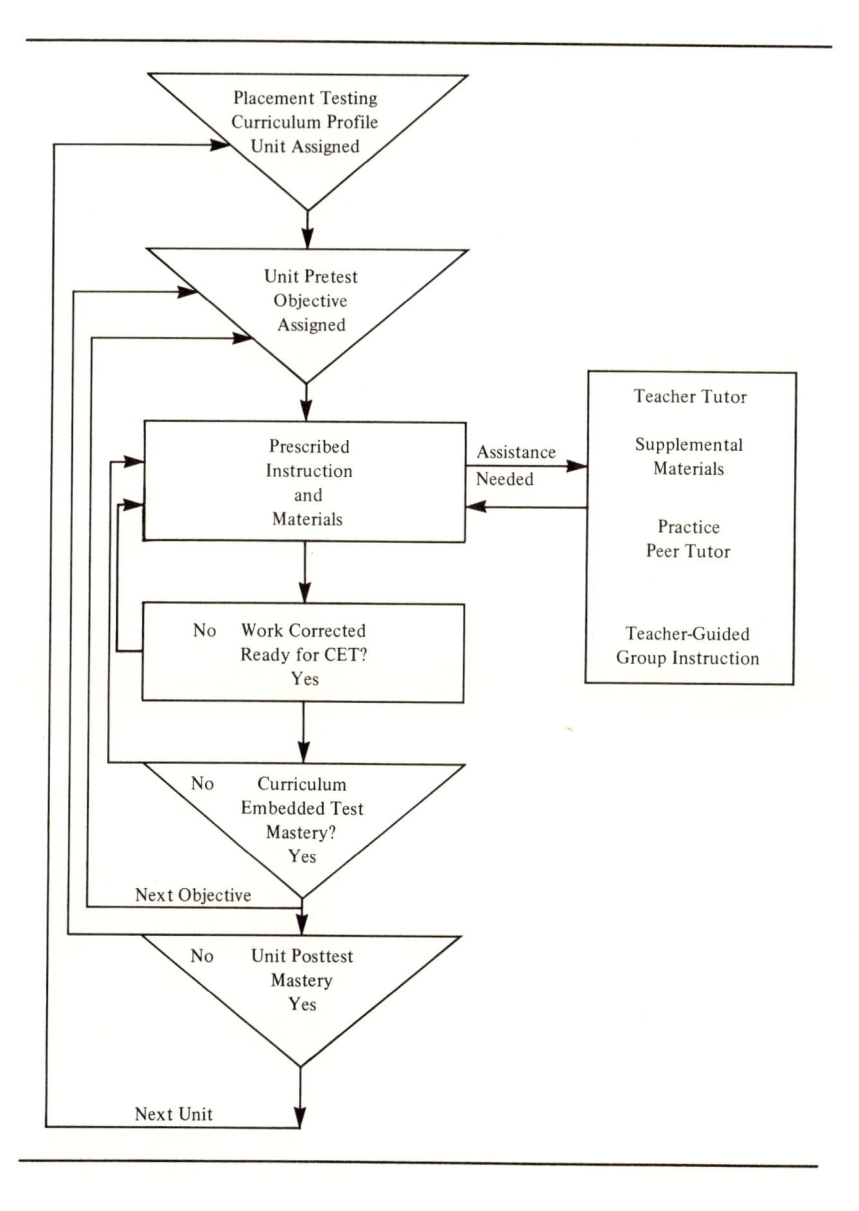

- Placement Testing / Curriculum Profile / Unit Assigned
- Unit Pretest / Objective Assigned
- Prescribed Instruction and Materials — Assistance Needed → Teacher Tutor / Supplemental Materials / Practice / Peer Tutor / Teacher-Guided Group Instruction
- Work Corrected / Ready for CET? No / Yes
- Curriculum Embedded Test Mastery? No / Yes
- Next Objective
- Unit Posttest Mastery No / Yes
- Next Unit

view of the program may be enhanced at this point by a cursory examination of the IPI classroom management plan. The schematic shown in Figure 6.2 provides an overall view of the IPI management plan and suggests the functions and relations of IPI elements.

Thus far, this section briefly touched on the psychology of IPI, its main elements, and the plan it provides for teacher management of instruction and learning. All of these are intended to support the teacher and his/her efforts to help students achieve a full set of IPI goals. It is true that IPI instruction is expected to lead students to mastery of content objectives, as has been frequently emphasized in the literature. It is also true that mastery of content is only one of a set of IPI instructional goals. Moreover, these goals represent the affective domain as well as the cognitive—and, indirectly, the attitudinal and feeling dimensions as well as the behavioral ones. However, IPI's developers felt that positive attitudes and feelings toward learning emerge as students experience success as self-managing learners and because behaviors are most amenable to direct measurement and facilitation, IPI's instructional goals focus on these behaviors rather than on attitudes and feelings, per se. These goals, reproduced from Lindvall and Cox (1970), appear below:

    I. Every pupil makes regular progress toward mastery of instructional content.
    II. Every pupil proceeds to mastery of instructional content at an optimal rate.
    III. Every pupil is engaged in the learning process through active involvement.
    IV. The pupil is involved in learning activities that are wholly or partially self-directed and self-selected.
    V. The pupil plays a major role in evaluating the quality, extent, and rapidity of his progress toward mastery of successive areas of the learning continuum.
    VI. Different pupils work with different learning materials

and techniques of instruction adapted to individual needs and learning styles (pp. 30-34).

However limited this section has been, hopefully it has conveyed a rough overall notion of the IPI program. Now, the additional comments that were promised on the IPI elements are in order. These comments elaborate the specific function of each element and clarify the prerequisite conditions and contingent relationships that bind the elements and provide the rational basis for the IPI management system.

Continuum of Behaviorally Specified Content Objectives. If there are content objectives that learners are expected to achieve, then it is a premise in IPI that learners will more likely achieve them if instruction is shaped by clear and specific statements of these objectives. Further, the adequacy of instruction will be more readily determined if the objectives are stated in terms of observable student behaviors. Finally, the progress of students will likely be more certain and steady if the "objectives" of a curriculum are so arranged that the learners are always in possession of the learning that is prerequisite to the achievement of the immediate objective they are attempting. Thus it is that IPI programs have been erected upon a base of content that has been carefully analyzed into subject matter and behavioral components, stated in objective form, and sequenced in a manner that assures the prerequisite competence of students as they progress in their learning.

Criterion-Referenced Curriculum Placement Tests and Unit Diagnostic Pretests. Two convictions are fundamental to IPI programs: (1) students ought not to be matched with instruction they have already mastered, and (2) they ought not to be matched with instruction for which they lack the prerequisite competencies necessary for learning success. Consistent respect for these convictions requires some means that teachers can use to determine the curriculum competency of entering students and their next instructional needs. The Curriculum Placement Tests and Unit Diagnostic Pretests, respectively, are typically used in IPI programs to assist teachers in matching students with appropriate instruction.

Because accurate placement is so critical in IPI programs, norm-referenced tests are of little value. Rather, IPI instruments are criterion-referenced measures with items related to specific objectives in such a way that test scores reflect the actual achievement specified by the curriculum objectives.

Of course, it would be presumptuous to suggest that content competencies and needs are the only pieces of information teachers need in order to appropriately match students with instruction. It would also be naive to assume that testing technology will ever be adequate to the task of providing all the kinds of information that are needed for appropriate matching. Hence, teachers are encouraged to use all of their personal and professional skills to acquire and use whatever information will assist them to match each student more accurately with individually appropriate instruction.

Provisions for Instructional Options. Glaser (1975) has noted that "teachers are trained to teach a class and have had much less experience in teaching individuals. Moreover, instructional materials, especially in the elementary schools, are designed to be used with groups rather than with individuals." It might be added that school materials typically depend upon teachers for translation and interpretation.

IPI instructional materials are not intended to be teachers' exclusive instructional resources. Indeed, teachers are encouraged to develop and locate materials to complement and supplement IPI materials. However, the IPI materials are intended to be a solid base of support—one that has been tested and found workable and effective. Of course, the IPI materials do not always work for every student, and, in these cases, teachers correctly depart from them to search for different learning approaches to mastery of the terminal objectives. Departures from this baseline are usually motivated by the need for additional practice or enrichment experiences, or to exploit interest-arousing opportunities.

In order to avoid the classroom conditions of confusion and/or "downtime" that may result from the inability of students to learn from materials frequently used in individualized classrooms, great care was taken in the preparation of IPI materials. In lieu of any known way to deduce effective instructional sequences (Lumsdaine, 1964), IPI developers subjected instructional materials to successive cycles of testing and revision until they achieved optimal effectiveness.

While books have been written about the practices and principles that were borrowed or developed in the preparation of IPI materials, here it is only necessary to provide a few illustrative descriptions of these to convey some notion of the thinking that guided the development effort. These examples have been selected from Lindvall and Bolvin (1967).

- To the extent possible, instructional objectives should be ordered in a sequence which makes for effective pupil progression with a minimum number of gaps or difficult steps, and with little overlap or unnecessary repetition.
- If pupils are to work through a curriculum on an individual basis, it is essential that instructional materials be such that pupils can learn from them without constant help from a teacher and can make steady progress in the mastery of the defined objectives.
- For individualized instruction, conditions must be provided which permit each pupil to progress through a learning sequence at a pace determined by his own work habits and by his ability to master the designated instructional objectives.
- If instruction is to be effective, it must make provisions for having the student actually carry out and practice the behavior which he is to learn.
- The final criterion for judging any instructional sequence

must be its effectiveness in producing changes in pupils, and feedback concerning pupil performance should be used in the continuing modification and improvement of materials and procedures.

Criterion-Referenced Curriculum Embedded Tests and Unit Diagnostic Posttests. According to IPI philosophy, there can be greater assurance that expected learning has occurred if students are able to demonstrate the performances they have achieved, and these performances match well with descriptions of the program's criterion performances. Further, IPI philosophy holds that students are more likely to progress satisfactorily the more accurately and securely they have achieved objectives that are prerequisites for achievement of subsequent objectives.

The formal means for monitoring students' progress in IPI are the curriculum-embedded-tests (CETs) and the unit posttests. CETs are measures designed to assess achievement of a single objective, and they enable the teacher and pupil to make short-term evaluations of the student's progress. Posttests also measure achievement, and, since curriculum units typically consist of several objectives, the posttest may be thought to comprise a set of measures that are parallel forms of the CETs in the units.

Before leaving this area, some attention must be given to two very important questions: (1) When to test? and (2) How accurate must a test performance be to be accepted as mastery? In IPI, tests are intended to be motivating experiences. It is intended that students will be successful in their test performances and that these successes will motivate them to persist in their study and progress. When to test, then, is really a matter of teacher and student estimating when sufficient learning has taken place to assure a high probability of student success on the test.

Ideally, 100 percent performances are desirable both from a student reinforcement point of view and from the view that students should be protected from future failures that are almost assured when they move through the program without first having secured

Individually Prescribed Instruction (IPI)

the prerequisite behaviors. However, as a practical matter, 100 percent test performances are not always necessary to assure that students have achieved adequately to support their future progress. Different kinds of objectives imply different standards.

Many people would acknowledge that different degrees of accuracy are in order depending upon whether the objective is to identify the numerals 0-9 or to demonstrate competency in adding two, two-digit counting numbers. Most likely, the critical importance of being able to correctly identify every numeral in any computational task would justify 100 percent standards for evaluating student performances on a numeral identification test. On the other hand, many people would regard 80 percent performance on a ten-item test of addition of two, two-digit counting numbers as sufficient evidence of addition competence, at least in this restricted domain.

Evaluating student performances involves large measures of judgment and considerable reflection upon expectations. Students do not need to perform according to Olympic standards in order to demonstrate a competence in figure skating. Neither does one expect the consistency and accuracy of an Olympic performance from the immature and developing learner. In any event, IPI provides for the teacher's judgment to override the system when it is appropriate.

Perspectives on Possible IPI Program Improvements

Just as IPI provides teachers and students with data-feedback for evaluating and improving students' learning, so has the system provided masses of data for its own evaluation for further improvement. These data have been accumulated by different teachers with different populations of students across a variety of contexts over many years. They clearly seem to indicate that the IPI program could benefit from several categories of improvements: (1) addition of more and different kinds of learning and instruction options, (2) elaboration of teacher preparation to include more emphases on teaching skills, and (3) reduction of user costs.

Options. It had been assumed that teachers and learners would, on their own, capitalize on opportunities to enrich and vary teaching and learning in IPI once the principles of individualized instruction were understood and a classroom environment conducive to exploration and experimentation was established. Experience has shown that this is not likely to occur so often as might be hoped unless special provisions are introduced into the program that will foster these behaviors.

In IPI, the program of learning and instruction is mostly linear. That is, the content objectives follow one-after-the-other as if the entire course of study was one standard prerequisite sequence. Of course, this is an inaccurate portrayal of knowledge in any field. Careful analysis of the sequence of IPI objectives could identify many points in the progression that might be "choice points." "Choice points" would be points in a student's learning when the student is in possession of sufficient prerequisite skills to undertake any of several follow-on sequences of learning. Revising IPI to make these instruction and learning alternatives explicit options for teachers and students could make the program more interesting and more individualized for students.

Usually, a variety of approaches will achieve the same terminal objective. Inclusion of some parallel sequences in IPI would also open additional options to teachers and learners. To the extent that parallel approaches might provide symbolic, iconic, and enactive paths to achievement of the same objective, the program could more readily accommodate a greater range of learner aptitudes. This should be particularly valuable for the education of some handicapped students.

Some exploration at RBS indicates that specification is also possible for some higher-order cognitive objectives—it just takes more skill and imagination. Increased richness and a greater variety of learning could be accomplished in IPI with the inclusion of such objectives. And, the introduction of specific affective objectives of the type described in Krathwohl *et al.* (1956), might well enhance the attainment of IPI instructional goals by all students. Nor is there any reason why developmental objectives of the type described by Hewett (1969) should not be included particularly for the handicapped. All of these enhancements of the IPI content would substantially expand instructional and learning options currently available to teachers and learners.

Teacher Preparation. The intent from the beginning was that teachers should employ their own skills and imagination to create tutorial presentations and small group instruction, as needed, using the IPI materials as a framework. But experience has indicated that such teaching is more likely to develop if opportunities for it are clearly identified in the instructional materials, if optional suggestions and directions for conducting the teaching are part of the teacher's guides, and if appropriate manipulatives and supplemental materials are deliberately coded by objectives.

However, even with these embellishments, the desired improvement in teaching is likely to occur only if the teacher training course is also elaborated. Indeed, the more options that are created and the greater the range of skills that is expected of teachers, the more pressing is the need for appropriate training. Past history has revealed that basic skills of diagnosis and prescription, alone, will require more effective training if all teachers are ever to achieve adequate competency in these areas. With the entry of the handicapped into regular classrooms, a whole new set of understandings and skills must be attended to in the teacher training component.

User Costs. Making IPI programs competitive in cost with traditional programs can help to make individualized instruction available for all students in all classrooms, as needed. Currently, IPI instruction is provided in booklets and/or packages prepared for each objective. As a rule, instruction is designed so as to require frequent student responses in the booklets. Although some of the instruction would be difficult to accomplish if students could not make their responses directly in the booklets, there is good reason to believe that most of it could be contained in reusable materials which should sharply lower materials costs.

The need for the publisher to warehouse many small and different booklets and then to assemble custom orders for shipment to customers is very expensive. Doubtless, redesign of the instructional "package" to require handling and managing of fewer units is feasible and would permit substantial reduction in users' costs.

With respect to the costs of using paraprofessionals, greater reliance on students for management of their own learning would help to reduce this cost and would be entirely consistent with the instructional goals of IPI. Even in the primary grade where assistance to teachers may be necessary, consideration should be given to the use of volunteer aides.

Degree of Structure. Advocates of unstructured individualized programs sometimes referred to as "open" or "informal" education will probably note that the proposed revisions do not include suggestions for removal of any of the structures that facilitate decision making in IPI. Such structures include the specified objectives, criterion-referenced tests, diagnostic and prescriptive procedures, and planned instructional sequences. Some critics of IPI claim that these structures are incompatible with individualization and that less structured open education is the proper norm.

There is no common definition of individualized instruction which might be used to resolve this controversy. According to Gibbons (1970), so many programs of such diverse character have been given the "individualized" label that the term is no longer a useful categorizer. However, recent work on classroom processes (Cooley and Lohnes, 1976; Cooley and Leinhardt, 1975; Stallings and Kaskowitz, 1974; Soar, 1973; and Valdes and Helms, 1975) suggests that the same instructional variables are common to all classrooms, and it is the degree to which these variables are effectively attended to for students, individually, that may be the best measure of individualization.

IPI-type programs are predicated on the assumption that instructional technology can be usefully employed by teachers and students to attain "best fit" matches between students and their instruction as the students pursue the achievement of predetermined objectives. Whether open or informal education can achieve more appropriate matches by relying upon unobtrusive measures, environmental shaping, and the students themselves has not been established.

In any event, there are reasons for believing that IPI-type technology and open education are compatible rather than mutually exclusive alternatives. Indeed, instructional technologies of the IPI-type may not only have a legitimate role in the open classroom (Resnick, 1972), they may be necessary. This view is predicated on the assumption that the challenge of correctly attending to the variety of learning and instructional options for each student, relative to the student's competence, needs, interests, etc., may exceed the capability of students and most teachers—unless they have effective assistance. Such assistance is the purpose of IPI-type technology.

Some Implications of the IPI Experience for Implementation of P.L. 94-142

1. The IPI experience has demonstrated that teachers can adapt instruction for individual students if they have been trained in the use of a plan and materials designed to assist the efforts—and if the feasibility and efficacy of the plan and materials have been established in the variety of contexts for which they are intended.

2. Any widescale effort to directly assist teachers to individualize instruction that will be evaluated in terms of its efficiency and effects should follow a comprehensive plan, i.e., a plan covering awareness activities, consultation, demonstration, training, technical assistance, evaluation, and data-based modifications.

3. Moreover, the assistance and participation of the relevant educational hierarchy needs to be secured for the effort.

4. Because of the mutual adaptations of the planned innovation and the adopting school that occur during implementation, school people need to be fully participating partners in the innovative process to assure the integrity of the innovation.

5. Individualization can be implemented for any number of students in a school or for the whole school at one time. However, care needs to be taken to assure an adequate range of materials for students receiving individualized instruction regardless of their administrative grade levels. Curriculum planning needs also to provide for students who do not receive individualized instruction and for both groups in the future as well as the present.

6. The planned effects of a program of individualized instruction are predicated upon an assumed implementation. Departures from the anticipated implementation need to be carefully weighed relative to the probable consequences of the departures and the needs of the students. School personnel must be the ultimate judges of what should be done.

7. Effective implementation of the program will depend upon the performance of committed and competent teachers whose efforts are coordinated by a supportive principal who is also a competent instructional leader.

8. Instruction for the handicapped appears to need to differ mostly in terms of the degree to which adaptation is required. Mastery standards and achievement expectations may need to be modified. The program must be especially interesting and rich in manipulatives. Learning increments and learning steps need to be small and time for learning needs to be adjusted to the need. Extra practice must be available. Finally, developmental objectives need to be included.

Conclusion

If experience confirms the need for individualized instruction in mainstream classrooms, it is likely that it will be more and more employed at the school level even if no guidance or support for its studied use comes from higher levels. Increased use could come about in a casual, almost random, and inconsistent way. It might take the form of gerrymandered adaptations of existing programs that were not designed for the handicapped. A more desirable and, in the long run, more efficient way of utilizing instructional technology for this special purpose should be through research and development, programmatically planned for the purpose.

Thus, it is recommended here that careful, comprehensive study be given to existing efforts to individualize education for the handicapped. This study should specify what is being done, why, and what needs to be done to more effectively provide for a variety of handicapped students, over the range of age/grade levels, and across subject areas.

Given the outcomes of the proposed study, it is further proposed here that the data be used to design and specify one or more prototype programs that would meet the needs of teachers and students. Perhaps there should be versions intended for commercial publication, versions that represent adaptations of existing programs, and versions that depend upon local capability for their completion.

Finally, it is proposed here that selected prototype designs be carefully and systematically tested in the variety of conditions for which they are intended. Moreover, all of these experiences should be carefully documented so that they can become part of a knowledge base. Perhaps, this course of action could help to vindicate the faith of the Congress that educators are able to provide an equal educational opportunity for all children if only they receive sufficient support and confidence.

References

Averch, H. A., Caroll, S. J., Donaldson, T. S., Kiesling, H. J., and Pincus, J. *How effective is schooling?* Englewood Cliffs, N.J.: Educational Technology Publications, 1974.

Cooley, W. W., and Leinhardt, T. *The application of a model for investigating classroom processes.* Pittsburgh, Pa.: Learning Research and Development Center, University of Pittsburgh, 1975.

Cooley, W. W., and Lohnes, P. R. *Evaluation research in education.* New York: Irvington Publishers, 1976.

Gibbons, M. What is individualized instruction? *Interchange,* 1970, *1*(2), 28-51.

Glaser, R. Toward a behavioral science base for instructional design. In R. Glaser (Ed.), *Teaching machines and programmed learning,* II. Washington, D.C.: National Educational Association, 1965.

Glaser, R., and Rosner, J. Adaptive environments for learning: Curriculum aspects. In H. Talmage (Ed.), *Systems of individualized education.* Berkeley, Calif.: McCutchan, 1975.

Helms, D., and Graeber, A. Problems related to children's acquisition of basic skills and learning of mathematics and some suggested R&D options for NIE support. In *Conference on Basic Mathematical Skills and Learning* (Vol. 1). Washington, D.C.: National Institute of Education, 1975.

Hewett, F. M. A hierarchy of educational tasks for children with learning disorders. In W. Otto and K. Koenke (Eds.), *Remedial teaching: Research and comment.* Boston: Houghton Mifflin, 1969.

Jamison, D., Suppes, P., and Wells, S. The effectiveness of alternative instructional media: A survey. *Review of Educational Research,* 1974, *44*(1), 1-67.

Krathwohl, D. R., Bloom, B. S., and Masia, B. B. *Taxonomy of educational objectives. Handbook II: Affective domain.* New York: David McKay, 1956.

Lindvall, C. M., and Bolvin, J. O. Programmed instruction in the schools: An application of programming principles in "individually prescribed instruction." In P. C. Lange, H. G. Richey, and M.M. Coulson (Eds.), *Programmed instruction* (66th Yearbook of the National Society for the Study of Education). Chicago: The National Society for the Study of Education (distributed by the University of Chicago Press), 1967.

Lindvall, C.M., and Cox, R.C. (Eds.) The IPI evaluation program. *AERA Monograph Series on Curriculum Evaluation.* American Educational Research Association, 1970, 5.

Lumsdaine, A. A. Educational technology, programmed learning, and instructional science. In E. R. Hilgard (Ed.), *Theories of learning and instruction* (63rd Yearbook of the National Society for the Study of Education). Chicago: The National Society for the Study of Education (distributed by the University of Chicago Press), 1964.

National Advisory Council on Education Professions Development. *Mainstreaming: Helping teachers meet the challenge.* Washington, D.C.: Author, 1976.

Resnick, L. B. Open education: Some tasks for technology. *Educational Technology,* 1972, *12*(1), 70-76.

Rosenshine, B. Classroom instruction. In N.L. Gage and K.J. Rehage (Eds.), *The psychology of teaching methods* (75th Yearbook of the National Society for the Study of Education). Chicago: The National Society for the Study of Education (distributed by the University of Chicago Press), 1976.

Soar, R. S. *Follow through classroom process measurement and pupil growth (1970-71): Final report.* Gainesville, Fla.: College of Education, University of Florida, 1973.

Stallings, J. A., and Kaskowitz, D. H. *Follow through classroom observation evaluation—1972-1973.* Menlo Park, Calif.: Stanford Research Institute, 1974.

U. S. General Accounting Office. *Training educators for the handicapped: a need to redirect federal programs. Report to the Congress by the Comptroller General of the United States.* Washington, D.C.: Author, n.d.

Valdes, A.L., and Helms, D.C. *A design to study the effectiveness of well-implemented individualized instruction in compensatory reading and mathematics programs.* Philadelphia, Pa.: Research for Better Schools, 1975.

Whipple, G. M. (Ed.) *Adapting the schools to individual differences* (24th Yearbook of the National Society for the Study of Education, Part II). Bloomington, Ill.: Public School Publishing, 1925.

Author's Note

The author wishes to express his appreciation to the following for their helpful comments on an earlier draft of this chapter: Mauritz Lindvall, Learning Research and Development Center, University of Pittsburgh, Pittsburgh, Pennsylvania; and Hugh Summers, The Conference of Executives of American Schools for the Deaf, Inc., Washington, D.C.

7.
The View of P.L.94-142 from the Classroom

Anna L. Hyer

Every teacher in every school in the United States is affected by P.L. 94-142, Education for All Handicapped Children Act of 1975. It is quite understandable, therefore, that teachers are vitally concerned that the implementation of the legislation be such that the philosophically projected advantages of widespread mainstreaming be achieved in actual practice.

Although all persons with roles in the educative process will share in the success or failure of P.L. 94-142, it is the classroom teacher who must make the day-to-day decisions and implement these. In the end, the teacher will be the one the parents and others hold accountable. Is it any wonder then that the classroom teachers, while endorsing the goals of the new legislation, have some serious questions and reservations about the speed and manner in which P.L. 94-142 is to be implemented?

Their anxiety is increased as they look at the current literature as represented in the ERIC bank which treat almost none of the classroom teacher's concerns beyond the skills and knowledge they must have in their new roles. The anxiety is fanned further by articles on topics such as "changing the teacher's attitudes" sometimes referred to as "selling" the teacher on mainstreaming (Leckie, 1973), or advocating the consulting teacher approach because "it is less costly and disruptive, avoids labeling and extensive testing, provides normal peer models, and trains regular teachers in special education" (McKenzie, 1971).

This chapter will discuss some of the anxieties of teachers and related problems which must be addressed if P.L. 94-142 is to achieve its intended goals.

Changing Role of Teachers

Until relatively recently, the role of the classroom teacher was fairly well established and understood as it related to physically and emotionally disabled students. Basically, it was to identify through rough screening, and then refer to specialists for diagnosis and treatment. Classroom teachers, administrators, and special educationists were prepared psychologically and educationally for this division of labor. Large amounts of time and money were invested in supporting this system with its special facilities and a variety of specially trained and certified educators.

During the past ten years, evidence has been mounting on the negative effects of labeling, of testing, of segregation, and faulty self-perception. During the sixties, the rights of minorities were actively defended; parents became actively involved in decision making; the "separate but equal" doctrine was destroyed; the federal and state governments mandated and/or funded programs at levels previously unattained; and the courts entered the picture. By 1975, the courts in 33 states had decreed that it is a state responsibility to educate handicapped children. In P.L. 94-142, the federal government's commitment to the education of all handicapped children is spelled out with a plan to ensure the rights of handicapped children to a free, appropriate, individualized, public education in the least restrictive environment.

As with most attempted massive innovations, it is easier to mandate, and even to finance, than it is to implement successfully a desired change. Changes tend to take place in one, or at most only a few, of the links in the system chain, whereas innovations usually require system-wide changes, many of which should take place simultaneously. As Pappanikou and Paul (1977) point out, it is necessary to mainstream the system before it is possible to mainstream children. An added problem is the lack of proven implementation models over any extended period of time. In fact, some experts doubt that mainstreaming will result in better education of the handicapped.[1] James L. Paul and Susan Rosenthal[2] state: "Mainstreaming is an important and a potentially dangerous educational innovation. It is important because it suggests providing, for the first time, full participation by handicapped children in the educational system. It is dangerous because, without appreciation of the complexity of the changes involved and without sufficient professional and technical support for implementing those changes, mainstreaming could sabotage the advances already made in providing educational service for these children."

The Teacher's Dilemma

This is the milieu; and the teacher sees himself/herself as the center of the storm, tossed about by mandates of legislators and bureaucrats, the expectations of parents and children, the pressures of school boards and school administrators, and the uncertainty of new relationships with those in the special education field. And yet the teacher is well aware of positive values that could be gained if mainstreaming and other features of P.L. 94-142 can be implemented successfully. They are probably more aware than most of the damage done by the unwise use of tests, of damage done by labeling, of the importance of self-concept, of the relationship of expectations to achievement, and of the importance of schooling in the socialization process. What the teacher needs, therefore, is not to be sold on the concept of mainstreaming, but rather assurance about an involvement in decision making concerning how the concept is to be put into practice.

Teachers know that they will be facing unfamiliar roles, ones for which many of them were not prepared in their preservice education or later experiences. They know they may be called upon to function in situations previously handled by specialists with months of special training. If they are given a few days of inservice education, will they be expected to do as well or better than the specialist did?

Teachers know that many of the students in their regular classes are not achieving as they or the parents would like for them to achieve. Part of the reason for this is lack of time to devote to individual students, the lack of appropriate teaching materials, and in some cases, lack of preparation for the individualization of instruction. Some teachers are fearful that the mainstreaming of handicapped students into the class will damage the educational opportunities of those already in their regular classes by reducing still more the time the teacher will have to spend with individuals because of the increased demands of the handicapped student.

Teachers also know that class sizes are increasing, and the support, both financial and attitudinal, of the public is decreasing. Will school boards and school administrators make adjustments in class size when handicapped students are mainstreamed into the classroom?

Teachers know that there is uncertainty and conflicting opinions about the appropriate goals for public education. One of the goals of mainstreaming is to put the handicapped child back into the school scene with the idea that he/she will later be more able to participate in the mainstream of life. This has been one of the goals that teachers have tried to achieve for the students in the regular classroom. But this, as we all know, has met with some criticism in recent years. There has been a strong "back to the basics" movement. The public has expressed concern over the decreasing test scores in areas such as reading, writing, spelling, and arithmetic.

The cartoon in the December 1976 issue of the *Phi Delta Kappan*[3] points up in a comic way the views of many employers, college teachers, and others. The caption of the cartoon is the conversation of two parents viewing their son in his graduation cap and gown stating, "It took four years and $20,000, but now we have a son who knows how to tie flys, survive while caught in a blizzard mountain climbing, enjoy folk music, skydive, make pottery ... ."

The same day I saw that cartoon, I read in the *Washington Post* an editorial by Henry Fairlie (1976) entitled "A Nation Unfit for Leisure?" In this article, he said, "the task of the public education system in America ... is to educate, in this case, not a class but a whole nation to the use and enjoyment of its leisure, to stock their minds for their own continuous pleasure and employments ... an education not only to fit them for a labor market, but to equip them for the increasing rewards of their leisure."

These two citations illustrate the divergent views held on the appropriate goals of education. Real conflicts may develop between the parents of the regular students and the parents of the handicapped over the goals of public education. Will the regular students and their parents view the handicapped students as assets or liabilities in the classroom?

As teachers look at P.L. 94-142, they see that the parents have rights of due process and appeal, but they do not see any similar rights or remedies for teachers. It is possible that teachers may be legally responsible for implementing programs of instruction which they know from the beginning are destined to fail due to lack of adequate resources, support staff, and the like. How is the teacher to cope with this lack of power of appeal or legal authority?

Teachers know that to some people P.L. 94-142 and mainstreaming in general should be front and center with teachers. Yet teachers know that there are others who feel the same about metric education, career education, return to the basics, drug education, environmental education, open schools, individualized instruction, multicultural-bilingual education, and on and on. To the classroom teacher, mainstreaming is but one of a hundred pressing problems and programs to which they are held accountable, many of which are mandated by federal or state legislation.

Heath (1974), in a prologue to his proposal to update teacher readiness, comments on the pressures under which teachers work. He mentions the necessity to completely update every ten years a teacher's repertoire of knowledge. He also mentions the strenuous evaluation of teachers based on student performance—not the mean performance of the class, but the performance of each individual child. He ends by stating, "Never in the history of mankind have children been expected to assimilate so much knowledge during school years. Moreover, the demands that the society places upon teachers go beyond the heroic to the Herculean."

In the preceding section of this chapter, considerable space has been spent on the features of mainstreaming and P.L. 94-142 that are anxiety-laden for teachers. What may appear to others to be rejection or footdragging by teachers may be only the outward manifestations of their inner anxiety. Just as we believe that the self-concept of others is important to their functioning, so are the attitudes of teachers important if they are to approach their new role with confidence, programmed for success and not failure. The proper approach to attitude change for teachers is, in my opinion, not that of brainwashing, but rather recognizing and facing the problems teachers have and involving them in planning for their alleviation.

Views of Teachers Associations

The National Education Association presented favorable testimony before the Senate on the Education for All Handicapped Children Act. The NEA takes an advocacy view on mainstreaming, but has spelled out the circumstances under which it should occur. Its position is stated in the following Resolution 75-26 as passed by the 1975 Representative Assembly (NEA, 1975):

> The National Education Association will support mainstreaming handicapped students only when:
> a. It provides a favorable learning experience both for handicapped and for regular students.
> b. Regular and special teachers and administrators share equally in its planning and implementation.
> c. Regular and special teachers are prepared for these roles.
> d. Appropriate instructional materials, supportive services, and pupil personnel services are provided for the teacher and the handicapped students.
> e. Modifications are made in class size, scheduling, and curriculum design to accommodate the shifting demands that mainstreaming creates.
> f. There is a systematic evaluation and reporting of program developments.
> g. Adequate additional funding and resources are provided for mainstreaming and are used exclusively for that purpose.

The AFT also adopted a position in 1975 that is similar in many ways to the NEA (Rauth, 1976). This resolution:

> 1. Supports mainstreaming of handicapped children both moderate and severe, to the degree recommended by psychologist, special educator, administrator, and classroom teacher.
> 2. Encourages locals to promote federal funding of special educator programs to provide mainstream settings, to train additional special education personnel, and to provide necessary support services for mainstreaming programs.
> 3. Urges that collective bargaining agreements have adequate provisions for viable class size and protection against diminution of special certificates or licenses for both special

education and regular teachers in the implementation of mainstreaming.

The remainder of this chapter will treat different aspects of these provisos of the teachers' associations with some views on how the anxieties of teachers can be alleviated.

Meeting Requirements of the Act

Five legislative requirements to P.L. 94-142 have particularly important implications for teachers. These sections deal with: personnel development, least restrictive environment, procedural safeguards for parents, individualized programs for handicapped students, and funding requirements. Careful attention to implementation procedures and adequate involvement of teachers in decision making will do much to alleviate teachers' anxieties and to insure a favorable climate from which to proceed with implementation.

Personnel Development

P.L. 94-142 §613(a) (3) "a comprehensive system of personnel development which shall include the inservice training of general and special educational and instructional support personnel, detailed procedures to assure that all personnel necessary to carry out the purpose of this Act are appropriately and adequately prepared and trained, and effective procedures for acquiring and disseminating to teachers and administrators programs for the handicapped children significant information derived from educational research, dissemination, and similar projects."

In view of the changing role of the classroom teacher, it is little wonder that teachers cite as their number one problem preparation to work in mainstreamed settings. This has been borne out in various surveys made among teachers throughout the United States and was verified by the NEA in its annual Teachers' Opinion Survey.

In a random sample of the 1.8 million members of the NEA in the spring of 1976, 62% of the respondents reported that handicapped children were being moved from segregated special education classes to regular classes in their school systems for some or all of their instruction. Lack of preparation of regular classroom teachers to handle a wide variety of handicapped children was cited as one of the biggest problems.[4]

Preparation of Teachers in Service

As teachers begin to plan toward mainstreamed classrooms, they perceive the gaps in their previous education and experience must be filled in order for them to function adequately in new roles. Among the needs frequently stated are:
1. Information about:
    (a) what mainstreaming is and is not, especially assurance that it does not mean wholesale return of all exceptional children now in special education classes to the regular classroom;
    (b) Public Law 94-142 and their own state plan;
    (c) materials support systems available to them;
    (d) support personnel: types, availability, and how to use them; and
    (e) models of successful programs which illustrate teacher involvement in planning, scheduling of the handicapped student in and out of the classroom, planning various uses of support personnel, etc.
2. Role definition—not only does the role of the classroom teacher need to be redefined, but the roles also of administrators and all types of support personnel including teacher aides. (Role relationships and lines of authority need to be understood by all.)
3. Team planning and working strategies—if mainstreaming is to succeed, it must be conducted as a collegial rather than an individualistic enterprise.
4. Diagnostic techniques and behavior management techniques.
5. Individualization of instruction—techniques, materials, curriculum designs, and the like.

6. Ways of preparing regular students for the introduction of handicapped students into the classroom. Children can be cruel to one another, not so much from maliciousness as from insensitivity to the feelings of others. Regular students also may resent the handicapped students for the extra attention they get and even for some of the materials of instruction, particularly the audiovisual tools, which may in some cases be reserved for the use of the handicapped.
7. Ways of preparing the handicapped student for integration into the regular classroom. Motivation is a major academic problem teachers face with all students, but there may be particular problems associated with the motivation of the handicapped, particularly with the mentally retarded child who may, because of past failures, be in special need of additional reassurance and approval.
8. Methods of evaluating handicapped students. This is often a special problem for teachers because of the special instruments required for evaluation; also in the setting of the appropriate goals with smaller than normal increments of success.
9. Parent liaison techniques. Parents and teachers have always worked together in the education of the children. In most cases, however, each observed, and for the most part understood, their "territory." Provisions in the new Public Law 94-142, however, require more, and a different kind, of parent involvement in the education of the handicapped than has been the case previously. Anxiety may exist for both parents and teachers. As Adleman[5] says, "teachers are often ill-prepared to play the role of parent liaison. Teachers are required to act as consultants to parents, advocate for the child, or negotiator for the school system to resolve differences of opinion between the parent and the school relative to program development or program placement for the student in question. Further, the parent liaison role is often further enacted within a context of parental ignorance of, fear of, or dissatisfaction with the school system."

Certainly not all teachers are going to need inservice education in all the areas listed above. Further, no two teachers are going to have the same needs. Teachers, like students, are individuals and need programs individualized to meet their own needs. A guide to needs assessment at the local school level for those beginning mainstreaming has been prepared by Paul, Turnbull, and Cruickshank (1977).

Not only should teachers be involved in assessing their own needs for teacher education, but also in determining the methods by which this instruction will be presented. The most usual forms of inservice education, such as college courses or local courses given by college faculty, workshops, and the like, are frequently not perceived by teachers to be the most useful methods of inservice education. Worthy of consideration are opportunities for observation, for visitation, one-to-one training opportunities, self-instructional materials, audiovisual media including television, and modularized instructional systems such as the one being completed at Indiana University (Thiagarajan, 1976). The interaction between classroom teachers and resource teachers is one of the best kinds of inservice education for both.

The NEA has set forth some general principles about inservice education which represent the opinions of teachers.[6] These principles can well be applied to inservice education for mainstreaming, and will do much to ensure teacher interest and successful learning experiences.

1. Base the instructional and professional development on the needs of teachers as teachers see them.
2. Give teachers a preeminent voice in determining the content of their own inservice education program, and in helping to find the ways and means for their learning that are most meaningful to them in acquiring new skills, in gaining new insights, and in acquiring relevant knowledge.
3. Relate the inservice education to day-to-day job needs.

4. Make the inservice education a part of the teacher's job assignment.
5. Finance from public funds the acquiring of institutionally required new skills. These are the responsibility of the public and should not be paid for from the teacher's own earnings.
6. Conduct inservice education during school time as part of the teacher's day.

Funds to pay for inservice education are available from many sources. Most school districts and state departments of education have funds available. There are also special federal funds available through such legislation as EPDA and the 1976 Amendments to P.L. 94-482, the Higher Education Act, which in Part B of Section 253 of the Amendment provides for Teacher Training Programs and Training for Higher Education Personnel.

To assure the effectiveness of mainstreaming, professional development activities should be provided for all school personnel, not classroom teachers alone. It should be recognized also that training cannot be accomplished in a one shot effort. It must be a continuous process.

Preservice Teacher Education

Although a very immediate concern is inservice education of staff for mainstreaming, in order not to be operating always from point zero, preservice education must be changed simultaneously. Much more seems to have been written concerning the inservice education needs of teachers than about the preservice training of teachers as regards aspects of special education.

One problem to be solved is to find time within the limited sequence of preservice teacher education to devote to developing the needed skills and knowledge. One way to solve this problem will be to search for core areas that cut across different areas in education, that is, are applicable in more than one area.

Another way in which the training of educators can be mainstreamed is through the field experiences and intern programs.

Special educators need the experience of working in team fashion with special educators in classrooms.

Another problem that is of interest to teachers is what will happen to state certification requirements. These do not now, for the classroom teacher, generally reflect any differences between teachers who are qualified to serve handicapped children and those who are not. Will there be a push to change the credentials, as has been the case in some places with classroom teachers who obtain special training to deal with the bilingual/bicultural education programs?

Least Restrictive Environment

P.L. 94-142 §612(5) (B) "procedures to assure that, to the maximum extent appropriate, handicapped children, including children in both public and private institutions or other care facilities, are educated with children who are not handicapped, and that special classes, separate schooling, or other removal of handicapped children from the regular educational environment occurs only when the nature of severity of the handicap is such that education in regular classes with the use of supplementary aids and services cannot be achieved satisfactorily."

To succeed, mainstreaming needs more than adequately prepared teachers and other personnel. It will not even succeed if facilities, equipment, instructional materials, and support staff are provided. For the handicapped child to succeed in that "least restrictive environment," many additional environmental factors must be dealt with.

One of the administrative concerns of teachers relative to mainstreaming deals with role definition. Usually the school institution is referred to as the school "system." It could be more readily described as a collection of systems of bureaucracies most of which jealously guard the decision making prerogatives in their own areas. When the problems of mainstreaming are added to the already ill-defined role situation, the interests of the child can become lost in the jockeying between departments.

The responsibility for instruction is usually assigned to the classroom teacher or a head teacher where team teaching is practiced. It is not clear, however, in the mainstreamed classroom who bears the responsibility for instruction and other needs of the handicapped. Is it the regular classroom teacher, a consulting specialist, or a team responsibility? Administrators must clarify this matter, hopefully with the involvement of teachers in the decision making process.

In addition to the clarification of roles, attention must be given to establishing and making known the lines of authority for instructional and supportive responsibilities. In the case of special educators, they are subject to the authority of their own bureaucracies as well as that of the principal. But who has authority over a mainstream program? Is it the classroom teacher, the principal, the special educator, the special education administrator, or combinations of the above? Also, what is the relationship between school district policy regarding mainstreaming and variations in practice at the school building level?

Some rethinking of traditional approaches to school management is also required to free up time for school personnel to engage in the new tasks associated with mainstreaming. Adequate staff time is an essential ingredient in successful mainstreaming. Mainstreaming requires more team work and team work depends on time for team members to get together for planning. Too, time is required for teacher involvement in inservice education, for diagnosis and evaluation of handicapped students, for designing and preparing for individualized programs, for the parent liaison required by P.L. 94-142, and the recordkeeping.

Individualized Programs
P.L. 94-142 §614 (5) "provides assurances that the local educational agency or intermediate unit will establish, or revise, whichever is appropriate, an individualized education program for each handicapped child at the beginning of each school year and will then review and, if appropriate revise, its provisions periodically, but not less than annually."

The law defines "individualized education program" to mean a written statement for each child developed in a meeting attended by a representative of the local education agency or intermediate unit, the teacher, the parent or guardian and, whenever appropriate, the child. The statement is to include the present levels of educational performance of the child, a statement of annual goals, including short-term instructional objectives, and a statement of the specific educational services to be provided to the child, the projected dates for providing the services, and appropriate objectives criteria and evaluation procedures.

Ideally, all education should be individualized, that is, appropriate to the needs of each individual child. We all know this does not occur. Why not? What are the deterrents? Major among these are lack of teacher preparation for individualized programming, lack of adequate classroom space and facilities, lack of time for teacher planning, student conferences and the like, and the lack of appropriate materials of instruction. These problems are not going to disappear with mainstreaming but rather will be intensified.

Teachers have a lot at stake and they want to be involved in the decisions relative to student assessment and placement, in the development of individualized programs which they will be responsible for carrying out, in making decisions relative to the amount and use of support staff, facilities, materials, and the like. The professional judgment of a teacher, who works with a child every day, over a period of time, should carry much weight in analyzing the needs and programs for a student.

A by-product of teacher involvement is good inservice training. Frank D. Taylor, supervisor of Special Services in Santa Monica, California,[7] states that in his school district, a regular teacher sits in on the School Appraisal team meeting, and that they have found that this is one of the best inservice training methods available because teachers have a real sense of participation in the special education program for the child.

Teacher Load

By law, individualized programs are required for the mainstreamed handicapped student. Therefore, if teacher time is not sufficient, it will be the average or regular students who will be required to share some of their educational benefits with the handicapped child. In other words, there's a limit to how widely the teacher can spread his/her time.

The problem in the beginning may be intensified because some teachers by training and experience will be able to work more effectively with special needs children than will others. Administrators and parents will be looking for the best placement for a child, and those teachers who are prepared to handle the handicapped student may find their classrooms overloaded with special needs students, particularly the more severe cases.

Certainly class size is not a good single criterion for determining teacher load, but although figured in a multitude of ways, it is the most used criterion. An NEA paper on class size[8] states: "All measures of class size are attempts at quantifying responses to the question, 'How many staff members are needed as related to given numbers of students to provide optimal conditions for achieving particular school objectives?' Thus, class size becomes one measure among several for quantitatively representing student-staff ratios."

With this definition, then, it is obvious that there are many ways to vary teacher load. One way is to put a smaller number of students in self-contained classrooms. Another is to add more teacher aides and support staff for teachers. Others are to provide materials for individualized instruction, engage in team teaching, and the like. Whatever method or methods are to be employed in a school district it is important that special consideration be given to teacher load when mainstreaming occurs.

Teacher groups are just beginning to deal with the problem of how to consider the handicapped student when figuring the teacher's load. One example of this is Lodi, California.[9] The local association became concerned about the quality of learning opportunities for each child regardless of special problems or deficiencies. Elementary classes ranged in size from 18-39, and mainstreaming was being introduced. The association developed a weight factor to be applied in the consideration of class load. The children's weight factors reflect the uniqueness of children and the demands upon teachers to work with such uniqueness. They established a weight factor of one for the normal functioning, 1.5 for the slow learner, 2.5 for the emotionally disturbed, etc. In Pittsburgh, the Federation of Teachers recommended that no more than five handicapped students be assigned as a part of any class. The AFT in New York City recommends that special education children not exceed ten percent of any class.

Some of the goals being sought through mainstreaming are ones that are affected by class size. McKenna and Olson (1975) presented nine generalizations which research on class size support. Some of these have particular implications in the mainstreaming situation. For example, Generalization 1: Teachers employ a wider variety of instructional strategies, methods, learning activities, and are more effective with them when they have fewer rather than more students; and Generalization 2: Students benefit more from individualized instruction when teachers have fewer rather than more students.

Support Services

Not only must adequate support staff be available, but also a close working relationship between regular and special educators must exist. Planning meetings should not be dominated by either classroom teachers or specialists. The ultimate product desired is an instructional program to benefit a particular child.

Individualized programs as defined by the Act, call for systematic instruction and the application of technology to the unique learning needs of the handicapped. These are areas in which many classroom teachers are ill-prepared, and inservice education will be required. The assistance of educational technologists, media specialists, and librarians will be required both in the training for and in the implementation of this systematic approach to individualized instruction.

Parent Involvement

P.L. 94-142 §615 (a) "to assure that handicapped children and their parents or guardians are guaranteed procedural safeguards with respect to the provision of free, appropriate public education by such agencies and units."

This clause goes on to specify that it includes the opportunity to present complaints, impartial due process hearings, and as a last resort, the right to civil action.

Siegel (1969, p. 122) discusses in some detail the negative attitudes which may exist on the part of both teachers and parents of handicapped children and which could interfere with harmonious team efforts. He summarizes by stating: "What is needed is mutual competence, respect, and empathy. In a majority of cases, both teachers and parents are working toward the same goal—the development and adjustment of the child. However, their efforts are hampered because of the inability to communicate and subsequent defensive thinking." Some of these anxieties of teachers can be relieved through informational and inservice educational opportunities.

The legislation and the courts have made clear the rights of the exceptional child and the parent, but the status of the teacher relative to substantive due process is at present very unclear. Weintraub and McKaffrey writing in *Public Policy and the Education of Exceptional Children* (Weintraub, Abeson, Ballard, and Lavor, 1976, p. 333) state: "The most critical relationship in the education process is between the professional and the child. The professional who serves an exceptional child may be employed by a bureaucracy yet his or her relationship to the child is the same as all other professionals. In this context, the professional is an individual with a unique expertise for serving the exceptional child." The authors go on to say "not enough attention is being devoted to the implications of those relationship changes to the professionals who directly serve exceptional children."

Another closely related issue is the position the teacher is in as he/she carries out the child advocacy role. How do teachers defend their professional opinion of what is in the child's best educational interest if this opinion is opposed by parents and/or school authorities?

Funding

P.L. 94-142 §614 (2) (B) "Federal funds expended by local educational agencies and intermediate educational units for programs under this part (i) shall be used only to pay the excess cost directly attributable to the education of handicapped children, and (ii) shall be used to supplement and, to the extent practicable, increase the level of State and local funds expended for the education of handicapped children, and in no case to supplant such State and local funds."

On the face of it, it would appear that if Public Law 94-142 is to be funded along the lines that the Act provides, that all the funding problems for the education of the exceptional child would be solved. However, in the statement of purpose in the opening portion of the Act, it is stated that there are approximately 1 million handicapped children in the United States that at the present time are excluded from the public school system. We also know that it costs an average of $400 to $800 more to educate the exceptional child than the normal child. If these 1 million not now in the public school system are returned to it, we are speaking of some massive financial needs beyond those now provided for handling the mainstreamed currently under the care of the public schools.

In many situations, school administrations and school boards see mainstreaming as a way to cut costs. Mainstreaming is doomed to failure when special education students are placed in regular classrooms with no provision for adequate support services, individualized instruction, or teacher and student preparation, and particularly when class sizes go even higher than they are today. In California, for example, some overzealous school districts have attempted to implement mainstreaming legislation without increased funding. They have closed special education classes, returned the students to regular teachers, and are spreading the special teachers as resource persons among a number of classrooms.

Teachers are anxious to see that all funds provided through the Act be spent for direct costs involved with the education of the handicapped—that is, not spent for indirect support such as administrative overhead. This would do much to ensure that funding really assists the intended client group.

Conclusions

As stated in the opening part of this chapter, teachers in general and teachers' associations are in favor of the concept of mainstreaming and particularly of the goals that it is expecting to achieve. The paper was prepared to point up some of the questions and problems which teachers are facing relative to the new public law, and which must receive attention if the goals desired are to be achieved.

In the opinion of the author, the following are some items that will in the future be discussed in bargaining sessions: (1) Mainstreaming's implication for teacher load/class size; (2) Assignment procedures which link student needs with teacher abilities; (3) Specialized support services; (4) Teacher rights and the due process when conflicts arise between parents and teachers or in the teacher's child advocacy role; (5) Provision of teacher time for parent meetings, teacher/specialists meetings, recordkeeping, and the like; (6) Teacher involvement in decisions relative to the placement of exceptional children into regular classes; (7) Provisions of an adequate supply of learning resources—resource centers, materials of instruction, regional systems for media support, and the like; (8) Adequate inservice education prior to mainstreaming; (9) Appropriate teacher involvement in decison making relative to the handicapped, including: student assessment, placement, program development, inservice education, and the like.

Notes

1. E. Zigler. Testimony before the Senate Labor-HEW Appropriation Subcommittee on the FY1977 budget for the National Institute of Child Health and Human Development.
2. J.L. Paul and S. Rosenthal. Mainstreaming schools. Unpublished manuscript, School of Education, The University of North Carolina, Chapel Hill, 1976.
3. *Phi Delta Kappan.* A cartoon, *58,* No. 4, p. 313.
4. National Education Association. Press Release. November 19, 1976.
5. P. Adleman. Mainstreaming and the classroom teacher. Unpublished manuscript, Massachusetts Teachers Association, 20 Ashburton Place, Boston, 1976.
6. R.A. Luke. The teacher role in inservice education. Paper presented at conference on inservice education sponsored by the Council of States on Inservice Education, 1976.
7. F.D. Taylor. Personal communication, December 10, 1976.
8. National Education Association. Class size. A working draft given limited circulation by Instruction and Professional Development, National Education Association, 1201 16th Street, NW, Washington, D.C. 20036, August, 1975.
9. V. Green, chairperson. Report of the class size committee, Lodi Education Association (CTA File No. 6). California Teachers Association, Burlingame, Ca., 1974.

References

Ashcroft, S.C. NCEMMH; A network of media/material resources. *Audiovisual Instruction,* 1976, *21,* 10, 46-47.

Brenton, M. Mainstreaming the handicapped. *Today's Education,* 1974, *63,* 2, 20-25.

Education of All Handicapped Children Act of 1975. Public Law 94-142. November 29, 1975.

Fairlie, H. A nation unfit for leisure. *Washington Post,* November 28, 1976.

Heath, E.J. *Inservice training: A proposal to upgrade teacher readiness.* Bloomington, Indiana: Indiana University, 1974.

Leckie, D.J. Creating a receptive climate in the mainstreaming program. *Volta Review,* 1973, 75, 1:23-7.

McKenna, B.H., and Olson, M.N. Class size revisited. *Today's Education,* 1975, *64,* 2, 29-31.

McKenzie, H.S. Special education and consulting teachers. Montpelier, Vermont: State Department of Education, 1971.

Meade, E.J., Jr. When a foundation goes to school. *Today's Education,* 1973, *62,* 3, 22-24.

National Education Association, *NEA handbook 1975-76.* Washington, D.C.: National Education Association, 1975.

Oldsen, C.F. The National Instructional Materials Information System. *Audiovisual Instruction,* 1976, *21,* 10, 48-49.

Pappanikou, A.J., and Paul, J.L. *Mainstreaming emotionally disturbed children.* Syracuse, New York: Syracuse University Press, 1977.

Paul, J.L., Turnbull, A.P., and Cruickshank, W.M. *Mainstreaming: A practical guide.* Syracuse, New York: Syracuse University Press, 1977.

Rauth, M. Mainstreaming. *The American Teacher,* Magazine Section, April, 1976, 1-4.

Siegel, E. *Special education in the regular classroom.* New York: John Day Co., 1969.

Thiagarajan, S. Coping with misfits in the classroom. Don't panic. *Audiovisual Instruction,* 1976, *21,* 10, 28-29.
Weintraub, F., Abeson, A., Ballard, J., and Lavor, M. (Eds.) *Public policy and the education of exceptional children.* Reston, Virginia: The Council for Exceptional Children, 1976.

Author's Note

The author wishes to express her appreciation to the following for their helpful comments on an earlier draft of this chapter: Frances Quinto, Program Staff, Instruction and Professional Development, National Education Association, Washington, D.C.; Frank Taylor, Supervisor, Special Services, Santa Monica Unified School District, Santa Monica, California.

8.

Short Term Inservice Programs

Donald P. Ely

When major new legislation pertaining to education is passed, the machinery for implementation is rarely spelled out. The Education for All Handicapped Children Act (P.L. 94-142) is no exception. As educators at all levels study the implications of the new law, plans will be developed to carry out its several mandates.

States and local school districts will develop plans to indicate how each will conform to the major requirements of the law. One section of the plan must spell out a comprehensive system to develop and train general and special education teachers and administrators to carry out the requirements of the law.

The purpose of this chapter is to consider short term training alternatives to implement the provisions of P.L. 94-142 which relate to teaching and learning. One successful national model (the Instructional Development Institute) will be reviewed as a possible prototype for personnel development as specified in the law.

For the purpose of this chapter, short term will mean a program of forty hours or less. It does not preclude possibilities for follow-up workshops and consultation. It could provide for 2-3 semester or quarter hours credit if the training is offered through a college or university.

The length, content, and intensity of training programs must, of course, be determined locally. Such factors as the current level of teacher and administrator competency, number of handicapped children, availability of time and resources, and leadership will determine appropriate configurations of the training program.

Existing Short Term Programs

Currently there are no short term training programs which are specific to the requirements of P.L. 94-142. There are, however, a number of training programs which are concerned with evaluation and the design of individualized instruction. The *Catalog of NIE Products* lists several programs developed and field tested by the regional education laboratories and the research and development centers. For example, "Design and Development of Curricular Materials" is a self-instructional course in individualized curriculum design developed by the Learning Research and Development Center at the University of Pittsburgh. "Classroom and Instructional Management" (CLAIM) is an inservice training program designed to help teachers acquire skills that will help them to reduce the frequency of behavior problems and increase the amount of academic work done by students. It was developed by the Central Midwestern Regional Educational Laboratory. The Far West Laboratory for Educational Research and Development has created several minicourses which are appropriate for inservice training, e.g., "Organizing Independent Learning." The Northwest Regional Educational Laboratory has developed "Modules and their Role in Personalizing Programs: A Workshop," a two-day workshop for inservice teachers.

Another program is the Instructional Development Institute (IDI), which was planned, developed, tested, and is now managed

Short Term Inservice Programs

by the University Consortium for Instructional Development and Technology (UCIDT).* The IDI is a 40 hour training program designed to provide teams of teachers, administrators, community members, and specialists with initial skills in applying an instructional system approach to developing practical solutions to critical teaching and learning problems. The purpose of the IDI program is to assist school systems with limited resources, substantial numbers of academically or culturally deprived students, and a desire to find innovative and effective solutions to problems related to teaching and learning.

Training programs developed by the regional education laboratories, the research and development centers, and the University Consortium go through an extensive (and expensive) process to produce a validated, replicable, and exportable program. The process usually takes one to three years, involves a team of several people with support personnel, and often requires three or four tryouts in field settings. The cost for the personnel, materials, and field testing can run as high as one million dollars for 40 hours of instruction by the time the process is completed.

The development of training packages usually involves a team of content specialists, evaluators, and instructional developers (educational technologists) who carefully design each element of the training program to insure attainment of each objective. The training package includes such materials as a leader's handbook, participants' notebooks and handout materials, slides, tapes, films, and programmed materials. It may contain videotapes, simulations, and games as well. To guarantee replicability and quality control, there is often a training program for leaders.

Since there is some urgency in preparing teachers to implement the provisions of P.L. 94-142, it would seem useful to build upon the experiences of those who have developed products similar to

---

*Members of the Consortium are: Indiana University, Michigan State University, Syracuse University, U.S. International University, and the University of Southern California.

those required for this new audience. It may be that some of the products already available could be adapted for the new mission.

Criteria for Short Term Training Programs

Experience with the Instructional Development Institute has yielded a set of criteria which could be applied to the selection and/or development of training programs for personnel who will be involved in the P.L. 94-142 programs.

1. The program should be adaptable to local needs and conditions. Each school district is different. Some teachers and administrators already have the skills to develop new and specialized programs; others need to start from scratch. Some communities have children with a wide variety of handicaps; others have limited numbers. No one program should be unilaterally instituted without a determination of needs.

2. The program should involve teachers, administrators, community members, and specialists. Cooperative planning helps to insure psychological ownership of the program. Wide participation helps to guarantee that all needs will be addressed. As new procedures and materials are introduced, they will have the support of several publics. Involvement of all who will be affected offers one of the best indicators of successful implementation.

3. The program should include follow-up after initial training is concluded. Mere installation is not sufficient to guarantee long term results. A plan for maintenance of the program once adopted is necessary. This step usually means that a person or team is given specific instructions to help individuals who have begun to use a new practice.

4. The program should specify new resources or reallocation of existing resources. Most new programs require resources beyond those which were required for previous instruction. If new monies cannot be made available, it may be necessary to reallocate funds from other sources. It is naive to expect a new program to flourish without adequate resource allocations.

5. The program should permit active participation on the part of all trainees. Educators have been talked at all of their professional lives. New practices require individuals to *do* something; to perform activities similar to those which are expected in the classroom. Simulations, games, and microteaching help to achieve this type of involvement.

6. The program should be conducted by competent, trained personnel. Leaders of short term training programs must be completely familiar with each material and procedure to adequately conduct a program. Leaders should have gone through the program as participants at some point and should have been thoroughly supervised during their initial instructional responsibilities.

7. The program should have been field tested with comparable populations, and evaluations of the field tests should be available. The process of instructional development should yield hard data about how the program works with specific audiences. This "learner verification" is the best guarantee that the expected outcomes will occur. No respected developer will offer a program without field tests, revision, and validation. Data regarding each iteration should be available.

8. The procedure advocated within the context of the program should, if appropriate, be demonstrated in the conduct of the program. The "practice what you preach" admonition is relevant here.

9. Outcomes should include a change of attitude in a positive direction as well as acquisition of specific knowledge and skills. While new knowledge and skills are probably the primary objectives of most inservice training programs, change of attitude is likewise important. Trainees should possess an "approach tendency" toward the new materials and procedures if the program is to be deemed successful.

Content of the IDI

The basic content of the IDI is a synthesis of various models of instructional development. A three-stage, nine-function model (see Figure 8.1) was developed which contains the components necessary for effective development.

It should be pointed out that while the UCIDT developers felt the model contained the critical elements for effective instructional development, they were aware that presentation of the model as nine linear lock-step functions was not an accurate representation of the instructional development process. The instructional development process is in fact a dynamic complex interplay among a vast number of variables which defies strict prescriptive interpretation. Experienced instructional developers point out that they seldom follow the model in lock-step fashion; rather, the model serves as a reminder that each of the component functions must be attended to at some stage in the development process to insure that validated results are produced.

The model is composed of three major stages—Define, Develop, and Evaluate—each of which is composed of three functions or tasks. In the *Define stage,* the three functions of instructional development are (1) Identify Problem, (2) Analyze Setting, and (3) Organize Management. "Identify Problem" requires a careful analysis of the present educational system, an equally sensitive delineation of the ideal system and, after noting the differences between the present conditions and the projected ideal state, a setting of priorities to determine which problem to tackle to move the system closer to the ideal. The second function, "Analyze Setting," calls for a thorough investigation of the audience (students) affected by the problem, the conditions or environment in which the problem exists, and the potential resources to help alleviate the problem. The goal of the next function, "Organize Management," is to effectively organize teams of teachers, administrators, specialists, and community representatives to work cooperatively to bring about the desired changes in the school district. Tasks and responsibilities must be assigned to

Figure 8.1

*The Instructional
Development System*

STAGE I: DEFINE

FUNCTION 1: **IDENTIFY PROBLEM**	**FUNCTION 2:** **ANALYZE SETTING**	**FUNCTION 3:** **ORGANIZE MANAGEMENT**
Assess Needs	Audience	Tasks
Establish Priorities	Conditions	Responsibilities
State Problem	Relevant Resources	Time Lines

STAGE II: DEVELOP

FUNCTION 4: **IDENTIFY OBJECTIVES**	**FUNCTION 5:** **SPECIFY METHODS**	**FUNCTION 6:** **CONSTRUCT PROTOTYPES**
Terminal	Learning	Instructional Materials
Enabling	Instruction	Evaluation Materials
	Media	

STAGE III: EVALUATE

FUNCTION 7: **TEST PROTOTYPES**	**FUNCTION 8:** **ANALYZE RESULTS**	**FUNCTION 9:** **IMPLEMENT/ RECYCLE**
Conduct Tryouts	Objectives	Review
Collect Evaluation Data	Methods	Decide
	Evaluation Techniques	Act

appropriate team members and time-lines must be established to organize the work.

The three functions in the *Develop* stage are: (1) Identify Objectives, (2) Specify Methods, and (3) Construct Prototype. "Identify Objectives" requires the development of behavioral objectives for the student so that when the desired behavior is performed it will serve as evidence that the instructional problem is moving toward solution. Objectives must be written in terms of both the desired terminal student behavior and the enabling or lower-level skills. The "Specify Methods" function suggests that appropriate teaching/learning strategies, including instructional media, can be identified which are likely to assist the student in mastering the specified objectives. Completion of the last function of the *Develop* Stage, "Construct Prototype," requires the actual production of a first draft version of the instructional materials and the evaluation instruments which will be used to test them.

The *Evaluate Stage* also has three functions, namely (1) Test Prototype, (2) Analyze Results, and (3) Implement/Recycle. The "Test Prototype" function specifies that evaluation data must be collected about the prototype instructional materials by testing them on a sample population of students for which the objectives and teaching/learning strategies were devised. In the next function, "Analyze Results," the data collected during the tests are analyzed in terms of objectives, methods, and evaluation techniques. The final function, Implement/Recycle, can be completed after careful analysis of all data collected during the prototype tryout. The decision is then made whether to recycle back through appropriate functions in the model or whether to implement the system on a full-scale basis. Recycling is necessary if all objectives have not been achieved at the desired level, while implementation raises the need for training and other activities necessary to integrate the new system into the existing one.

Briefly described, the model of instructional development outlined above is characterized by a careful analysis and identification of the instructional problem; an assessment of manpower and resource requirements; the formulation of specific objectives to meet the problem; the selection of viable teaching alternatives; tryout, revision, and retesting of the alternatives; and continuous monitoring of the new instructional system as a whole as well as evaluation of the separate components of the system. Only through such systematic procedures can the goal of instructional development be realized, namely, to improve each learner's opportunities to obtain a high quality education.

Organization

In operation, the IDI is usually offered in a five day configuration although it is divided into eight separate units which can be pursued over a longer period of time. A new version of the Instructional Development Institute has been developed and fully tested which follows the same basic model but offers six distinct days which can be used separately or in any combination. They are: Needs Assessment, Managing Instruction, Developing Instructional Objectives, Planning Instructional Strategies and Media, Evaluating Instruction, and Dissemination and Implementation. In either version, a modular approach permits adaption to local needs and conditions.

Participant Teams

The participants are required to come in teams from individual schools and school districts. There are usually 50 individuals in each IDI. Each team is composed of teachers, administrators, school board members, or community representatives and specialists (in curriculum, library, guidance, etc.). This mix is necessary for beginning cooperative planning resulting in the definition of a specific local instructional problem and a feasible plan for resolving the problem. The ultimate goal is commitment of time, personnel, money, and physical facilities by the school district with the support of teams consisting of teachers, administrators, board or community representatives, and specialists.

At the conclusion of the instructional phase of the IDI, the agency conducting the IDI is asked to complete a three-step follow-up consisting of: (1) a three week post institute telephone contact with the school district administration, (2) a six week post institute interview with each team, and (3) a nine week collection of team plans by mail. Gathering data is one purpose of the follow-up but professional consultation to encourage continued progress and to insure completion of the plan are concomitant objectives of the post-IDI activity.

Nature of the IDI

The IDI experience includes large and small group activities. Large group settings are used for major presentations while small groups are used for discussion and interaction. Activities include simulations, games, planning sessions, and practice in evaluation. A variety of films, slide/tapes, and recordings is used as appropriate. Each of the instructional activities is designed to require active responses by each participant.

Training of Coordinators

The IDI is conducted by two coordinators and a technical support person. Each of the coordinators is required to go through a unique training program to become "certified" as trainers.

First, personnel from an agency (state education department, local or regional school districts, colleges, and universities) are required to attend an IDI as participants. Second, they participate in a formal three day training session to learn the organization and management of the institute. Third, they assist in the conduct of an IDI as staff members. Finally, they conduct an IDI with a trained monitor in attendance for back-up support. Following completion of the four stages of training, they are certified to conduct their own IDI's. During the initial period of active dissemination (1970-1974) over 300 people from 77 agencies in 38 states were trained to conduct IDI's.

Field Testing. After initial development of the IDI, three field tests were held in Detroit, Michigan (for inner city teachers), Phoenix, Arizona (for Bureau of Indian Affairs teachers), and Atlanta, Georgia (for city teachers). Each field test used the results of the previous Institute as data for improvement. As IDI's were offered first across the nation in 1971-1972, approximately 40 Institutes were held and each provided evaluative data which were used to make minor adjustments in procedures. An evaluation by the University Consortium for Instructional Development and Technology gathered further data to determine the effectiveness of the IDI with its designated audience. The results of the study revealed the following strengths of the IDI at that time:

- provides a systematic procedure which is easy to implement and is applicable in most situations;
- a smooth-operating Institute which has been carefully conceived and expertly prepared for dissemination on a large scale;
- a high quality development effort capable of influencing school districts who are interested in applying system procedures;
- easily transportable and sufficiently detailed to allow inexperienced personnel to conduct successful Institutes;
- combines a variety of instructional techniques which demonstrates actual use of the I.D. model; and
- brings together all levels within a school district for greater awareness of problems and better communication.

There were weaknesses as well. Conceptual continuity was lacking, concern for the learner was minimized, some technical errors were observed, and follow-up procedures were not considered to be adequate. After this evaluation, each weakness was analyzed and changes were made in the materials and in the total IDI design based on the problems identified during the evaluation.

Impact. Over 400 IDI's have been conducted in 38 states with more than 20,000 participants completing the training. More than 300 individuals have been certified as trainers. The cost per participant is about $20.

The IDI is now being offered in the Philippines. An Iranian version has been prepared in Farsi. In each case the original design of the IDI was retained but examples were changed to local educational contexts.

Some examples of the range of products produced by IDI participants are provided in the following report of activities in participating school districts.

- The Gwinette County School in Lawrenceville, Georgia developed completely new handbooks for implementing a K-12 Career Education program.
- In the East Lebanon School District, Pennsylvania, IDI teams developed an instructional program for faculty moving into a new open classroom middle school.
- In the San Antonio, Texas, schools, a new elementary reading program entitled "I Am" was produced.
- Teachers in the Bryon School District near Houston, Texas, were given released time to receive university instruction to implement an individualized instruction program.
- In rural Idaho, teachers in the Pocatello elementary schools worked with community representatives to set up after-school enrichment programs for students who had to wait at the school for buses at dismissal time.
- IDI participants in San Jose, California, submitted eight proposals for instructional improvement developed during the Institute to the Board of Education; over half were approved by the Board.

This list is only a sample of the many team plans for improvement which grew out of participation in the IDI.

Implementing the Training Program

The IDI is offered as a model of a short term training program which could be used to help educators implement the instructional aspects of P.L. 94-142. There are other programs covering certain aspects of evaluation and developing individualized instruction programs which could be considered for short term inservice training. It is not envisioned that all programs could be embraced without some modification but it is possible to consider adaptation of existing programs since many are modular in fashion. For example, it would be possible to adapt or prepare new modules which would aim at different classes of handicapping conditions; for classroom management problems; for use of the network resources; and for the design and use of diagnostic testing procedures. A modular short term inservice program would permit customized programs responsive to local needs. Whatever program is selected, developed locally, or requested from an agency, it should meet the criteria for short term programs delineated earlier.

While selection or development of the short term program is one essential element of inservice education, the limitations of short term training should be considered. Workshops can help individuals to develop positive attitudes toward new information or techniques; they can even provide opportunities to learn basic skills. But unless there is an opportunity to *practice* the new skills in "real world" settings, the newly acquired skills are likely to fade. Insufficient follow-up through consultation and team support can diminish the effectiveness of the training. Lack of adequate resources and wavering commitment by the administrator and/or board can overcome the teacher's commitment to use newly gained skills in the classroom.

Guidelines. The implementation of the training program must consider ways to overcome these limitations as part of the total inservice design. There are several guidelines which should be addressed to insure effective inservice education:

1. Representatives of all groups who will be affected by the

results of the program (teachers, parents, learners, board members, administrators, and specialists) should be involved in the planning.

2. At the beginning of the inservice program the chief administrative officer should express his/her commitment to the effort and indicate specifically the resources to be made available.

3. One person should be designated to coordinate the entire program. This person should be available after the short term training to assist in the follow-up.

4. Instructional planning on a team basis should be organized. Individuals on teams are supported by each other. Multi-disciplinary efforts considering one problem are likely to yield better solutions than the individual working alone. Such teams usually focus on the individual learner rather than on the teacher. Teams usually divide the work load, which makes each person dependent upon the other.

5. Time lines for completion of plans should be established. This procedure helps individuals to stay "on target" and meet deadlines as they move toward completion of each task.

6. The training should be conducted in a school setting, i.e., in a building within the school system or in a teaching center. The environment of the actual setting where instructional development will be practiced is usually better than such locations as university classrooms, hotels, or retreat centers. The fact that resources which may be required in the future are close at hand is an additional asset.

7. The training should be offered during "school time" or during a period when salary is paid to all personnel. If the program is considered desirable for all involved and if it is important for each person to attend, released or paid time as an indicator of administrative support is mandatory.

These guidelines stem from extensive observations of the Instructional Development Institute and other short term inservice training programs. If followed, the likelihood of success will be enhanced.

9.
Needed Changes in Preservice Education of Regular Classroom Teachers to Prepare Them to Teach Mainstreamed Children

Patricia H. Gillespie

As a result of the proposed rules and regulations implementing P.L. 94-142, regular class teachers will be placed on interdisciplinary teams involved in the development, implementation, and evaluation of individual educational plans for handicapped children. There is reason to question, though, whether regular class teachers, as currently trained, are prepared to deal successfully with the mainstreamed child. Teachers' attitudes toward special children and their integration into the regular class have been significantly less than positive (Harasymiw and Horne, 1976; Reynolds, 1976; Shotel, Iano, and McGettigan, 1972). Furthermore, in studies involving teachers' perceptions and interactions with the children in their classes, investigators have concluded that teachers are less tolerant of low-achieving, "acting-out" children, especially low-achieving boys (Brophy and Good, 1974; Lee and Gropper, 1974).

If children who have been previously placed in special classes are to be instructed in the regular class for part or all of the day, teachers must be provided training in the skills which will enable them to be actively involved in the educational decision-making process (Harasymiw and Horne, 1976; Kaufman, Agard, and Semmel, 1973). General education must become "special" (Gilhool, 1976), and teachers must be provided with a wider range of instructional alternatives in order to have the confidence to deal with the unique learning characteristics of *all* the children in their classes.

Needed Changes in Preservice Education

The necessary changes in teacher training programs for regular class teachers must extend beyond the addition of one or two courses to present training programs. Although expensive to implement, major alterations are necessary (Corrigan, 1976). The development of effective teacher training programs will require a serious commitment to the changing of attitudes of teacher trainers, higher education and school administrators, and preservice and inservice teachers (Lortie, 1976; Martin, 1976). No program will be successful unless teacher trainers view special educational services as an integral part of regular educational training (Corrigan, 1976).

Realistically, such a goal will not occur quickly. Traditionally, colleges and universities (like school systems) are resistant to changes which may cause a break with established programs. Moreover, the bureaucratic structures of higher education are "ever-present," and change is typically "slow" and "diluted" (Sarason, 1971, p. 17). Nevertheless, with the advent of the activities generated in public education by the proposed regulations of P.L. 94-142, teacher educators will not be able to "bury their heads in the sand." They will need to (1) restructure their organizational settings in order to respond to "individual and societal needs" (Corrigan, 1976, p. 48); (2) develop responsive and relevant programs; (3) develop and implement a systematic instructional process for the training of regular class teachers; and (4) train teachers in effective decision-making skills which are based on ecological analyses.

Organizational Changes

At the present time, most special education programs in higher education are separate from regular education. Most often, because of their responsibilities for training their own students, special education professors are not in positions to communicate with regular educators in their own institutions. To ameliorate this problem, changes can occur on a continuum which extends from the development of interdisciplinary teams or *ad hoc* committees (Reger, 1974; Wiegerink, 1974) to a radical departure in the present structuring of teacher education programs (Corrigan, 1976).

Attempts to examine alternatives in the organization of teacher training programs have occurred within the framework of the Deans' Projects funded by the Bureau of Education for the Handicapped. These projects have permitted special and regular educators to study and change the training sequences and curricula for regular class teachers. One of these projects, at the University of Vermont, Burlington, has advocated a reorganization of the university in order to respond to the needs of "mainstreamed children" and their teachers. Corrigan, Dean of the University of Vermont's College of Education, describes their reorganization:

> The most significant interaction in any kind of helping service relationship is teaching-learning. One of the most exciting things that has happened to our College is that we are now a College of Education and Social Services. We are moving toward an organizational approach that conceives of everyone who comes into the college as a 'human service educator' ... If you have a goal of improving total learning environments in homes as well as community action centers, museums, schools, industrial establishments, and old folks homes, you have some opportunity to work through the total environment notion of the helping service idea. Shuffling courses about, then, is not the answer; a major shake-up is needed in professional education, beginning with the introduc-

tion to the profession—as early as a person thinks he wants to become a helping services professional—and continuing throughout the entire professional career (p. 48).

Corrigan suggests the development of core competencies for all people going into the helping services professions. The development of such competencies requires that all educators engaged in the training of teachers work together to develop, implement, and evaluate programs. In order to facilitate cooperation, the University of Vermont has eliminated departments, and faculty in various disciplines work closely to develop a mainstream delivery system.

Special educators will not be able to change training programs for regular class teachers on their own. They will need to work on teams which include curriculum specialists, e.g., reading, math, social studies educators, educational psychologists, social workers, and other professionals involved in the human service delivery training programs. For training programs for regular class teachers to be successful, such activities will require administrative decisions from deans, division directors, and department chairpersons.

Relevant Programming

Training programs in higher education have often been criticized for not being relevant. This has been a particular concern of special education (Reger, 1974). A lack of attention to the concerns of teachers, administrators, special service agencies, and parents occurs if teacher trainers do not consider themselves to be part of the total human services delivery system.

Establishing relevant training programs must not be the mere addition of advisory committees to university and college training programs (Wiegerink, 1974). Often these advisory groups are nothing more than "window dressing."

The proposed rules and regulations for P.L. 94-142 provide emphasis on the role of local educational agencies (LEA's) in the identification and programming for handicapped children. Also, the law requires that each state develop and implement comprehensive personnel development at the preservice and inservice levels for general and special educators; therefore, faculties in special and regular education must work closely with state and local agencies to develop programs that will meet the needs in the field. Furthermore, the Division of Personnel Preparation, United States Office of Education, has required cooperative state planning for personnel preparation funded by Title V-D, Bureau of Education for the Handicapped. Universities, colleges, state department personnel, and local educational agencies have met in each state to plan the most appropriate utilization of resources for training special educators. These statewide planning efforts have also recognized the issues of mainstreaming and the responsibility of regular educators toward the education of special children. These joint meetings of state department personnel, local educational agencies, and training institutions should encourage the development of more relevant special education training programs as well as the training of regular class teachers to meet the needs of mildly handicapped children in regular classes.

Teacher trainers must "reach out" to local, state, and national parent groups, e.g., National Association for Retarded Citizens (NARC), Association for Children with Learning Disabilities (ACLD); state department personnel; administrative organizations, e.g., National Association of State Directors of Special Education, Inc. (NASDSE); local administrators; teachers' organizations, e.g., National Education Association (NEA); social service agencies; professional organizations in the helping services, e.g., Council for Exceptional Children (CEC); American Speech and Hearing Association (ASHA); and federal agencies. Through "shirt-sleeves" conferences (Gillespie and Middleton, 1976) and planned, continuous sessions, faculty and representatives of various interest groups can define the problems, identify available resources, and plan training competencies and components for regular preservice teachers. Such planning will require much time and money; however, these activities will be more beneficial than the present practices of isolationism of most teacher-training programs.

Systematic Instructional Programming

During the last two decades the accelerating expenses of public education and the disenchantment with the education of the economically disadvantaged, racial and ethnic minorities (Coleman *et al.,* 1966; White, 1973) have forced educators to become more accountable for their instructional programs. Specifically, in the area of special education, litigation involving the efficacy of special education programming for minority children (Cohen and DeYoung, 1972; Ross, DeYoung, and Cohen, 1971) and placement and individual programming for handicapped children, e.g., Pennsylvania Association for Retarded Citizens (PARC) vs. State of Pennsylvania (1971) have given impetus to the demand for accountability (Semmel, Semmel, and Morrissey, 1976). Relevant tools for carrying out the needed planning and evaluations of programs are increasingly visible (Thiagarajan, Semmel, and Semmel, 1974). This critical examination of training programs has created a demand for systematically developed instructional strategies and materials.

If special and regular teacher trainers are to provide training programs that reflect quality instruction, they are unlikely to attain it through a piecemeal approach to the problem. One alternative is to adopt an instructional development approach. This approach, an application of systems theory and systems analysis to instructional management (Banathy, 1968; Kaufman, 1972), has been increasingly employed by military, business, and educational programs. In the early 1960's educational technology had an impact on training programs, and educators have developed a new discipline, instructional systems technology. According to Stolovitch (1975) this technology is:

> ... a method of developing instructional materials and/or programs through a rational process involving a clear definition of a

problem, the development of a solution based on clearly stated objectives, the evaluation of the solution in terms of the objectives, and provisions for feedback and revision until the problem is solved (pp. 1-2).

There is a plethora of instructional systems models from which to choose (Stolovitch, 1975; Twelker, Urbach, Buck, 1972); all possessing the similar characteristics enumerated by Stolovitch (1975). Three models which have been found useful in practice and which teacher trainers may find helpful in developing their programs are the Michigan State University Instructional Systems Development Model (Barson, 1967); Instructional Development Institute Model (National Special Media Institute, 1970); and the 4-D Instructional Development Model (Thiagarajan, 1974). From the steps provided in these models, teacher trainers are able to systematically plan, implement, and monitor programs. Each model offers unique features for the planning of a total program for regular preservice teachers. For example, the Michigan State University model was developed for college faculty to use in designed courses, and the IDI and 4-D Models are particularly useful for designing courses, modules, games, simulations, and other instructional materials. The application of the instructional development approach holds out promise not only for solutions which are logically related to real problems but also solutions which are replicable—having a consistent and demonstrable effect on learners at different times and in different places. The payoff for the effort invested in this strenuous process is shareability of new programs and materials across institutions (Molenda, 1977). For example, the Center for Innovation in Teaching the Handicapped (CITH), Indiana University, has developed a series of teacher training materials for special and regular educators which can be used in other training institutions. Because of a shortage of special education teacher trainers, these materials can be useful supplementary materials for teacher training programs.

Total Program Development: Competency-Based Programs. No

matter what instructional model a teacher training program chooses, its members are going to be faced with the responsibility of identifying competencies and training components. Furthermore, training will need to be sequenced in such a manner to maximize experiential opportunities. An outgrowth of the systems approach to education is the development of performance or competency-based teacher education programs (CBTE). Principles of task analysis and the establishment of behavioral objectives are integral parts of competency-based programs (Semmel, Semmel, and Morrissey, 1976). The elementary teacher training models projects funded in 1968 by the U.S. Office of Education are examples of initial competency-based programs.

In their review of CBTE programs in special education Semmel, Semmel, and Morrissey (1976) cite strengths and weaknesses of extant programs. One major problem, as they view it, is the establishment of valid training competencies. At the present time there is a paucity of empirical evidence regarding the necessary competencies for working with handicapped children. This is especially true of those skills needed by regular educators in order to deal with mainstreamed children. This limitation gives cause for a closer examination of CBTE rather than an abandonment of it (Semmel, Semmel, and Morrissey, 1976). If we are to isolate necessary competencies, behaviors must be described in specific, discrete operational terms rather than conducting gain score research that utilizes a "homogenized labeling" approach. Within the framework of CBTE, special and regular educators have a vehicle for needs assessments, teacher-training research, and research of teacher-pupil interactional variables most effective for the programming of handicapped children in regular educational settings.

Scope and Sequence. All those involved in programming must, via needs assessment and empirical studies, identify competencies necessary for regular class teachers to instruct mainstreamed children. However, the process does not stop here. Teacher trainers must select training components that can be validated and sequenced in such a manner as to allow flexible programming.

One criticism of many training programs is that preservice teachers do not have the opportunity to utilize the skills they have acquired until the end of their training program (Corrigan, 1976). The opportunity to practice skills in realistic settings can be offered across a spectrum of activities, culminating in supervised field experiences. Planning instructional sequences that begin with an awareness of needs of handicapped children through the use of self-instructional modules, games, simulations, e.g., *Mainstreaming: Upset in Polymer* (Briggs and Guskin, 1976), is one alternative. Early access to the schools and communities as aides and observers will allow preservice teachers to *systematically observe* handicapped children in educational and other settings. Innovative training experiences that provide pacing, individualization of instruction for trainees, alternative methods of instruction, e.g., simulations, practica, seminars, team teaching, are also necessary for total programming.

Controlled Interaction. While most educators agree that practical experience with handicapped children is necessary, most of this training (often due to lack of trained supervisory personnel) has been relatively "laissez-faire" and not carefully or intensively supervised (Martin, 1976, p. 7). Merely placing students with handicapped students in natural settings is not sufficient. These experiences must be on a continuum in order for trainers to more effectively guarantee skills development. Prior to and during practical experiences, simulations, games, and role-playing, give the trainee the opportunity to try out newly acquired skills in controlled settings (Fink, 1974). According to Fink (1974) the "time-honored tradition in which the future teachers will experience and learn about education by interacting with real children in real setttings must be examined" (p. 4). Furthermore, observing teachers interact with handicapped children in controlled and natural settings (Lynch, 1976) will provide an empirical base for the establishment of necessary competencies for working with handicapped children.

The use of observational techniques in teacher training has been an integral part of several training programs, e.g., Lynch, 1976; Semmel, 1972; Semmel and Thiagarajan, 1975. The analysis of the interaction of trainees with children in cognitive and affective areas can serve as excellent training experiences, avenues for evaluation of training strategies, and bases for research on teacher performance.

Technology such as the computer for data-gathering and feedback has been employed by the Center for the Innovation in Teaching the Handicapped (CITH), Indiana University, Bloomington. The Computer-Assisted Teacher Training System (CATTS) (Semmel, 1972) is utilized for preservice training of special education trainees, inservice training, and follow-up of graduates. The software for the training program is the use of observation systems in cognitive and behavioral teacher-pupil interactions (Semmel and Thiagarajan, 1975). Trainee performance is observed systematically, and codified behaviors are fed back to trainees (Semmel, 1972, p. 5). Computers are used for data collection and feedback via hard-copy printouts immediately after a training session, and/or responses are reported almost simultaneously for the student on television screens. Many of the activities utilized by CATTS can be employed by institutions who cannot afford the technology involved. For example, hand-scoring of interactional behaviors (although an arduous task) or the use of videotaping are alternatives.

Training Strategies in Natural Settings. As stated, there appears to be an agreed upon emphasis on the importance of practicum experiences in natural settings. Steps for the evaluation of effective teaching skills in natural settings have been offered by Peck and Tucker (1973). Important in the steps are the identification of specific training objectives, feedback to trainees, and recycling to criterion. The Peck and Tucker model or other instructional models can serve as guides for planning of practica and/or student teaching. Furthermore, during such experiences educators can provide seminars and supplementary training experiences, e.g., simulations and self-instructional modules. This type of programming should maximize the use of closely working teams of regular and special educators.

Follow-up of Graduates. In any systematic instructional model, evaluation of the program and recycling or modifying it on the basis of evaluation data are important. Follow-up of trainees into the field is necessary in order to validate teacher training programs. If representatives of those involved in human services delivery systems are utilized as planners of competencies and training components, follow-up will occur more naturally. The evaluation of trainees' utilization of skills can begin in practica and continue through their beginning years of teaching. Changing certification requirements, e.g., year long internships prior to certification (Wiederholt, 1974) or working closely with schools designated as teacher centers (Mahan, 1974) will allow trainers to evaluate the relevance of their training programs.

Training Teachers in Decision-Making Skills

Teachers are more effective programmers of instruction for the handicapped if they are integrally involved in the development of educational plans (Kaufman, Agard, and Semmel, 1973); therefore, teacher trainers should be engaged in providing training in skills that will enable a teacher to work "through any problem but not to be dependent on that solution for dealing with future situations" (Garfunkel, 1974, p. 45). Such an approach is particularly important in light of recent concerns for non-categorical education of handicapped children (Hobbs, 1975; Reynolds and Balow, 1972). Rather than using a strict pathological model which assumes the deficit lies within the child (Bartel and Guskin, 1971; Mercer, 1973; Sagor, 1972), educators are studying the effects of environmental interactions, e.g., teacher-pupil interactions, on the labeling and programming of handicapped children (e.g., Gillespie and Fink, 1974; Rhodes, 1970; Swap, 1974). Labeling is presently being viewed by some researchers (e.g., Mercer, 1973; Rowitz, 1974) as occurring in the context of social organization and social control. According to Rowitz (1974), deviance is determined by the judgment of others and is not a property inherent in the actions of a given individual.

If teachers and the environments they create can be responsible for "creating or exacerbating" educational problems of children, teachers should be trained in decision-making skills that are based on *ecological analyses* (Carroll, 1975; Gillespie, 1976). Training programs in decision-making exist in the field of special education (see Gillespie and Sitko, 1976). Among the competencies for programming are an ecological analysis of the interactions in the regular class setting including (1) peer-peer interaction; (2) teacher-pupil interaction; and (3) material-pupil interaction. Observing the child in other settings such as the home is important. Vehicles for interactional analysis are available (see Fink, 1971; Lynch, 1976; Semmel and Thiagarajan, 1975; Simon and Boyer, 1970). If teachers are trained in decision-making skills, they will not view handicapped children as a homogeneous group and they will be more flexible in their programming.

Summary

Needed changes in preservice education for the training of regular class teachers to work with mainstreamed children must be ones that are comprehensive and systematically planned. The piecemeal addition of courses to present training programs will not be in spirit with the mainstreaming of handicapped children; nor will it lead to effective training programs. A total re-organization of training programs, with special education programs viewed as an integral part of the total human service delivery system, is necessary. Moreover, teacher trainers will need to develop or utilize skills in instructional design for the assurance of quality training. Also, teachers should be trained in assessment and programming techniques that analyze the effects of teacher-pupil interaction, peer-peer interaction, and materials-pupil interaction. If teachers are able to assume some of the responsibility of the mis-match between instructional programming and instructional need, perhaps educators will not feel the need to label children. In order for the mandate of P.L. 94-142 to be met, special education must be viewed as an integral part of a regular class teacher's training program, and teachers must be trained to program for the unique learning characteristics of *all* the children in their classes.

References

Banathy, B. H. *Instructional systems.* Palo Alto, California: Fearon, 1968.

Barson, J. Instructional systems development: A demonstration and evaluation project. East Lansing: Michigan State University, U.S. Office of Education, Title III-B Project, OE-3-16-025, 1967.

Bartel, N. R., and Guskin, S. L. A handicap as a social phenomenon. In M.W. Cruickshank (Ed.), *Psychology of exceptional children and youth.* Englewood Cliffs, N.J.: Prentice-Hall, 1971.

Briggs, A., and Guskin, S. Upset in polymer: An experience in mainstreaming. Bloomington: Center for Innovation in Teaching the Handicapped, Indiana University, 1976.

Brophy, J.E., and Good, T.L. *Teacher-student relationships: Causes and consequences.* New York: Holt, Rinehart, and Winston, 1974.

Carroll, A. W. The classroom as an ecosystem. In E. Meyers, G. Vergason, and R. Whelan, *Alternatives for teaching exceptional children.* Denver: Love Publishing Co., 1975, 318-337.

Cohen, J. S., and DeYoung, A. The role of litigation in the improvement of programming for the handicapped. In L. Mann and D.A. Sabatino (Eds.), *The First Review of Special Education, II.* Philadelphia: JSE Press, 1972, 261-286.

Coleman, J. S., Campbell, E. Q., Hobson, C. J., McPartland, J., Mood, A.M., Weinfeld, F.D., and York, R.L. *Equality of educational opportunity.* Washington, D.C., USGPO, 1966.

Corrigan, D. Discussion. In M. Reynolds (Ed.), Mainstreaming: Origins and implications. *Minnesota Education*, 1976, 2(2), 47-51.

Fay, L., and Shuster, S. Reorganization of the Division of Teacher Education and the institutional grant. Indiana University *Teacher Education Forum*, 1973, 2(1), 1-13.

Fink, A. H. Manual for observers: Fink interaction analysis system. Bloomington: Indiana University, Center for Innovation in Teaching the Handicapped, 1971.

Fink, A. H. Behavior management training through simulation and roleplaying. Bloomington: Center for Innovation in Teaching the Handicapped, School of Education, Indiana University, 1974.

Garfunkel, F. Render to the schools what is theirs. *The Journal of Special Education*, 1974, 8(1), 43-46.

Gilhool, T. K. Changing public policies: Roots and forces. In M. Reynolds (Ed.), Mainstreaming: Origins and implications. *Minnesota Education*, 1976, 2(2), 8-13.

Gillespie, P. H. *Ecological checklist.* Merrimac, Mass.: National Learning Disabilities Assistance Project, 1976.

Gillespie, P. H., and Fink, A. H. The influence of sexism on the education of handicapped children. *Exceptional Children*, 1974, 41, 155-162.

Gillespie, P. H., and Middleton, T. Conference on learning disabilities: A review of Rule S-1, 1976.

Gillespie, P. H., and Sitko, M. C. The training of preservice teachers in decision making skills. Bloomington: Center for Innovation in Teaching the Handicapped, Indiana University, 1976.

Harasymiw, S.J., and Horne, M.D. Teacher attitudes toward handicapped children and regular class integration. *The Journal of Special Education,* 1976, *10*(4), 393-400.

Hobbs, N. *Issues in the classification of children,* Volumes I and II. San Francisco: Jossey-Bass, 1975.

Kaufman, M., Agard, J.A., and Semmel, M.I. Project PRIME: interim report—year I, 1971-72, U.S. Office of Education, Bureau of Education for the Handicapped, January, 1973.

Kaufman, R.A. *Educational system planning.* Englewood Cliffs, N.J.: Prentice-Hall, 1972.

Lee, P.C., and Gropper, N.B. Sex-role culture and educational practice. *Harvard Educational Review,* 1974, *44,* 369-408.

Lortie, D.C. Changing public policies: Roots and forces: Discussion. In M. Reynolds (Ed.), Mainstreaming: Origins and implications. *Minnesota Education,* 1976, *2*(2), 16-17.

Lynch, W.W. Guidelines for applied uses of observation instruments in teacher education. Bloomington: Center for Innovation in Teaching the Handicapped, Indiana University, 1976.

Mahan, J.M. Alternative student teaching experiences: Emerging characteristics and encouraging payoffs. *Teacher Education Forum,* 1974, *2*(15).

Marker, G., and Shuster, S. Teacher education at Indiana University: A look at the future. *Teacher Education Forum,* Indiana University, 1973, *2*(1), 1-9.

Martin, E. Integration of the handicapped child to regular schools. Mainstreaming: Origins and implications. *Minnesota Education,* 1976, *2*(2), 5-7.

Mercer, J. *Labeling the mentally retarded.* Berkeley: University of California Press, 1973.

Molenda, M. Personal communication with the author, February, 1977.

National Special Media Institutes. What is IDI? The Instructional Development Institute Program for School Districts (Brochure), 1971.

Peck, R.F., and Tucker, J.A. Research on teacher education. In R.M.W. Travers (Ed.), *Second handbook of research on teaching.* Chicago: Rand McNally, 1973, 940-978.

Pennsylvania Association for Retarded Children vs. Pennsylvania, 334F. Supp. 1257 (E.D. Pa. 1971). Also 343F. Supp. 297 (E.D. Pa. 1972).

Reger, R. How can we influence teacher-training programs? *The Journal of Special Education,* 1974, *8*(1), 7-14.

Reynolds, M. Addendum. Mainstreaming: Origins and implications. *Minnesota Education,* 1976, *2*(2), 68-72.

Reynolds, M.C., and Balow, B. Categories and variables in special education. *Exceptional Children,* 1972, *38,* 357-366.

Rhodes, W.C. A community participation analysis of emotional disturbance. *Exceptional Children,* 1970, *36,* 309-314.

Ross, S.L., DeYoung, H.G., and Cohen, J.S. Confrontation: Special education and the law. *Exceptional Children,* 1971, *38,* 5-12.

Rowitz, L. Sociological perspective on labeling (a reaction to MacMillan, Jones, and Aloica). *American Journal of Mental Deficiency,* 1974, *79,* 265-267.

Sagor, M. Biological bases of childhood behavior disorders. In W. Rhodes and M. Tracy (Eds.), *A study of child variance,* Vol. 1. Ann Arbor: University of Michigan, 1972, 37-94.

Sarason, S. *The culture of the school and the problem of change.* Boston: Allyn and Bacon, 1971.

Schwartz, L. A clinical teacher model for interrelated areas of special education. *Exceptional Children,* 1971, *37,* 565-571.

Semmel, M. *Toward the development of a computer assisted teacher training system (CATTS).* Bloomington: Center for Innovation in Teaching the Handicapped. School of Education, Indiana University, 1972.

Semmel, M., Semmel, D., and Morrissey, P. *Competency-based teacher education in special education: A review of research and training programs.* Center for Innovation in Teaching the

Handicapped. School of Education, Indiana University, Bloomington, 1976.
Semmel, M.E., and Thiagarajan, S. Observation systems and the special education teacher. In E. Meyen, S.A. Vergason, and R.J. Whelan (Eds.), *Alternatives for teaching exceptional children.* Denver: Love Publishing Co., 1975, 205-224.
Shores, R.E., Barney, J.O., and Wiegerink, R. Teacher training in special education: A review of research. In L. Mann and David A. Sabatino (Eds.), *The third review of typical education.* New York: Grune and Stratton, 1976.
Shotel, J.R., Iano, R.P., and McGettigan, J.F. Teacher attitudes associated with the integration of handicapped children. *Exceptional Children,* 1972, *38,* 677-683.
Simon, A., and Boyer, G.G. *Mirrors for behavior I; An anthology of observation instruments.* Philadelphia, PA: Research for Better Schools, 1970.
Sitko, M. Undergraduate special education program. Indiana University, 1972.
Stolovitch, H. *Systems and alternative models for instructional development.* Center for Innovation in Teaching the Handicapped, School of Education, Indiana University, 1975.
Swap, S.M. Disturbing classroom behaviors: A developmental and ecological view. *Exceptional Children,* 1974, *41,* 163-172.
Thiagarajan, S. The teacher trainer as an instructional designer. *Teacher Education Forum,* Bloomington, Indiana University, 1974.
Thiagarajan, S., Semmel, D., and Semmel, M. *Instructional development for training teachers: A sourcebook.* Council for Exceptional Children (CEC), 1974.
Twelker, P.A., Urbach, F.O., and Buck J.E. *The systematic development of instruction: An overview and basic guide to the literature.* Stanford, California: ERIC Clearinghouse on media and technology, 1972.
White, L.R. PBTE in a multicultural society. *Journal of Teacher Education,* 1973, *24,* 225-231.

Wiederholt, J.L. Influencing change in special education. *Journal of Special Education,* 8(1), 1974.

Wiegerink, R. A reaction to how to influence teacher-training programs. *The Journal of Special Education,* 1974, 8(1), 23-24.

10.
How Can the Evaluation of Instructional Materials Help Improve Classroom Instruction Received by Handicapped Learners?

P. Kenneth Komoski

I want to begin with some observations that have to do with the role of instructional materials in classroom learning and with the evaluation of such materials, both of which are matters that deserve special attention from those concerned about the successful implementation of P.L. 94-142 at the classroom level.

First observation: As evidence continues to mount about the importance in classroom instruction of active, sustained involvement of learners in learning tasks (Bloom, 1976), and on the importance of the role played by instructional materials in organizing classroom learning tasks, it will become increasingly important to evaluate instructional materials in relation to how effectively particular materials engage the attention and sustained activity of individual learners.

Second observation: Although instructional materials are constantly being evaluated by materials producers, by state and local materials committees, as well as by the teachers who choose and use materials with learners, these evaluations seldom have as their primary focus the issue of a material's actual instructional effectiveness with learners.

Third observation: There are quite discernible reasons why many have ignored the issue of effectiveness of materials with learners.

Fourth observation: While these reasons, and the evaluations they spawn, ought to be changed, they cannot and will not be changed until the values that dominate most of today's decisions about instructional materials become less dominant and are superseded by values more centrally related to the essential (instructional) role of such materials in classroom learning.

All four of these observations are directly related to what I believe promises to emerge as a major frustration to those attempting the successful implementation of P.L. 94-142 at the classroom level. Unless there is (1) a supply of appropriate (effective) instructional materials from which teachers can select those materials which will best sustain the energy of individual learners on relevant learning tasks, and (2) unless teachers know how to make effective use of such materials, the P.L. 94-142 mandate requiring classroom teachers to design and to implement an "individual educational plan" (IEP) for each handicapped learner in his or her classroom is unlikely to be met.

Having made these observations, let me say that I am well aware that there are many more factors influencing the sustained attention of handicapped learners to classroom learning tasks than the availability, selection, and effective use of appropriate instructional materials. However, I leave the discussion of those factors to others. It is time to focus on instructional materials if for no other reason than because instructional materials are such a "given" in the classroom—so much a part of the "woodwork," as it were—that the role they play in the day-to-day, moment-to-moment business of classroom learning is simply taken for granted. As a

Evaluation of Instructional Materials

result, the underlying values of the process that delivers to, and that maintains the use of these materials in, the regular classroom have hardly been examined. I firmly believe that, in light of P.L. 94-142's implications for instruction in the regular classrooms of this country, the failure to examine this process and the values that currently dominate its workings would open those responsible for the implementation of P.L. 94-142 to the charge of irresponsibility.

Therefore, one purpose of this chapter is to focus the reader's attention on aspects of that process of material development, selection, and use that has particular relevance for P.L. 94-142 and to which the reader may not, as yet, have given much thought. Another purpose is to help the reader to understand how certain shifts of focus in the values and the criteria used in evaluation during the development, selection, and use of instructional materials can lead not only to needed improvements in materials, per se, but also to the possibility that the instructional demands of P.L. 94-142 can be successfully implemented at the classroom level. The final purpose of this chapter is to review some current efforts to improve the development, selection, and use of materials for handicapped learners, and to help the reader to think about some strategies that can help assure that these efforts are sustained.

Let us begin by focusing on the importance of time-on-task and relevance-of-activity-to-task in any effective learning situation. With these things clearly in focus, let us then concentrate on what is known about the percentage of classroom time and activity that is structured by the use of instructional materials. Surprisingly, until recently, no hard data existed on this rather important question. And now that the question has been asked, the answer turns out to be rather startling. It is that in regular classroom instruction in reading, mathematics, social studies, and science (at both elementary and secondary school levels), some 90 to 95% of classroom instructional time involves the use of some type of instructional material. Unfortunately, this research (based on data gathered from approximately 12,000 teachers during the 1974-75 school year by EPIE) does not provide very much information on how much of that 90 to 95% of classroom time (1) individual students spend actually attending to those aspects of the materials that are instructionally relevant to them as individuals at any given instructional moment, and (2) how instructionally relevant any given material is for any given learner at any given moment of instruction. Nevertheless, the reported percentage of materials use time as calculated by more than 12,000 teachers and corroborated by independent observations of representative classrooms does throw some important light on what until now has been an overlooked aspect of classroom activity. Yet despite the absence of empirical data regarding either actual learner time on task or the relevance of the materials being used to the actual instructional needs of individual learners, the survey does provide data that invite some reasonably strong inferences about whether the regular classroom teacher has either the time or the expertise (or, indeed, the freedom) required to choose and to prescribe those specific instructional materials which would result in an individual learner's working in a sustained manner on relevant learning tasks. These data have to do with what these 12,000 teachers have to say about teacher involvement, time, and training in relation to the selection and use of those materials.

To begin with, 45% reported that they *had not* been involved in the selection of the instructional materials that are most used in their classrooms. Second, the remaining 55% (those who had been involved in selecting their most-used materials) reported that on the average they had spent about *one hour* annually in selecting such materials. Finally, of this same 55%, less than half had received any training in the effective instructional use of the materials in question. (Some of these materials are large, complex instructional systems having many components and providing for a variety of instructional strategies new to many teachers.)

It does not seem unreasonable to infer from these findings that in many cases the probability is rather low that regular classroom teachers are in a position to select and use those instructional materials that will (1) best insure that an individual learner will be regularly using materials that will be appropriate to that student's learning needs and (2) will be likely to provide for that student's sustained activity on tasks relevant to those needs. Just how low this probability might be, is, of course, difficult to say, but these findings do provide an insight into the reality of materials selection and use in classrooms across the country that is a far cry from what is probably best described as the current mythology of instructional materials usage. This "mythology" (propagated by both producers and adopters of materials alike) paints a picture in which each student is actively involved in what for him or her are highly relevant learning tasks using an entirely appropriate material that has been carefully and knowledgeably selected by a teacher who has the freedom, the time, and the training required to make all the necessary materials-related decisions for a class of 30 students. This is a picture in which something is, indeed, "myth-ing."

With these findings regarding the role of regular classroom teachers in material selection and use clearly in focus, we may now properly raise what I have come to think of as the "P.L. 94-142–'IEP'–question." This question can be framed as follows: "If most regular classroom teachers are so ill-equipped (because of lack of training, time, and, in many cases, involvement) in choosing instructional materials that will best fit their own teaching requirements and the *specific learning needs of each individual student in their classrooms*, how can *regular* classroom teachers be expected to create an 'individual educational plan' that will result in effective instruction for each handicapped learner who is mainstreamed into their classrooms?"

This is the question that I kept foremost in mind as I set out to familiarize myself with how the *special-education* teacher (in contrast to the *regular* classroom teacher) relates to these same issues of instructional materials selection and use. I have come to some tentative answers based on interviews with what of necessity has been a small but not atypical group of people involved with the education of the handicapped. Among these were special-education teachers, supervisors, local instructional resource personnel, university-based researchers and teachers of special-education teachers, personnel at an Area Learning Resource Center and at a state-sponsored center, school principals, and last, but certainly not least, a number of handicapped learners. I also observed a regular classroom in which handicapped learners were being "mainstreamed." No doubt more time and more interviews would refine what I have to say at this point; however, here are my tentative conclusions.

First of all, I think that it is fair to say that, by and large, the teacher of handicapped learners rarely has had any more training in the selection and use of instructional materials than the regular classroom teacher. Nevertheless, I think that it is also fair to say that the teacher of the handicapped tends to give much more attention to, and is much more concerned about, the effectiveness and appropriateness of a specific instructional material than is the regular classroom teacher. I found teachers of the handicapped actively concerned with the appropriateness of a particular material for a particular learner in their classes. Not surprisingly, they wanted to know more about how to select (or adapt) a material to match their diagnosis of an individual learner's needs (and many wanted training in diagnosing those needs).

In particular, the special-education teachers I talked to were concerned with knowing how to select materials *that would help them bring about the specific behavioral changes needed for the growth of an individual learner*. In fact, special-education teachers seem to seek out materials that approach classroom instruction as *behavioral change*, and they seem to be convinced that some materials help do this better than others. On the other hand, regular classroom teachers tend to feel that most materials that cover the same subject matter are pretty much alike. (The 12,000 regular classroom teachers surveyed indicated that if the materials they were using most in their classes were no longer available, they would simply turn to other readily available commercial alternatives.) To put it perhaps unfairly, but at the same time fairly accurately: Whereas the special-education teacher expects to have to look for materials that will help the teacher shoulder the responsibility for successfully bringing about specified changes in behavior for each learner, the regular classroom teacher is more apt to operate on the assumption that all materials are pretty much alike and that some learners will learn well from them, others not so well, and still others not at all (an assumption that is reinforced by the nature of most teacher-made as well as standardized tests).

Perhaps this at least partially explains why I also found that special-education teachers seem to spend more of their own personal funds on purchasing instructional materials for their classes than do regular teachers. One special-education teacher I interviewed told me that when she had been a regular classroom teacher she never really thought much about the instructional materials she used. "I just used what the school provided." (She is from a state with a very narrow statewide materials adoption policy.) Now, however, as a special-education teacher, she is able to order and does order materials on her own. Nevertheless, she said when her classroom budget gets low, she buys materials with her own money ("about $100 worth a year"). This same teacher reported that as a regular classroom teacher, "I felt almost any material they (the state committee) had selected could be adapted to work for any group I had, but when I started working with handicapped learners I found out differently." She went on to say that, "At first, whenever I found a material that worked well with one of my group I couldn't wait to try it with another of them. But gradually I learned that this doesn't always pan out. Sometimes I have to adapt a lot, sometimes I have to find another material, and sometimes I have to develop my own. It takes time."

So it seems that the answer to my "P.L. 94-142–'IEP'–question" is that the *regular* classroom teacher is hardly in a position to develop and carry out an "individual educational plan" for individual handicapped learners because of a lack of training, time, and awareness of what is involved in an effective matching of instructional tools to learning tasks. The *special-education* teacher is somewhat better off.

This question and this answer speak directly to the issue of what must be changed for regular classroom teachers if the individual learning needs of handicapped and, indeed, of regular learners are to be met.

But to say that one thing that must be changed in order to give P.L. 94-142 a success in the regular classroom is to provide teachers with the training and the time to select and to use instructional materials appropriate to the individual needs of handicapped learners is to recognize only part of what must be changed. I say this because one might be tempted to agree that were that single change to be achieved, and classroom teachers were given both the training and the time to effectively fit materials to individual students needs, then improved instruction for handicapped learners, indeed for all learners, would be inevitable.

However, providing for these pressing teacher needs is not the only change required. This necessary change must be paralleled and supported by initiatives that result in long overdue changes among those who develop and market instructional materials and among those who establish the policies that govern the adoption, selection, and purchase of instructional materials. If these long overdue changes do not occur, teachers may find that no amount of time, training, or freedom to choose and use materials can prepare them to fulfill the P.L. 94-142 mandate to design and follow an "individual education plan" for each individual learner. If these parallel initiatives are not forthcoming, the materials being developed and adapted by producers, and reviewed and adopted by state and local materials screening committees for handicapped learners, will simply not be well enough developed and carefully enough screened to enable teachers to meet the exacting demands of that mandate. Put another way: If P.L. 94-142 is truly enforced, not only will classroom teachers find themselves in need of the skills and techniques that will enable them to build "individual education plans," but they will also need materials that have been appropriately developed and screened which help them to turn those plans into a reality for each handicapped learner.

In order to discuss the changes called for in these parallel sets of initiatives in a more focused manner, it is useful to note that each of these needed initiatives relates to changes in the "how" and "on what basis" instructional materials are "evaluated" as they pass through each level of decision-making during their entire life-cycle as usable classroom resources. I shall argue that there is a close connection between the task of improving classroom instruction and some long overdue improvements in the evaluation of instructional materials at each of the major decision points in a material's life.

Let us begin by asking why the tools of teaching needed by these classroom teachers who are being asked to develop and carry out individual educational plans for handicapped learners are not readily available and thoroughly tempered to the task now faced by those teachers. It is one thing to note that the materials used with regular students in regular classrooms have not been evaluated, revised, and, if necessary, redesigned in order to better facilitate learning for such students. It is quite another matter that materials in use with special-education students having one or more specific handicaps are, by and large, no more carefully evaluated, revised, or adapted to meet the needs of such learners. Nevertheless, this was what I found to be largely the case as I talked with special-education teachers and examined materials in special-education classrooms and in district and regional instructional materials centers that served teachers in those classrooms.

In most cases, I found shelves of materials that are currently being marketed for use in regular classrooms and teachers who were doing their best to adapt these materials to the specific needs of learners with specific handicaps. Occasionally, I found materials (mostly produced by the same two or three publishers) that had been developed specifically for use with the types of handicapped learners found in that class. This was clearly the exception rather than the rule. It goes without saying that what I observed does not bode well for the successful implementation of P.L. 94-142 in *regular* classrooms by *regular* teachers.

I have no doubt that there are many regular classroom teachers who will manage to provide helpful social environments for many learners with physical and other handicaps that have heretofore kept them apart from students who are rightfully their classmates. However, unless regular classroom teachers (and special-education teachers, as well) are given the appropriate time, training, and materials for dealing with specific learning handicaps, I see nothing but frustration ahead for all who are involved with P.L. 94-142 as far as instruction is concerned.

Having made these comments, I now want to return to the four observations made at the outset of this chapter. Taken together, these observations are designed to alert the reader to the fact that teachers are reporting: (1) that instructional materials are the essential structuring factor of both time and, hence, activities in classrooms across this country; (2) teachers have neither the time nor, in many cases, the expertise needed to select and to use these materials that will best help them to structure classroom time and activities for individual learners in order to meet the needs of their students; (3) while materials are constantly being "evaluated," "screened," and "selected" at every step, few of these evaluation activities help to deliver materials that assist classroom teachers to provide learners with learning tasks that are appropriate for and relevant to their individual needs; and (4) unless we reevaluate and reorder the values that undergird these current evaluative activities, there is little likelihood that the changes needed to help teachers carry out the mandates of P.L. 94-142 will ever be made.

Evaluation of Instructional Materials

Now, it may seem odd, or at best tangential, to maintain that the way to improve classroom instruction is by improving the evaluation of instructional materials. But this position is neither as aberrant nor as tangential as it might seem, if we remind ourselves of the purpose of such evaluations, or indeed of any evaluation. The ultimate purpose of any evaluation is, of course, to provide information with which to make a decision. Conversely, every time a decision has been made regarding one or another aspect of an instructional material, we may rest assured that some sort of "evaluation" of that material has been made. In many instances these decision-generating "evaluations" may not, and indeed, are not, recognized for what they are by those who conduct them. Nevertheless, it is important for us to realize that every time corporate decision-makers in an educational materials company decide to develop or not to develop, to market or not to market, to revise or not to revise a particular instructional material, *that material has been evaluated*. And every time an editorial director decides to shape a material one way rather than another, that material *has been evaluated*. Similarly, every time a company sales representative decides to recommend or not to recommend a particular material to a prospective purchaser, *that material has been evaluated*. In addition, every time USOE, NIE, or any other public or private funding agency decides to fund either the development or the dissemination of one material and not other materials, *those materials have been evaluated*. Furthermore, every time a member of a state- or local-level materials-adoption or screening committee decides to include or exclude a particular material from its list of approved materials, *that material has been evaluated*. Likewise, every time a teacher chooses a material for classroom use from such a list, or from a publisher's catalog, or at a commercial exhibit, *that material has been evaluated*. And every time that teacher uses a material for a specific purpose or decides not to use it again, *that material has been evaluated*. Finally, although hardly ever recognized for what it is, *every time a learner uses a particular instructional material in a purposeful way or fails to so use it, that material is undergoing an evaluation that is far more important than those evaluations it has undergone prior to that moment.* For it is only at this moment of instruction, this ultimate bottom line as it were, that it becomes possible to come to something approaching a valid decision as to the effective *instructional value* of a particular instructional material.

When we reflect on the pervasiveness of "evaluation" throughout the life of an instructional material, we can begin to see that key decisions are constantly being made, on the basis of these evaluations, that can and do have a direct bearing on how effectively a given material will function at the "moment" of instruction as it happens in a given classroom for a given learner. The long evaluative line of decision-making that caused that particular material (rather than some other one) to be produced, marketed, screened, adopted, chosen, and used in that particular classroom for that particular learner has all been aimed at the "moment" of instruction. Or has it?

To answer this question properly it becomes necessary, as I suggested at the outset, to examine the values that are operating beneath each of these evaluative decisions. For it is only by examining the values that ultimately dominate the decision-making at each one of the key decision-making points in the life of an instructional material that we can both answer the question and reach a clearer understanding of how instrumental the evaluation of instructional materials is, and can be, in shaping the success or failure of a given material during these "moments" of instruction which together add up to the ultimate bottom line of learning.

As we shall see, there are some other bottom lines that can often take priority over the learning considerations at one or another decision point in the life of an instructional material.

There is simply no escaping the fact that the outcome of a particular evaluation is controlled by dominant *values*, and that the act of evaluating is always an extension of the act of *valuing*. And

Evaluation of Instructional Materials 199

what can, unfortunately, be all too easily demonstrated is that the values underpinning most evaluations of instructional materials today have little to do with more essential values that give ultimate purpose to the materials of learning. These essential values are, by definition, related to the effective delivery of instructional assistance to learners.

If the essential concern of an instructional material is the effective delivery of instructional assistance to individual learners across all those instructional "moments" which taken together add up to the "bottom line of learning," then the values underpinning that concern must relate to *clear, effective* instructional communication that keeps learners on task and that provides feedback to each learner as he or she proceeds through a sequence of learning tasks. But in order to insure that clear and effective instructional communication has, in fact, occurred there must be constant feedback gathered during these instructional moments to those who develop and to those who assign the materials to learners. Instructional theory and empirical research on instructional practice (Anderson, 1969; Anderson, 1976; Bloom, 1976; MacDonald, 1976; and Tyler, 1950) increasingly corroborate what instructionally effective teachers have always known intuitively: that careful attention to communicating to learners so that one is sure the learners understand in such a way that it becomes thoroughly and demonstrably internalized (*in-structured*) are the essential elements of the learning (*in-structuring*) process. However, when one examines the values that underpin most current evaluations of instructional materials, these essential learning (in-structuring) criteria and values are hardly in a central position.

For instance, we have pointed out that, whenever an educational materials company decides to develop or to market a material, an evaluation of that particular material takes place. This is certainly as it should be. However, evaluations made at this phase of an instructional material's life tend to be those values that operate in any highly competitive market atmosphere. These values are implicit in the major question asked of any product development or marketing effort. First among these questions is, "Will the product sell in sufficient quantity or with a high enough profit margin to justify a development or marketing effort?" If a product fails to pass this evaluation, it never makes its way to the classroom. Often these questions are answered on the basis of the intuition or experience of one person, but more often, answers are based on information gathered from sales representatives, from classroom teachers, from curriculum directors, and from school administrators. This being the case, it should be noted that the product's ultimate users—learners—are not considered to be relevant sources of information on which to base a judgment about the potential value of a particular instructional material.

However, a question must sooner or later be asked as to whether learners are, in fact, able to learn from a product, no matter how marketable, and profitable, it may prove to be. This question is not answered as often as one might think. In fact, for most materials currently being used by learners, this question has never been asked or answered by those who are marketing (and, in most cases, who have developed) the material. This fact has been aphoristically underscored at the outset of an article, "The Trouble with Textbooks," by Broudy (1975), which points out the standard reason learners are not used by publishers in evaluating the effectiveness of their textbooks: "kids don't buy books, teachers do."

Given this fact of an instructional material's life, it is not at all surprising to find that education companies place great *value* on what educators say they want a material to be like, rather than on direct research with learners on what it needs to be like. As a result of this valuing of what educators want to be able to find in a material, there is no question that publishers and other producers of all types of instructional materials pay close attention to what is put into every one of their products. They also pay close attention to what they should not put into (or what they should take out of) a specific product. But the overriding, operating assumption is that all one needs to do is to check with educators on what they think about a material, and then to develop the sort of material that they say they need (i.e., will buy). This is an assumption that deserves to be seriously questioned.

There are times when a developer/producer does seek an answer to whether learners have, in fact, learned what was included in a particular material they have published. But when they do this, producers—rather than gathering information and evaluating how well their product functions, instructional *moment* by instructional *moment*, with representative individual learners—base evaluations on the statistical mean-score gains achieved by groups of learners. Such "field tests" give a teacher who must prescribe a particular material for a particular learner no real help. Nevertheless, in these cases both producers and educators alike are usually satisfied if the field test produces a statistically significant gain in the mean achievement score of a large, undifferentiated group of learners (usually the larger, the better). These data, if favorable, tend to satisfy the educators' need to know that the materials "work." They are also useful to the producer as an aid in advertising and marketing the product. If the data are not favorable, they can be conveniently ignored.

Only in exceptional cases do producers gather data carefully enough and analyze them thoroughly enough to discover where and why a material is instructionally strong or instructionally weak, how it might be improved, or how and why the material might be particularly useful in meeting the specific needs of individual learners (i.e., just the sort of information that a teacher would require to develop an effective individual educational plan for a handicapped learner). In sum, most producer evaluations ("field tests") are in effect market tests, conducted to establish the fact that the materials have been used by as wide an array of learners as possible, thereby establishing as wide a market as possible. It is not uncommon in the nonprint media area to find films, filmstrips, and cassettes listed in catalogues with no designation whatsoever as to the age or grade level for which the materials might be well suited—and with no hint that the materials were ever as much as tried out with learners—let alone revised before entering the market.

Despite this situation (or perhaps because of it), more and more educational materials companies are claiming their products to be well suited for use with handicapped learners. As one trade association announcement recently put it to its member companies: "Looking for money? How about five hundred million dollars?" The flier goes on to describe a guide to help media producers "participate in this funding" for the handicapped (NAVA, n.d.). There is little or no mention about how to *develop appropriate* products for that special market, or about how to evaluate them so as to insure their appropriateness. The few companies that do design and sell their materials targeted specifically for handicapped learners must face the prospect of a smaller market than do the designers and marketers of "buckshot" materials that are claimed to be useful for all types of learners. They may pay a high cost for limiting themselves in the marketplace because purchasers are not always willing to pay a higher price for especially targeted products. This is to be expected, however, in a market in which products look pretty much alike until carefully examined, a market in which few buyers look under the "instructional hood" as it were, or give a product a trial run to see how it has been put together and how well it works. Far too few educators, given their lack of time and their lack of professional training in examining products, really know what to look for either under the hood or during a trial run. Consequently, they continue to be influenced by the instructionally less-essential characteristics of material such as packaging, prestige (of the author or developer) and, of course, the "new" approach to the content. Seldom do they ask the "bottom line of learning" question, "Will this material help a teacher (either myself or the teacher I'm selecting this for) to change a learner's behavior more effectively, more efficiently, or more humanely than the material I am now using?" Yet it is somewhat encouraging to find that *special-education* teachers seem to ask these bottom line questions a bit more frequently than do the majority of regular classroom teachers.

But the fact is that P.L. 94-142, with its explicit mandate for individual educational plans, is dependent upon that majority of teachers who aren't looking under the instructional hood. Thus, those responsible for helping schools to carry out this mandate should at least know that they ought to be looking more carefully at the materials they are considering using with handicapped learners. But in order to do this, it is important for those who hope to implement P.L. 94-142 to understand the values and valuing that underpin the current "evaluations" that are used to justify a material's presence in the educational marketplace and in the classroom. This means understanding the values being applied not only by decision-makers in the educational materials industry but also at state, local, and school building levels as well.

They must also understand that the values applied by these decision-makers at particular times will depend, to a very great extent, on where in the life cycle of a product the decision is being made. If the decision is being made when a product is being screened at the state level (usually by a committee of lay persons, teachers, parents, and curriculum as well as subject matter experts), the values given priority are usually of two sorts. First, there are such social values as ethnic, racial, religious, and sex fairness. In many states, legislatures have made the application of these values into legal requirements. Second come the most ubiquitous of all values applied at this level: the long-term social/educational values on which criteria related to content coverage and treatment are based. These are criteria applied by the committee (and its local subcommittees) in order to decide which materials currently offered by the educational materials industry best fit the curriculum content that has been agreed upon as most appropriate for the schools of that particular state. Here again, in some cases, state legislatures have legally mandated that certain content must be included (or omitted from) materials selected for classroom use. At the present time, these social/educational values and the criteria they generate take up a major portion of the time and energy of state level decisions about instructional materials.

Surely, no one would argue that the social values and the long-term educational integrity of a material are unimportant. But what of values related to a material's *current instructional integrity,* its instructional effectiveness, and its specific appropriateness in relation to the specific instructional (in-structuring) needs of specific learners? In most states where there is state-level screening of materials (there are presently statewide screening or adoption committees in about half of the 50 states), the application of criteria generated by such performance-focused values is left largely to local curriculum committees, who in many cases pass the responsibility on to the individual classroom teacher. Even in the two states that currently mandate attention to values concerned with a material's instructional performance (California and Florida), the generation of specific criteria for materials screening is a matter of local responsibility. But on what basis can this responsibility be exercised when teachers have never been trained either in the development of or in the application of criteria that will help them to decide the extent to which a particular material will be likely to meet the needs of particular learners? Yet this is precisely the expertise that is needed to carry out the mandate of P.L. 94-142 for the development of individual educational plans.

Therefore, even though a state, county, or large district has done the work of screening for curriculum content coverage with an appropriate emphasis on social awareness and fairness, the values that must eventually be applied, if a material is to be evaluated in terms of its ability to facilitate the in-structuring of specific competencies into the behavior of individual learners, are very seldom found articulated in the form of operative evaluative criteria. This difficult task is left largely to classroom teachers at the elementary school level and to department heads, along with teachers at the secondary school level.

On the face of it, it seems reasonable to leave this task to those who have the most direct contact with the learners for whom materials are to be chosen, but at the risk of over-reiterating a point, I submit that the key question is how well are they (those regular classroom teachers) prepared to make operative these important instructional values to carry out this task? The answer, once again (to reiterate another point), is that most classroom teachers are not only ill prepared, but also they do not have the time either to develop or to apply criteria generated by these often-neglected instructional values.

For the most part, to whatever extent instructional values are made operative is done largely on an experiential or intuitive basis, and, even then, only by the more able, more concerned teachers in a group. This is not to say that there aren't teachers who have developed an excellent sense of how to choose materials that fit not only their own teaching preferences, but also the needs of specific learners as well. However, these teachers tend to be in the minority and their sense of how they, in fact, do what they do is not only *not* shared systematically with their colleagues, it is something that they, themselves, do so unconsciously that they would have a difficult time sharing it, even if required to.

Thus, other teachers, with whom the experienced chooser of materials might serve on a materials selection committee, don't necessarily learn new skills from those who are better at the task. As anyone who has served on, or observed the workings of, such a committee knows, the short time, the lack of agreed-upon procedures, and the absence of "shareable" techniques often result in heavy dependence of the entire committee on the judgments of one or two of its members. These are those teachers who seem to have a better intuitive grasp, more prestige, more energy, or more hard-earned experience in judging the quality and appropriateness of the materials being considered. (And if, as is often the case, the committee lacks such people, its members are very often heavily influenced in their decision by which company's sales representative happens to be most readily available at the time.)

Unlike their counterparts at the state and district levels, teachers who serve on school or departmental materials selection committees (or who are simply serving their own classroom needs) would hardly ever describe what they are doing as "screening" materials (i.e., evaluating them in order to decide which among a group of materials are, and which are not, compatible with those broad-based educational and social values mentioned above). Teachers at the classroom level will describe what they are doing as looking for (and finally choosing) materials they feel will "fit" or be "right" for their particular students. But, as we have already noted, this is a basically intuitive judgment that may or may not be informed by past experience indicating that a particular material (or type of material) will work well with a particular learner (or type of learner). Whether intuition or experience is operating at this "choosing level" in a material's life cycle, the classroom teacher's operative values generate a different emphasis and a different set of questions than those which predominate at the state or district "screening level." A teacher's questions are primarily related to how successfully a particular material will help that teacher to develop specific psychomotor/cognitive/affective structures within specific learners. Few teachers articulate what they are about in precisely those terms; but for teachers concerned with *in-structuring* learners, these questions take precedence over the broader-scale curriculum, social, and legal questions, and values that operate at other levels of decision-making.

Teachers evaluating materials are concerned with questions such as: "Is this what my pupils need?" "Will they understand it?" "Will they like it?" "Are the examples and exercises clear, and varied enough, and are there enough of them?" "Is the material easy to use?" "Will it last?" "Is it easy to keep track of?" "Will the pupils get bored with it?" Teachers are less apt to ask: "Does the material conform with the state's/district's curriculum framework?" "Does it represent and treat all groups fairly?" "Does the binding and packaging and price conform with state/district regulations?"

In sum, the questions teachers tend to ask about a material are generated by values related to instructional teaching/learning concerns. And, as we have seen, these questions (especially those directly related to how well learners understand specific aspects of the material) are given a lesser priority by state/district and by producer/marketer materials "evaluators" who feel justified in leaving the "instructional questions" to classroom teachers. Yet, as we have seen, down at the classroom level the answers to these all-important instructional questions are more apt to be based on intuition and arrived at hurriedly under the pressure of time on the basis of no objective analysis of the instructional integrity of a material's design or empirical evidence of its actual performance.

The result of this state of affairs seems to be a noticeable lack of accumulated, "shareable" information, knowledge, technique, and skill in materials evaluation among regular classroom teachers. Each teacher seems destined to learn (or destined not to learn) what he or she knows only from his or her own limited individual experience. State and district agencies, publishers, and nationwide marketers do very little to change this condition, for, as we have seen, their priorities tend not to be the priorities of the classroom teacher. Their specific evaluative criteria and the values underlying those criteria differ because the day-to-day decisions they have to make at their particular levels of the instructional materials world are different from those made at the teachers' level.

Figure 10.1 is a schema illustrating the four major levels of evaluative decision making that operate during the life cycle of an instructional material. The four levels are labeled: (1) developer/producer; (2) screener/adopter; (3) chooser/prescriber; and (4) user/student. At each level, the "evaluations" that take place, the

Figure 10.1

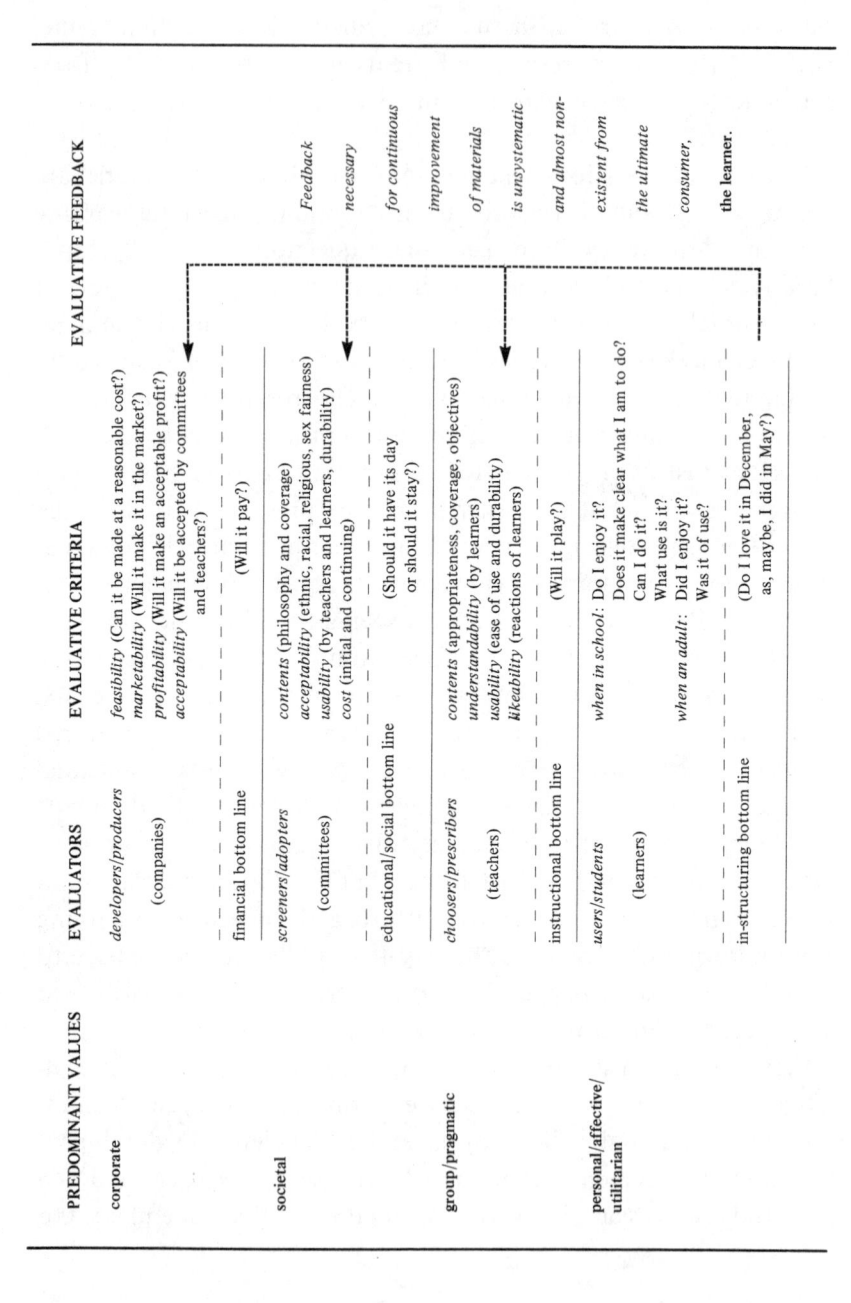

PREDOMINANT VALUES	EVALUATORS	EVALUATIVE CRITERIA	EVALUATIVE FEEDBACK
corporate	developers/producers (companies)	*feasibility* (Can it be made at a reasonable cost?) *marketability* (Will it make it in the market?) *profitability* (Will it make an acceptable profit?) *acceptability* (Will it be accepted by committees and teachers?)	
	financial bottom line	(Will it pay?)	
societal	screeners/adopters (committees)	*contents* (philosophy and coverage) *acceptability* (ethnic, racial, religious, sex fairness) *usability* (by teachers and learners, durability) *cost* (initial and continuing)	Feedback necessary
	educational/social bottom line	(Should it have its day or should it stay?)	for continuous improvement
group/pragmatic	choosers/prescribers (teachers)	*contents* (appropriateness, coverage, objectives) *understandability* (by learners) *usability* (ease of use and durability) *likeability* (reactions of learners)	of materials is unsystematic
	instructional bottom line	(Will it play?)	and almost non-existent from
personal/affective/ utilitarian	users/students (learners)	*when in school:* Do I enjoy it? Does it make clear what I am to do? Can I do it? What use is it? *when an adult:* Did I enjoy it? Was it of use?	the ultimate consumer,
	in-structuring bottom line	(Do I love it in December, as, maybe, I did in May?)	the learner.

criteria that are applied, the decisions that result, and the implications of those decisions are different.

At level one, developers/producers ultimately must be concerned with corporate values. Individuals in the industry may have a sincere desire to help handicapped learners, or to introduce a new approach to teaching a particular subject, or even to revise totally the school curriculum. But corporately, they must be guided by the criteria of product marketability, purchaser acceptability, and financial feasibility. Their eyes, as individuals concerned about education, may be on the "In-structuring Bottom Line" which appears beneath the fourth, or learner/user level, of the schema, but their corporate eye must be on the "Financial Bottom Line" for each particular instructional material they develop, produce, and market. In addition to watching that bottom line for each individual material, they must also constantly watch their overall *"corporate* bottom line"–the annual profit and loss statement. (A recent example of this fact of corporate life in the educational materials industry is a report in the press that a major producer of instructional materials had decided to invest a good portion of its available capital not in producing more, or better, instructional materials but in buying a profitable tourist attraction.)

At the second (screener/adopter) level of an instructional material's life, we find that fewer decisions are influenced predominantly by economic criteria although, as indicated, the high cost of a material is a factor, but not usually a major one. At this second level, however, the values undergirding decisions tend to be the broad-ranged, social/educational ones discussed above, and the criteria generated by these values are, as we have already pointed out, usually expressed by screener/adopter committees in such questions as "Does the material's *content coverage* fit our state's or our district's educational goals?" or "How *acceptable* is the material regarding major current social issues (e.g., racial, religious, sex bias; social and work attitudes toward the handicapped)?" or

"Can the material be used with ease by teachers and learners?" A material that is rated low on *usability/durability* will be screened out and fail to be among those materials from which decision-makers at the chooser/prescriber level are permitted to select. As shown at this third level, the dominant criteria of the individual teacher are *not* the broad educational and social criteria that are uppermost in the minds of those who serve on level-two screening committees. At level three, the individual classroom teacher is much closer to the "In-structuring Bottom Line" of the *ultimate user* of instructional materials: *the learner*.

The values that undergird level-three decisions result in a heavy emphasis on instructionally focused criteria for *regular* classroom teachers. As noted, special-education teachers focus even more tightly on those criteria. As mentioned earlier, special-education teachers focus on criteria they feel will help them to identify a material that will be useful *in-structuring* a particular learner who has a specific handicap or other disability. These criteria are represented in the schema as *Usability* (can and will learners use it?), *Understandability* and/or *Readability* (can learners understand it?), and *Likeability* (do learners like it?). The individual classroom teacher/chooser is also shown in the schema to be concerned with *Contents*. But this concern is not whether the contents of a material cover the broad scope of curriculum concerns that are usually the focus of level-two screeners/adopters. A teacher's concern about content is usually expressed as a demand that a material contain *objectives* needed by specific learners to help them master a specific weakness at a specific time. Finally, as we approach the bottom of the schema, we arrive at the fourth level (learner/user), which gives meaning to and reminds us of the purpose of the "In-structuring Bottom Line." At this fourth level, it is difficult to speak as confidently about the values and the criteria that undergird a learner's all-important, evaluative decision to say "yes" or "no" to a material, to open or to close his or her affective, psychomotor, cognitive receptors to it—to be *in-structured or not* by a material.

Evaluation of Instructional Materials 211

Learners I interviewed seem to base their *initial* evaluative decisions as bottom line evaluators of materials predominantly on affective criteria. The first question seems to be, "will I, or do I, like using it?" Often, the very young learner doesn't realize that the material is a learning material at all; however, when learners do reach that realization (or are made to realize it) I sense that there is more of a concern with questions like, *"does it make clear what I am to do?"* and *"can I do it?"* Later, during adolescence, the basis of the student/user's evaluation seems to shift to criteria related to usability. But this is usability of a very different sort from the usability criteria applied by decision-makers on the three prior levels of materials' evaluation. The student/user's concern at this point seems best summed up in the question, *"What use is it to me?"* There is even some willingness to forgo affective criteria (*"Do I enjoy it?"*) if there is some sense that the hard work that may have to be put into using the material can be of some identifiable use now or in the forseeable future. These affective and utilitarian values that seem to undergird evaluations of instructional materials made as ultimate consumers are using the materials are also applied by these users after they have left school. These ultimate evaluations are made at some later point in a learner's life and are likely to be part of a largely unconscious evaluation of their whole school experience, or, at best, of a particular type of instructional material (e.g., "dry textbooks," "make-work workbooks," and "Friday-afternoon-time-filling films"). But the overriding criteria still are, *"did I enjoy it?,"* and, *"was it of use?"*

One gets the sense in these days of "back to basics" that some of the concerned citizens who have campaigned for and won appointments on state and local materials' screening committees (or who, failing that, have formed self-appointed 'screaming committees') are convinced that most of the materials used in school teach nothing useful; at worst, slick and wrong—at best, colorful but frivolous, "fun"-oriented materials. To others "back to basics" also means back to what they see as basic moral and spiritual values, which they believe should be applied to the evaluation of instructional materials. Whichever orientation they have, most of these concerned citizens, as well as the concerned educators who serve on the screener/adopter committees, make assumptions about how their committee's decisions eventually will be evaluated by student/users at the "In-structuring Bottom Line." But very few ever make use of feedback from that point of ultimate evaluation. This is equally true for corporate level decision-makers in the education materials industry.

Before leaving the schema, I would like to point out that its purpose is not to precisely define each decision-making level and to specify *all* the values and criteria operating at each level. In reality, the levels, the values, and the criteria are, of course, less neatly stratified. The purpose of the schema is simply to help illustrate what I believe to be some truths that are frequently overlooked about the central and rather complex role that "evaluation" plays in the life course of all instructional materials.

In reality, it would also be more accurate to speak about the interrelated, and sometimes conflicting, roles that are played by (or assigned to) evaluation, when decisions are made about instructional materials at the different levels of a material's life cycle. For evaluation at each level is predominantly influenced by four inexorably related, but different, "bottom lines": the *financial bottom line* of the developer/producer, the *educational/social bottom line* of the screener/adopter, the *instructional bottom line* of the teacher chooser/prescriber. It is the last of these which is the closest to the ultimate consumer—the learner—but all three impinge on an even more final bottom line that has to do with the ultimate value of what each individual learner feels he or she has received from the years spent in the classroom. The *in-structuring bottom line* (what stays with each individual learner, rather than what stays or doesn't stay in the curriculum or what pays or doesn't pay in the materials marketplace) *is what matters in the end.*

Evaluation of Instructional Materials

As we can now see, the question, asked in the title of this chapter—"How can the evaluation of instructional materials help improve classroom instruction received by handicapped learners?" has within it the questions, "evaluation of what sort?" "by whom?" "for what purpose?" and "at what points in a material's life?" As we can also see, the answers to these questions are far from simple, but they are discernible. And they all point to the overriding fact that most of the evaluative questions being asked today of instructional materials are not very directly focused on the issue of improving the quality of classroom instruction being delivered to individual learners. For in order to do that these evaluations would have to pay much greater attention to values related to what we have labeled "the moments of instruction" and the "in-structuring bottom line."

Of course, there will always be those (and not only commercial developers and producers) who will claim that the in-structuring bottom line is best evaluated by whether or not a material continues to be purchased and used by schools over time. Thus, success in the competitive marketplace economy, they say, while not perfect, is the best measure of a material's instructional value that we can hope for. For them, the financial bottom line is an indirect but perfectly adequate measure of all the other bottom lines. As just mentioned, this view is held not solely by corporations in the commercial sector. It has also been espoused recently by a representative of one of the federally-sponsored educational laboratories that have been heavily involved in materials development during the last decade. His statement was made at a symposium dealing with minimum evaluative criteria for instructional products held at the 1976 convention of the American Educational Research Association. At that symposium, John E. Hopkins (1976) Director of Planning and Evaluation, Research for Better Schools, Inc., took the position that as long as an instructional material is not found to be obviously harmful to learners (e.g., socially fair, free of bias and stereotyping), "... there should be no further requirements, and the marketplace should simply be allowed to work its will." Whether or not one agrees with this position, it is one that is obviously broadly held. But even if one were to accept it as valid, the position does not address the question being dealt with in this chapter, which is that improvements in the evaluation of instructional materials can help to improve the quality of classroom instruction being received by individual handicapped learners. This position simply fails to come to grips with the fact that there is a need to be concerned with the improvement of even those materials that have been "evaluated" positively on the basis of their having been accepted in the marketplace.

In contradistinction to this "let the marketplace decide" position, the position being taken in this chapter is that the continuous, ongoing improvement of all products used by handicapped learners is a necessary component of the successful implementation of P.L. 94-142 at the classroom level. Implicit in this position, and in the schema just presented, is the assumption that such improvement would be forthcoming if developers/producers were to focus more directly on the in-structuring bottom line by using feedback from handicapped learners/users of their materials via direct observations, testing, and, where appropriate, interviews of such learners and their teachers in an effort to improve the effectiveness of specific materials.

Given the fact that so few producers of regular classroom materials historically have used this sort of direct consumer feedback as a basis for product improvement, there is a need to press all developers (both private and federally funded) to do this as their products are used with handicapped learners. This need is underlined by the fact that an estimated 90-plus percent* of the materials currently included in NIMIS (National Instructional Materials Information System), designed as an information resource for teachers of the handicapped, are in fact regular classroom materi-

---

*Personal interview with the director of NIMIS.

als that have not been designed for and developed on the basis of direct feedback from handicapped learners/users (or, for that matter, on the basis of direct feedback from learners/users of any sort).

It may, at this point, appear to the reader that most of the ground covered thus far adds up to a discouraging prognosis for the success of P.L. 94-142's instructional mandate for regular classroom teachers. What then, are we to conclude? Are we to say that P.L. 94-142 may very well have such social and emotional benefits for both handicapped and nonhandicapped children in regular classrooms that we should be willing to tolerate something less than success on the instructional side of classroom life? Are we to conclude that, after all, instructionally, things may end up being no better, but then again no worse, for the handicapped learner who is "mainstreamed" than they have been all along for the regular learner in the regular classroom? Can we tolerate such a "head in the sand" conclusion?

To come to such a conclusion is perhaps a tempting alternative to heading down the difficult road of instructional improvement which lies ahead. But as alternatives go, it would be a sorry "cop out." For despite the fact that there is an enormous job to be done, and too few people who are being given too little time in which to do it, the nature of the job does become clearer the more we analyze the task of instructional improvement. We are now at that point, where our own "time on task" is essential to our learning what we need to learn. And we can be mildly encouraged by the fact that there are actually some people, in the educational materials industry, in the federal government, in independent agencies, in universities, in regional centers, and in classrooms that are "on-task" trying to solve the problem. But, as yet, they are too few in number.

As mentioned earlier, there are a few companies in the educational materials industry making substantial investments of time and effort in the development of materials designed specifically for learners with specific handicaps or disabilities. Some of these companies are concentrating their efforts primarily on designing materials in a particular learning mode, or in a medium that is most appropriate for learners with a particular problem, such as in hearing, speaking, or seeing. It is clearly to the credit of these producers that they are making this investment. However, there are also companies that are doing more. These companies are putting an equal amount of time and effort into continuously monitoring how well a particular material is accomplishing its instructional (*in-structuring*) task with handicapped learners who are representative of those for whom the product has been developed. A few of these companies even provide inservice teacher training that seems to face head-on those instructional problems that other teachers have run into when using the product with individual learners. This sort of honest, straightforward dealing with the problem of instructional improvement is as commendable as it is exceptional.

Many more companies must begin to provide evidence that they too are paying this sort of attention to the in-structuring bottom line before any substantial progress toward instructional improvement for handicapped learners can be made in regular classrooms under the mandate of P.L. 94-142. The necessary adjustments in values and evaluative criteria by decision-makers in the educational materials industry has not yet occurred. As the schema illustrates, the feedback loop is not complete. But, there is some movement.

Concomitant with this mild movement within the educational materials industry have been a number of federal initiatives. These initiatives have managed to stimulate a variety of activities, all aimed at improving the selection and use of instructional materials for handicapped learners. To date, these initiatives include a national needs assessment project, interactions with companies and trade associations in the education industry, help to noncommercial developers, a set of "standard criteria" for the selection of materials, and a National Instructional Materials Information System. Particularly important among these initiatives was the role played by the National Center on Educational Media and Materials for the Handicapped (NCEMMH) at The Ohio State University. The Center had been instrumental in stimulating commercial and noncommercial developers to pay more attention to the development of materials targeted to the needs of handicapped learners. The Center had also functioned successfully as "broker" between special educators engaged in designing their own materials for specific handicapped learners and commercial companies interested in producing and marketing such materials. In particular the *Developers' Guide* created and distributed by NCEMMH as a guide for materials developers pays commendable attention to "the in-structuring bottom line."

Another product of this federally funded initiative is related to two other levels in the life cycle of instructional materials at the screener/adopter level and the chooser/prescriber level. This is a document entitled "Standard Criteria for the Selection and Evaluation of Instructional Materials." The criteria are comprehensive and are clearly aimed at helping decision-makers at both the screening and chooser levels to arrive at a reasonably good teacher-materials learner "fit" or "match." I should point out that the system employed by the document to arrive at such a "match" was viewed as being hard to use by the few special education teachers I asked to react to it. However, given the fact that teachers have so little time in which to examine and to choose materials, any approach that takes time to master is apt to be viewed as unnecessarily complicated. However, because these "Standard Criteria" are aimed at matching a material to both teacher requirements and learner characteristics, their underlying values are more directly focused on the schema's "instructional bottom line" than are many other available lists of criteria. Another effort worthy of mention (somewhat parallel to the "Standard Criteria" document) related to our present concern is the Materials Analysis Project (MAP) of the Northeast Area Learning Resources Center, begun in the fall of 1975. To date the project has produced materials' screening and review forms and has drawn heavily on NCEMMH's "Standard Criteria" as well as the materials analysis reports published by Educational Products Information Exchange (EPIE). The MAP materials' review form does ask the reviewer to search for evidence that the materials under review have worked successfully with handicapped learners, but because the MAP project is basically a screening and review process it, by definition, falls short of what teachers need to know in order to deal successfully with the classroom level tasks expected of them under the individual educational plan strategy mandated by P.L. 94-142.

However, it must be noted that, even in these very comprehensive approaches to the screening and choosing of materials for classroom use, there are no specific questions addressed to whether a material has been developed or revised on the basis of direct learner feedback, and no advice to the teacher about the value of simply trying a material with a learner or two as a way of empirically establishing its instructional level, effectiveness, and appropriateness. Such a suggestion along with some guidance as to how to check out a material during such a trial run would counterbalance these instruments' dependence on what the producer states as being the "instructional level," "interest level," and "appropriateness," etc., of the material. Yet despite this obvious shortcoming and their rather *potpourri* approach to materials' analysis, NCEMMH's "Standard Criteria" and MAP are going to be a help to those interested in improving the screening and the choosing of materials for handicapped learners.

In addition to its work on stimulating materials developers, and helping screeners and choosers of materials, the National Center NCEMMH) also developed an information system (NIMIS)* that can be used by screeners and choosers to find appropriate materials for handicapped learners. Here again, while there are specific

---

*Now NICSEM and located at the University of Southern California.

shortcomings of the system in its present, still embryonic state, the concept is sound and the simple fact that it exists in its present form and size is impressive. NIMIS clearly has great potential as a help to teachers who are willing to invest time and energy to find out about materials that they otherwise might not know exist. One of NIMIS's strong points is that one of its major information categories, "Evaluation Information" gives evidence of the use of each material in the system with handicapped learners. At present, the information provided is a bit lean, but there is no reason why it must remain so. Indeed, there is every reason to believe that this is the category that will increase most in breadth and depth over time.

The one shortcoming of NIMIS may be its inability to have its information get through to the chooser/prescriber level of decision-making on any large scale. As alluded to above, a teacher has got to be willing to invest time and effort.

It is clear that teachers want more immediate and easier access to information on materials. Another shortcoming of NIMIS in its present state of development is that it does not provide teachers with information that helps them to interrelate the use of materials in the system, either with one another or with larger "instructional systems" type materials that are not included in NIMIS.

For instance, teachers need to know whether a particular multimedia material, simulation game, kit, etc., has been, or may easily be integrated into the use of the larger instructional program they may be using with a particular group of learners. They also need to know how the smaller mediated materials that are included in NIMIS relate to one another. And teachers need to have that information at their fingertips. This means that there is a need for well-integrated descriptive information and evaluative data on materials for the handicapped immediately accessible to teachers *at the building level.* This would seem to be an essential element in the successful implementation of P.L. 94-142 by classroom teachers. The few scattered entrepreneurial efforts in the commercial sector that are aimed at supplying this sort of building-level information to teachers (some of which were originally developed under Federally-funded projects for the handicapped) are each severely limited in one way or another and fail to deal effectively, if at all, with a teacher's need for integrated information about the value of specific materials described by the system within a comprehensive framework of instructional design.

There are two statewide projects, one in Ohio, and the other in Texas, and a regional center in Connecticut, that seem to be moving toward meeting these two closely related teacher needs. The Ohio HELPS project, with its origin as a local ESEA Title III activity, has been expanded to cover about 80 percent of Ohio school districts. It seems to have something of a complementary, informal relationship to NIMIS in that it goes beyond NIMIS in the information it provides about suggested student activities and objectives. However, the amount of materials information accessible through HELPS is about half that of NIMIS. HELPS, like NIMIS, is a fairly sophisticated computerized information system that requires teachers to be willing and available to be trained in its use or that requires an intermediary to assist teachers in using the system. However, HELPS has developed an extensive cadre of local "linking agents" who do provide this aspect of the service.

The Special Education Resource System (SERS) of the Texas Education Agency calls for:

- professional leadership in the evaluation, selection, and development of special instructional materials, media, and books and other supplies; and
- inservice training for special education personnel in the better utilization of instructional materials, media, books, and other supplies.

The intent of the plan is "the development and maintenance of

Evaluation of Instructional Materials 221

the Special Education Resource System at the local level" (Texas Education Agency, 1976).

This plan, now underway, would seem to hold great promise as a comprehensive and thorough model for the successful implementation of P.L. 94-142. Its criteria for the selection of materials are aimed very clearly at the "In-structuring Bottom Line": The chief consideration *in the choice or selection* of instructional materials and its collateral parts is that it *brings about desired changes in the behavior of the learner as stated in the objectives* for the use of the material (Texas Education Agency, 1976) [Emphasis added].

What bears watching in the Texas SERS is (1) the amount and quality of training that gets through to the regular classroom teacher confronted with the P.L. 94-142-IEP mandate; (2) the accessibility and quality of materials information available to the regular classroom teacher; and (3) the arrangements made for teacher-time available to implement P.L. 94-142.

There is a noteworthy effort connected with a regional, state-sponsored agency in central Connecticut. At this SERC (Special Education Resource Center) an individual trained in instructional materials analysis by EPIE Institute is giving a course for classroom teachers in materials evaluation. Using an adaptation of the EPIE Materials Analysis System (EPIEform A) he requires teachers to develop their own selection and purchasing criteria and then to *justify* each of their purchases against competing products. Given the evidence that teachers of handicapped learners do spend considerable amounts of their own—as well as their schools'—money on materials, this approach has much to recommend it.

However much potential these last three state and regional efforts add to the national efforts mentioned earlier, there still remains the very practical problem of (1) multiplying their effects; (2) maintaining quality control as this multiplication develops; and (3) delivering both materials information to teachers—where they sit—in an easily accessible, integrated fashion and training them to apply it productively in their classrooms to help individual learners.

The importance of meeting these two teacher needs—and of meeting them right where teachers sit—through local inservice training, cannot be overemphasized. Based on my interviews of classroom teachers, I believe that this is an essential element, if there is to be success with P.L. 94-142 in classrooms across the country. This means, of course, that teachers will need the released time to be trained. And I am well aware that teacher's time — just like everyone else's time—means money. But this is one case where money can go a long way toward insuring the success of something that is worth more than money to a lot of Americans. Teachers need to know how to do a better job of evaluating a material's instructional quality before, during, and after using it. Teachers also need to know how to better "fit" or "match" materials to their teaching style as well as to the specific needs of individual learners. Finally, teachers need to know how to integrate their use of many materials into well-designed instructional plans that they can learn to observe and analyze as they implement—and improve upon—as they carry them through to completion.

A project recently undertaken by EPIE Institute and a national network of school districts, while not specifically designed to serve teachers of the handicapped, *is* aimed at creating the sort of thoroughly integrated approach to providing teachers with information on materials described above. This building-level information is being designed to enable teachers to interrelate the use of materials within their own classroom-developed instructional designs. It would seem feasible to link its work to NIMIS and to employ it as a grass roots building-level extension of NCEMMH's work. The project as currently designed calls for going beyond the delivery of an integrated building-level materials information system to include a building-level/classroom-level inservice training package in Instructional Design Decision Making for classroom teachers. This aspect of EPIE's work might also be adapted to the need of teachers confronted with dealing with the P.L. 94-142-IEP question. But, as made painfully clear throughout this chapter, the successful implementation of P.L. 94-142 in classrooms across the country is not going to be achieved simply by supplying teachers with information and training that may be useful to them in designing and carrying out the Individual Educational Plans called for in that Law. There are a number of necessary parallel developments that must also occur—each a large undertaking in and of itself. But each parallel strand must be accomplished if the full potential of P.L. 94-142 to help handicapped learners in U.S. classrooms is to be realized. In this chapter I have tried to deal with these parallel strands somewhat systematically by showing how the inevitable process of valuing and evaluation (although not always recognized as such) impinge on each strand separately and as they relate to each other.

I began with four observations, and I will end with four recommendations. The general thrust of these recommendations has been, I think, more or less apparent in what has already been said about each of the decision-making, evaluation levels described in the schema; nevertheless, it may be useful to state them explicitly:

First of all, I recommend that present initiatives such as the national needs assessment survey and NCEMMH's efforts to stimulate the development, production, and distribution of materials targeted for handicapped learners be continued, but that greater attention and incentives be given to commercial and nonprofit developers, to develop and revise their materials with greater attention to the use of direct learner/user feedback. Incentives should also be given to developers/producers of major instructional systems to provide appropriate inservice training to teachers in the effective use of the materials—particularly if the materials are being marketed as a "system." These incentives could be made available as (1) direct subsidies for research and development to any developer who is willing to make a major commitment to respond immediately to high priority product needs as identified by the National Needs Assessment Project by developing materials on the basis of learner feedback, and (2) reimbursements to schools and to classroom teachers who have purchased products that have been developed or revised on the basis of documented feedback from learners and teachers.

My second recommendation is that there be a major federal/state supported funding for the inservice training of classroom teachers (perhaps related to the recent "teacher center" legislation, perhaps independent of it) related to the choosing and using of instructional materials within a teacher generated instructional design.

My third recommendation is that a series of regional conferences to be attended by materials developers/producers/screeners/adopters be held for the purpose of focusing attention on "The Instructional Bottom Line" to examine ways in which feedback from handicapped learners/users of the products they develop and/or adopt for learner use may be integrated into their decision-making (evaluative) processes.

My fourth recommendation is that ways be established to systematically interrelate (and continuously evaluate) all extant materials information, screening and training projects, networks, and systems relevant to the implementation of P.L. 94-142 so that their impact may be collective and self-corrective in responding to the needs of teachers and learners.

References

Anderson, R. C. The comparative field experiment: An illustration from high school biology. Proceedings of the 1968 invitational conference on testing problems. Princeton, N.J.: Educational Testing Service, 1969.

Anderson, J. R. *Language, memory, and thought*. Hillsdale, N.J.: Lawrence Erlbaum Associates, 1976.

Bloom, B. S. *Human characteristics and school learning*. New York: McGraw-Hill Book Company, 1976.

Broudy, H. The trouble with textbooks. *Teachers College Record, 77*(1), 1975.

Hopkins, J. E. Criteria acceptable to the educational developer. Paper presented at the annual meeting of the American Educational Research Association, San Francisco, California, April 26, 1976.

MacDonald, F. J. Report of a study of teacher effectiveness, conducted by Educational Testing Service, undertaken at the request of California Commission for Teacher Preparation and Licensing, funded by National Institute of Education, 1976.

NAVA. Flier promoting a NAVA Special Report—*Education of the handicapped*—published by the Education Department of the National Audio-Visual Association, n.d.

Texas Education Agency. Special Education Resource System. Bulletin 766. Austin: Texas Education Agency, 1976, p. 1.

Tyler, R.W. *Basic principles of curriculum and instruction*. Chicago: The University of Chicago Press, 1950.

11.
Teacher Selection of Instructional Materials for Use with Handicapped Learners

Diane Dormant

This chapter addresses the problem of selecting instructional material for teaching the handicapped learner. It assumes that individualization of instruction is one of the educational goals of the teacher, and that, in a classroom—whether special or regular—that includes handicapped students, the unique configuration of strengths and weaknesses of each handicapped student increases both the need for individualization and the difficulties of achieving it. And, it assumes that instructional materials will be used and that both the effective individualization of instruction for a single student and the effective management of the classroom instructional system for all students can be enhanced through systematic selection of those instructional materials.

Specifically, first the teacher's role in selecting instructional materials is considered, as well as some of the problems involved in selecting materials. Then, some of the existing selection systems and their relevance to teacher-selection of materials are discussed.

With an emphasis on adaptation, a systematic selection procedure is presented. And, last, some questions are raised and some suggestions made.

The Role of the Teacher in Selection

A number of studies suggest that teachers spend little time in the selection of material, as noted by Komoski in the previous chapter. Furthermore, neither teachers themselves nor teacher-trainers gave the selection of instructional materials a high priority. Although, in fairness to these professionals, it should be noted that many school systems do not allow, let alone expect, classroom teachers to select materials. Such selection is more often carried out by administrative committees which may or may not include teacher representatives.

However, even when teachers do select instructional material, their competency in evaluating effectiveness has been questioned in a number of studies (Rothkopf, 1963; Lucas, 1974). While these studies themselves have methodological problems (Markle, 1973), they do suggest that teachers do not have the necessary skills to select effective instructional material. To the contrary, it would seem from both empirical and subjective data that teachers often select material primarily on two bases: availability and attractiveness. That is to say, if the material is on a shelf down the hall, it has a higher probability of being chosen than material which is in the downtown materials center or the state university film library—regardless of the relative quality of the material. Additionally, if non-evaluated material looks "slick," it has a higher probability of being chosen than less slick-looking material which has been field tested and found to be instructionally effective. This latter point has, of course, long been known to commercial manufacturers and publishers.

In the face of the legislative mandate as well as the professional desire to individualize instruction for all learners in a classroom which has an increasing range of individual needs, teacher-selection of materials seems to have new importance. Yet, at first glance, the status of teachers regarding selection seems dismal. However, I would point out that (to the best of my knowledge) the teachers studied are those in regular classrooms, and that in fact the points made above regarding both selection activity and selection competency may not apply to most experienced special education teachers. Based largely on a decade of direct experience, I believe that special education teachers do, in fact, spend a great deal of time evaluating, selecting, and adapting instructional materials to the individual needs of their handicapped learners. The pedagogic descendants of Anne Sullivan have long searched toy stores, hardware stores, and libraries, as well as basements and backyards, to find materials which meet the unique needs of their blind, deaf, retarded, or otherwise handicapped students. And, where organized information and materials have been made available to them, special education teachers have made enthusiastic use of them.

Therefore, I would suggest the potential usefulness of examining the needs, attitudes, and behavior of special education teachers with regard to the selection of instructional materials. Such an investigation might yield useful information regarding the directions which pre- and inservice training of regular classroom teachers might take. In fact, it is possible that training efforts associated primarily with the goal of individualizing instruction for handicapped learners might also result in individualizing instruction for non-handicapped learners as well.

The following section discusses some of the problems a teacher *actively* involved in selection processes may meet.

Selection Problems

Finding out what's available. When a new teacher first looks for what's available in instructional materials, the initial reaction is likely to be one of being overwhelmed by sheer quantity. The materials displays—even at local CEC meetings—are so crowded as to remind one of the county fairs, which they are often named after.

Tables are loaded with books, ditto master sets, kits, games, and manipulative materials; walls are alive with moving and still pictures, posters, and announcements of still more materials to come. And, should the new teacher decide to investigate the availability of materials by requesting information by mail, he or she will soon be swamped by advertisements, brochures, catalogues, directories, bibliographies, and even bibliographies of bibliographies—information from commercial publishers and manufacturers, government agencies, and professional organizations. Instructional materials seem to exist in infinite quantity and in infinite locations. So what's the problem?

First of all, infinity is not easy to deal with. How can so much information be processed? Against what criteria should judgments be made? Which claims of excellence and usefulness can one believe? And, if no material at all is found, does that mean that no material exists? Information retrieval and processing are general problems characteristic of our times. Among the current responses to these problems are a number of systems specifically related to instructional material for the handicapped. These will be discussed in a subsequent section.

A second aspect of the problem is that the infinity of materials is more apparent than real. The applicability of most of the material to any specific instructional need may be small. In fact, as the instructional need is clarified, the questions are likely to be more like these: "Where can I get material to teach addition skills to a 6-year-old blind child?" "What is available to help me teach driving skills to the deaf?" "What information is available to teach retarded adolescents to get sexual satisfaction in a socially acceptable way?" When such questions as these are asked, the quantity of available materials may abruptly diminish, sometimes to one or even none.

Finding out what's available and also *useful* involves specification of an instructional need, and that involves analyses—of the learner, of the subject matter, and of the instructional environment. While such analyses are not the province of this chapter, it might be useful to note here that the kinds and the extent of the analyses should be appropriate to the student performance desired. Three months spent in analysis when the performance desired is tying shoes may be appropriate for the learning psychologist; it is not for the classroom teacher. In any event, some instructional analysis is required to determine the instructional need, which is critical to making a satisfactory match between need and material.

Matching available materials to instructional needs. If you have ever bought a replacement part—a ribbon for your typewriter, a bag for your vacuum cleaner, a fuse for your lighting system—you know some of the problems of matching materials to needs. The first problem involves an adequate analysis of the need and an adequate description of the material satisfying that need. With instructional materials, this means not only knowing what the learner's instructional needs are, but also knowing what materials are available to respond to those needs, where they can be obtained, and so forth.

Many teachers get this kind of information by word of mouth from their peers or directly by examination of materials which exist in their school environment. With adequate implementation, more formal information systems can also become workable for teachers. For this to happen, however, it is critical that these sources be readily available to teachers and viewed as helpful by the teachers.

Evaluating the evaluation. One of the recurrent problems in descriptions of material has been the difficulty, even when the intent is honest, of communicating accurately what the material is for, who it is for, under what conditions it should be used, etc. With the advent of the specification of behavioral objectives as well as the emphasis on both formative and summative evaluation, the reliability of material descriptions is going up. Nevertheless, teachers need to make their own evaluation of the dependability and usefulness of information from commercial publishers and manufacturers, professional services, and information systems.

A shortage of time. If a shortage of time is not the most ubiquitous problem, it is (next to money) the one most frequently used to excuse all manner of omissions and shortcomings. A teacher can spend the better part of an entire weekend searching the library for material which will be consumed by the student in 30 minutes; or spend hours in finding, previewing, and ordering a film which, when it arrives, does not satisfy the instructional need. Some systematic procedure that will make the teacher's time count for more in the selection process seems to be in order.

Not finding anything suitable. A problem adding insult to injury occurs when an extensive search has been made and preliminary selection has been promising, but after all that, nothing seems suitable.

A Systematic Selection Procedure

It seems inevitable that if instruction is to be effective, teachers are going to be faced more and more frequently with selecting material appropriate to the individual needs of their handicapped students.

Efforts have been made to provide guidelines for selection activities. Even when such efforts emphasize the importance of prescriptive instruction and point out the difficulties of finding a common ground for analyzing needs and materials (e.g., Ensminger, 1972), they are seldom usable by the classroom teacher. Similarly, while evaluation is clearly an underlying factor in effective selection procedures, evaluation models do not lend themselves to the classroom teacher's situation.

The following procedure is logically developed to provide a teacher (or other user) with a sequential system for selecting material. Such a procedure can be useful whether or not it is always, or ever, rigorously applied. In addition, familiarity with such a procedure seems likely to increase teacher involvement in selecting materials, reveal problem areas, suggest alternatives, and increase the efficiency and effectiveness of the materials chosen. The usefulness of this suggested procedure remains to be validated.

Overview. The five phases of selection include activities related to the instructional need, information on materials, matching the materials to the need, expert appraisal, and student try-out.

Phase 1: Instructional Need. Preliminary selection activities include the identification and specification of the instructional need and the development of a checklist of materials' attributes related to the need.

To begin with, the teacher must *identify the instructional need*. At first, this may be a rather general statement, e.g., "I need some kind of instructional material to provide oral language training for the deaf boy who was just mainstreamed into my fifth grade classroom." However, the instructional need should then be made more specific; this can be done by making appropriate instructional analyses of the learner, the instructional task, and the environment in which the instruction will occur. Questions at this level of analysis might be "How old is this deaf student chronologically and functionally? What is his general language ability? What, exactly, would I like him to be able to do in oral language? Will this instruction be carried out in the regular classroom? Can an individual tutor be used?" The outcome of these analyses should be a clear statement of the performance objectives for the unit of instruction. As emphasized earlier, the extent of such analyses should be appropriate to the instructional objective. When teachers, or others, are discouraged by elaborate procedures and lengthy forms, they tend to avoid the task altogether.

The result of these preliminary selection activities should be a *checklist of instructional attributes* which the material must have. These attributes might usefully be classified into three groups: essential, adaptable, and preferred attributes. *Essential attributes* are those absolutely critical to the instructional need. *Adaptable attributes* refer to those aspects of an instructional material, although essential to the instruction, suppliable in some adaptive way. *Preferred attributes* reflect simply those attributes it would be nice for the material to have but which are not essential, for example, a filmstrip medium rather than a slide-sound set medium (when projectors of both types are available).

Phase 2: Information on Materials. Systematic, effective selection is dependent upon *information* collection. Information about existent materials can be obtained by *word-of-mouth* (professional peers, supervisors, university faculty, parents of the handicapped), by *demonstration* (professional conferences, in-service training sessions), from *print* sources (commercial catalogues, professional journals), and from *information retrieval systems* (NICSEM, ERIC).

It is important to note that whether the information source is complex or simple, the method of searching and particularly of saving information can be systematic. Computer printouts, bibliographies, catalogues, and card indexes are the read-outs of complex systems. However, classroom teachers may benefit from developing their own library and card catalogue on materials sources, even though the "library" may consist of a cardboard box of miscellaneous publications and the "card catalogue" may consist of a few index cards in a rubber band. This growing collection can reduce the time and effort involved in retrieving again what has been retrieved before: for example, the name and address of some small and obscure manufacturer of writing materials for the cerebral palsied.

Phase 3: Matching Materials to Need. This phase consists of two parts. The first quick-and-dirty, but comprehensive, scan of the sources for the purpose of selecting any and all materials which might with any stretch of the imagination be useable. One looks at everything, but one does not look very hard at anything. The result is a set (empty or otherwise) of instructional materials, evaluated at this early stage of selection to be potentially useful.

The second part of this phase involves a systematic, careful comparison of the attributes of the materials found with the attributes specified in the checklist devised earlier. This comparison process is broken into three levels. At the first level of comparison, if the instructional material does have the attributes classified as "essential" on the checklist, it is accepted; otherwise, it is rejected. At the second level of comparison, if the material has the attributes indicated as "potentially adaptable" or if it has other attributes which could be adapted to be equivalent with these attributes, then the material is accepted; otherwise, it is rejected. At the third level of comparison, information on whether or not the material has the "preferred" attributes is simply noted.

The major part of this phase is an annotated *preview list* of instructional material apparently worthy of expert appraisal. However, another result, one aimed at conserving information, is an annotated *list of rejections*. The advantage of this latter list (perhaps on index cards in another rubber band) is that the descriptive and evaluative information collected so far need not be wasted. Should an instructional need arise later which matches one of the evaluated materials, the item can be retrieved with relative ease.

Phase 4: Expert Appraisal. Before trying out material on students, it should be submitted to the appraisal of experts, particularly for an assessment of content accuracy and appropriateness. The teacher who is going to use the material is often an adequate content specialist. However, this is not to discourage collaboration, particularly not if the teacher is inexperienced with the handicapping problem. Then expert appraisal by resource teachers or special education teachers may be important to the selection of effective instructional material. The initiating teacher would do well to figure out ahead of time what is wanted; a simple one-page sheet or card with specific questions may be useful. And, occasionally, a check with a higher authority may be advisable. Sometimes, local citizens who are experts in a given content area are happy to serve as content specialists, provided little of their time is involved. Legitimate areas of consideration for the experts include the adequacy of the previously determined match of attributes; the feasibility of adaptation; and the selection of one from among several comparable materials. Also, teacher preference should be considered, if not slavishly followed.

Ultimately, each item is judged by the expert(s) to be accepted, adapted, or rejected. Three lists are then compiled. One list is the student try-out list made up of items which were accepted as they were by the experts. Another list is the adaptation list made up of items which must be adapted before they can be submitted to students for try-out; this list should include recommendations for adaptation. The last list is the list of rejections. All three lists can profitably be annotated and this information saved for future reference.

Phase 5: Student Try-out. No matter how highly the experts value a piece of instructional material, it is the students' performance that counts.

Students upon whom materials are tried should be as much as possible like the students for whom the material is intended. In fact, they will usually *be* the students for whom the material is intended. Why call it a "try-out" then? Because calling such student use of materials a "try-out" tends to keep the system flexible and subject to improvement. Material which fails to meet evaluation standards is more likely to be set aside if it was just being "tried out." Such try-outs can be considered as a form of criterion-referenced evaluation.

This is the appropriate mode of evaluation for a classroom teacher to use in evaluating materials. The main question this kind of evaluation deals with is simply "Does the material teach what it's supposed to teach?"

The classroom teacher is engaged in decision-oriented inquiry of the most pragmatic type. Trying to apply the techniques of carefully designed conclusion-oriented inquiry is not likely to reveal any "truths" but is likely to cause teachers to abandon all evaluative efforts.

Teacher Selection of Instructional Materials *237*

Figure 11.1

Five Phases of Selection

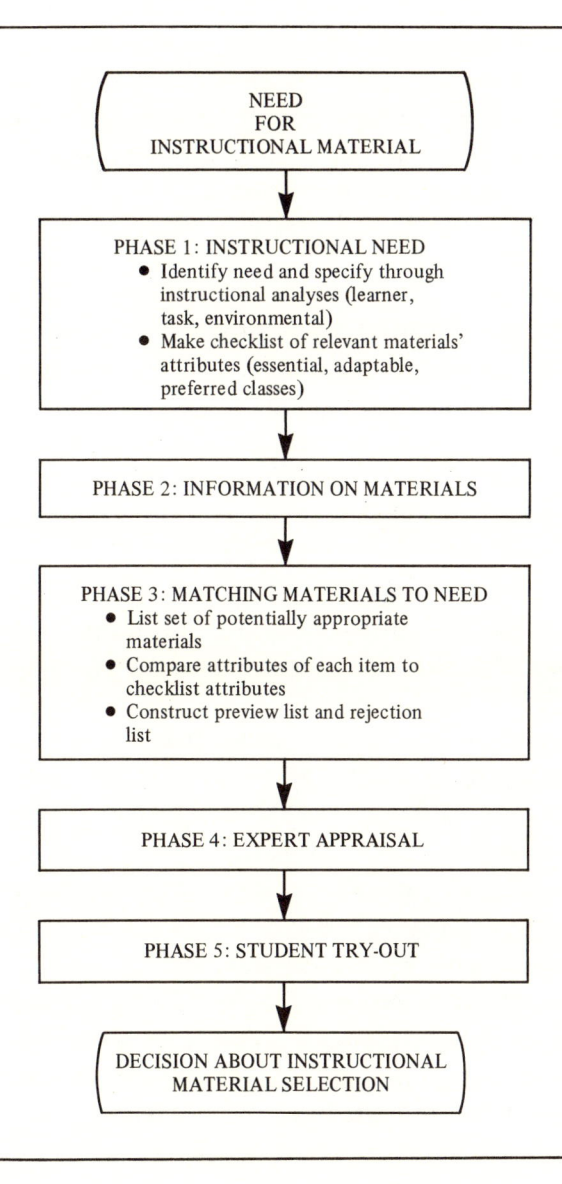

```
           ┌─────────────────────────┐
           │         NEED            │
           │         FOR             │
           │  INSTRUCTIONAL MATERIAL │
           └───────────┬─────────────┘
                       ▼
┌──────────────────────────────────────────┐
│ PHASE 1: INSTRUCTIONAL NEED              │
│   • Identify need and specify through    │
│     instructional analyses (learner,     │
│     task, environmental)                 │
│   • Make checklist of relevant materials'│
│     attributes (essential, adaptable,    │
│     preferred classes)                   │
└───────────────────┬──────────────────────┘
                    ▼
┌──────────────────────────────────────────┐
│ PHASE 2: INFORMATION ON MATERIALS        │
└───────────────────┬──────────────────────┘
                    ▼
┌──────────────────────────────────────────┐
│ PHASE 3: MATCHING MATERIALS TO NEED      │
│   • List set of potentially appropriate  │
│     materials                            │
│   • Compare attributes of each item to   │
│     checklist attributes                 │
│   • Construct preview list and rejection │
│     list                                 │
└───────────────────┬──────────────────────┘
                    ▼
┌──────────────────────────────────────────┐
│ PHASE 4: EXPERT APPRAISAL                │
└───────────────────┬──────────────────────┘
                    ▼
┌──────────────────────────────────────────┐
│ PHASE 5: STUDENT TRY-OUT                 │
└───────────────────┬──────────────────────┘
                    ▼
           ┌─────────────────────────────┐
           │ DECISION ABOUT INSTRUCTIONAL│
           │    MATERIAL SELECTION       │
           └─────────────────────────────┘
```

Upon completion of the student try-out phase, the final output of the entire selection procedure is again a judgment of acceptable, adaptable, or unsuitable. If the material can be used with students as it is, it is accepted. If it shows promise for adaptation, it may be adapted and later brought back for another student try-out. If the material is wholly ineffective, it is rejected. In all cases, keeping records of student performance data will provide information which may be useful at some later date. Figure 11.1 presents a flow-chart of the selection procedure.

Summary Comments

What training would be useful to teacher-selectors? Recently, during the needs analysis of a project on tutoring for mainstreamed students (Maguire, 1977), teachers who had had mainstreamed students in their classrooms for about two years were interviewed. One of the interesting bits of information that came from these interviews was that, while mainstreamed students were often instructed in subjects such as mathematics by resource teachers outside of the regular classroom, these same students were expected to participate in the scheduled mathematics lesson going on within the classroom. The problem for the teacher was one of scheduling, e.g., if everyone was doing math, then the mainstreamed student must do math, regardless of individual needs. As the project director suggested, her job in providing tutoring materials to assist the teacher involves more than just tutoring; it involves training in the concept underlying tutoring— that is, individualizing instruction.

Influenced by the impact of the current legislation, perhaps individualizing instruction will move from the theoretical realm to the practical domain of teacher-training.

How can information systems be responsive to teacher needs? I have no doubt that teachers are going to be looking for more and more information regarding instructional materials for handicapped learners. As indicated earlier, in order for that information to be useful to the teacher, it must be readily available and effective in producing the desired instructional outcomes.

Commercial manufacturers have long been effective at making information about their materials readily available. With sales as the measure of their success, marketing departments have seen to that. However, on the negative side, users have often questioned the accuracy of product information supplied by commercial organizations, whose claims sometimes exceed instructional outcomes.

An additional problem for the user is that, by and large, commercial manufacturers have never produced much for the thin market of specialized materials for the handicapped learner. Aside from the teacher's own cut-paste efforts, materials for handicapped learners have generally been funded for development at universities and R&D Centers. Here, sizeable financial and personnel resources have often resulted in materials of excellent instructional quality. Unfortunately, and (from a logical point of view) somewhat incredibly, materials so-developed often go to their permanent resting place on a shelf in the center where they were created. The reason? Dissemination has not in the past been emphasized by either the developers or the funding agencies. Happily, this situation is changing.

References

Armstrong, J. R. *Minimum Guidelines Used in Consumer Information Analyses*. Paper presented at the annual meeting of the American Educational Research Association, San Francisco, California, April 19-23, 1976.

Ashcroft, S.C. NCEMMH: A Network of Media/Material Resources. *Audiovisual Instruction,* 1976, *10,* 46-47.

Ensminger, E. E. A proposed Model for Selecting, Modifying, or Developing Instructional Materials for Handicapped Children. In E. L. Meyen, G. A. Vergason, and R. J. Whelan (Eds.),

Strategies for Teaching Exceptional Children: Essays from Focus on Exceptional Children. Denver: Love Publishing Company, 1972.

Lance, W. D. What You Should Know About P.L. 94-142. *Audiovisual Instruction*, 1976, *10*, 14-15.

Lucas, R. J. The Relationship of Training and Experience Variables to Teachers' Skill in Judging the Effectiveness of ITV Programs. *AV Communication Review*, Spring, 1974.

Maguire, M. *Mainstream Tutoring Project*. Center for Innovation in Teaching the Handicapped. Bloomington: Indiana University, 1977.

Markle, S. M. It figgers. *Improving Human Performance*, 1973, *2*, 169-174.

McNeil, D. C. Developing Instructional Materials for Emotionally Disturbed Children. In E. L. Meyen, G. A. Vergason, and R. J. Whelan (Eds.), *Strategies for Teaching Exceptional Children: Essays from Focus on Exceptional Children*. Denver: Love Publishing Company, 1972.

Oldsen, C. F. The National Instructional Materials Information System. *Audiovisual Instruction*, 1976, *10*, 48-49.

Rothkopf, E. A. Some Observations on Predicting Instructional Effectiveness by Simple Inspection. *Journal of Programmed Instruction*, 1963, *2*, 19-20.

Worthen, B. R., and Sanders, J. R. *Educational Evaluation: Theory and Practice*. Worthington, Ohio: Charles A. Jones Publishing, 1973.

Author's Note

The author wishes to express her appreciation to the following for their helpful comments on an earlier draft of this chapter: Alan M. Hofmeister, Director, Outreach and Development Division, Exceptional Child Center, Utah State University, Logan, Utah; and Don Perrin, Audiovisual Services, California State University at Northridge, Northridge, California.

12.
How Commercial Producers Can Systematically Develop Effective Instructional Materials for the Handicapped (and Still Make a Profit)

Sivasailam Thiagarajan

Providing the least restrictive environment for handicapped learners will require, among other things, increased availability of effective instructional materials. While some amount of local production by teachers does take place in the schools, the exportability of these materials is limited and their impact, negligible. The major sources of instructional materials for the handicapped at this time may be grouped into academic institutions (federally-funded R & D Centers, universities, and learning resource centers) and commercial organizations (publishers and media producers). There is an obvious difference in the instructional and motivational quality of teaching materials developed by these two types of organizations: usually, academic instructional development is reportedly based upon careful analysis and systematic validation, while commercial media production results in highly motivating and technically slick products. Based on my schizophrenic professional experiences between the worlds of academic instructional development and commercial media production, I have come to the conclusion that these differences in the products are due to different contingencies that control the processes. In this chapter these differences are briefly examined and the relative strengths and weaknesses of commercial producers as a source of instructional materials for the handicapped are identified. This is followed by a presentation of strategies for obtaining more effective instructional materials from commercial producers. These strategies include symbiotic collaboration between academic developers and commercial producers, financial support for those deserving activities with low probability of commercial payoffs, and the evolution of an intermediate technology for instructional development which adapts academic systems approach models to the resources and constraints of a commercial producer.

Different Strokes for Different Folks

The way in which an academic institution develops instructional materials for the handicapped differs from that of a commercial organization. Some of the major differences are presented in high-contrast fashion in the following discussion. Obviously, in real life, there are many gray areas, but this exaggerated discussion enables us to identify the relative strengths and weaknesses of commercial producers.

Fame and fortune. The primary reinforcement for a scholarly special-educator instructional developer is peer approval and recognition. To the commercial producer, it is the profit on the bottom line. The academic instructional developer usually obtains fairly large sums of money from some external sources. Within limits, the developer's costs are prespecified with nothing gained by saving money. The price of the product—if and when it becomes available to the field—is unlikely to reflect these developmental costs; even if it does, the developer is unlikely to gain any monetary benefit from commercial exploitation. Therefore, there is no need for the developer to minimize the development cost. In contrast, commercial producers operate under the control of profit-loss statements. They would prefer to take the cash and let the credit go, and not invest any money which does not improve the quality and *marketability* of the instructional material. These differential reinforcers for the two types of developers force them to emphasize different elements of the instructional-development process.

The question of accountability. Ultimately, both the fame for the scholar and the fortune for the entrepreneur are linked with the instructional effectiveness of the material in terms of gains for the handicapped learner. However, there is a difference in the immediate group to which these organizations are accountable. Academic instructional developers are responsible to their funding agencies, their project officers, the site visitors, and their colleagues. They are reinforced for indulging in research-like activities and writing, presenting, and publishing professional articles dealing with the analysis and evaluation of the instructional material. The actual design of the material is seldom considered to have scholarly respectability. This crucial task is often delegated to graduate assistants. Peers and panels seldom have the patience to go through the actual instructional materials; they prefer to evaluate the product in terms of the final report and statistical tables. In contrast, commercial producers are accountable to administrators and teachers in the field. They know that administrative gatekeepers and teachers make adoption decisions and control the purse strings. Commercial producers are thus closer to the classroom, but they are not necessarily responsive to the needs of the handicapped learner. Their consumer is the teacher. What the teacher wants may very often be different from what the learner needs. The commercial producer may turn out extremely colorful and attractive material which is appealing to the teacher but without any evidence of appeal to the learner. If the teacher wants a series of mimeograph masters to keep the handicapped learner busy in a minimally meaningful way, the producer is happy to provide them. If administrators are willing to accept instructional materials which are correlated to popular tests on the basis of their face validity without checking their treatment validity (Hofmeister, 1976), the commercial publishers will not waste any resources in conducting learner verification or field tests.

Parts of the process. Neither the competencies nor the contingencies encourage academic instructional developers to emphasize the writing and production of the material. There is greater payoff for the faculty member in conducting systematic needs, learner, task, concept, and other analyses and documenting them. Controlled evaluation, collection of multivariate data, and sophisticated statistical analyses form another set of respected and reinforced activities for the academic. As a result, these analyses and evaluations become ends in themselves in many funded projects. Detailed analyses are extremely useful and laudable exercises, but of limited value in the instructional materials development process unless they are directly translated into prescriptions for instructional design. Similarly, many academic instructional developers spend a considerable amount of resources in coming up with controlled experimental studies using a nationwide stratified random sample for the evaluation of the instructional materials. The amount of data collected and the sophistication of statistical analysis are extremely superfluous. Partly because of their incompetencies in the area, academic instructional developers affect a disdain for slickness in media production. They spend minimal money for improving the appearance or appeal of the material, e.g., selectively citing research evidence to support that color does not add anything to the amount of learning from a television program. In doing so, they deliberately and systematically disregard the fact that before handicapped learners can learn from the material they have to attend to it. And long before that, the material has to be selected by a teacher or an administrator, who usually associates sloppy production with ineffective instruction.

Commercial Producers

In contrast to all of these, commercial producers spend most of the resources in the design of the instructional material. They hire competent and creative writers, artists, photographers, and narrators to turn out attractive and appealing packages. The analytic efforts of the producer are usually limited to surveying the market, and the evaluative efforts to collecting testimonials from experts. The commercial producer knows that learners, teachers, and administrators instinctively and unavoidably judge a book by its cover and a television program by its color. To such a producer, analytic and evaluative activities have very little payoff because they are invisible in the final product. Very few administrators and teachers ask for or study the data on the process by which the instructional material was produced, even if they are offered free of charge.

Big projects and small. Few commercial producers are interested in the instructional materials for the handicapped under the assumption that the market is too thin to guarantee appropriate return for investments. Academic instructional developers have little problem with rushing into the areas where commercial producers fear to tread because subsidies from funding agencies take care of the heavy costs involved with the basic research, analysis, and evaluation procedures. Most of the large-scale instructional development projects in special education are generally supported by such funding which permits developers to select alternative media combinations. Commercial producers, on the other hand, are more likely to stay with their favorite medium because of heavy investments in equipment and talent. In the case of many commercial producers, the media selection procedure is likely to be of the inverted variety in which suitable problems which lend themselves to a specific medium are sought, instead of working the other way around. Commercial producers are also keenly aware of the problems of multimedia packaging and marketing. They know that the probability of an instructional material being used is inversely proportional to the number of instructional components and pieces of media hardware.

It is obvious that academic and commercial organizations have different strengths and weaknesses when it comes to producing instructional materials for the handicapped. The focus of this chapter is on getting better instructional materials from commercial producers. Hence, a summary of the relative strengths and weaknesses of commercial producers is useful at this time:

Strengths

1. Commercial producers are less likely to indulge in expensive, superfluous activities such as writing elaborate reports and sophisticated statistical analyses. Hence, they keep the development costs down.

2. Commercial producers are close to administrators, teachers, and classrooms. They receive immediate feedback about their production through changes in sales and profits. Hence, they develop materials practical and feasible for use in the classroom.

3. Commercial producers can design instructional materials with high levels of technical and aesthetic qualities.

4. Commercial producers are constantly interested in the marketability of the materials. Because they cannot afford to leave their finished products idle on the shelves, they have developed effective networks for large-scale dissemination.

Weaknesses

1. Commercial producers are unlikely to enter relatively thin markets, which includes instructional materials for the handicapped.

2. With notable exceptions, commercial producers tend to concentrate more on the attractiveness and the appeal of the materials than on the instructional effectiveness. As a result, their materials may motivate the learner, but teach inefficiently.

3. Many commercial producers help teachers fight the day-to-

day problems of managing the classroom rather than attending to long-term learning gains on the part of the handicapped.

4. Commercial products are likely to have a high face validity but they may undergo very little learner verification or validation. The feedback from the field is usually reserved for changes between editions.

5. Commercial producers cannot afford to invest a long period of time or a large percentage of their resources in preliminary analyses. Established publishers use established authorities to provide them initial guidelines, but these do not supplant the outcomes of systematic analysis.

A Productive Partnership

There are obviously no representative commercial producers who possess all these strengths and weaknesses strictly according to the list. But most producers agree that these statements are true of their mode of operation without feeling defensive about what they are doing. They will point out that academic instructional developers have the time and the resources to indulge in areas of limited utility. Because of the complementary emphases between these two types of organizations, it is obvious that one way to obtain more effective instructional materials is to form a partnership based on efficient and cost-effective division of labor. Instructional materials produced through such collaborative interaction are likely to be more appealing and exportable than those produced by the academic alone and more theoretically sound and valid than those produced by the entrepreneur. Such an arrangement enables the academic to carry out analyses before and evaluation after the commercial producer designs and produces the material. The producer then follows up with wide distribution of the material.

The field of special education is replete with successful case histories of this type of collaboration between academic centers and commercial distributors. Among the various projects funded by BEH, Project LIFE materials, originally designed under the direction of Dr. Glen Pfau, are now being commercially distributed by General Electric. Dr. Janet Wessel's programmatic research in physical education for mentally retarded children and youth has resulted in the I CAN materials being distributed commercially by Hubbard. The mediated operational research for education project under Dr. James Lent has yielded a series of highly successful commercial products for Edmark Associates. Dr. Herbert Goldstein of Yeshiva University directed the Social Learning Curriculum Project, the products of which are now being produced and distributed by Charles E. Merrill Company.

At its best, this type of collaboration between the academic instructional developer and the commercial media producer can result in more attractive *and* effective instructional materials for the handicapped. At its worst, such a marriage of convenience may result in a combination of weaknesses. The commercial product may assume unlimited editorial liberties such that any resemblance between the field test material and the commercially produced material is purely coincidental. This results in a total waste of the investment in the prototypic production by the academic instructional developer. While, in general, refinements by the producer result in improvements, there have been cases where the slicker version produced significantly inferior learning in comparison to the sloppier prototype. Unless coequal checks and balances and some validation with actual learners are built into the conversion process, the collaboration may result in negative consequences.

Increasing the Probability of Successful Collaboration

Guidelines for ensuring successful coequal collaboration between academic and commercial organizations in the production of effective instructional materials include the following:

1. Funding agencies should encourage joint production efforts with an appropriate division of labor between the two types of organizations. While proposals from commercial producers usually

include an impressive list of academic consultants, real evidence of meaningful inputs from them must be required in order to avoid this arrangement from becoming a purely political maneuver.

2. Proposals for academic instructional development projects should be required to specify plans for commercial distribution of the materials. Just as evaluation has reached its current level of significance through insistence from the funding agencies, commercial diffusion can also be elevated in its importance by being made an essential element of any instructional development project. Academic institutions should be funded to consult with potential commercial distributors at the early stages of their project.

3. Directors of academic instructional development projects should be educated on the legal and technical requirements for reproduction and commercial distribution of their materials. This can avoid, for example, violations of copyright that prevent commercial distribution.

4. The process of converting prototype materials from academic sources into commercial packages must be streamlined and simplified. The current red tape and administrative obstacles work against the ultimate goal of wide distribution of publicly funded projects. In conjunction with simplifying legal requirements, more opportunities for commercial producers to make honest profits should be worked out.

Incentives for Commercial Producers

Partnership between academic institutions and commercial organizations will result in increased instructional effectiveness of mediated materials for the handicapped. However, not all commercial producers are able or willing to acquire a compatible academic partner. Many of them would prefer to go it alone, and they must be helped to upgrade the instructional effectiveness of their products. As a prior step, we have to encourage more commercial producers to enter the thin market for the handicapped through various incentives.

Commercial producers should be encouraged to respond to RFPs from federal and other funding agencies. External funding ensures that such activities as analysis and evaluation are subsidized. In extremely thin markets—such as those of multiple handicapped—proposals for the development of instructional materials may extend to dissemination and distribution activities to enable handicapped learners to achieve their fullest potential through the availability of free instructional materials where they are needed. Commercial producers may also be encouraged to write separate proposals to organizations associated with different handicapping conditions to fund the free or cost-of-reproduction distribution of validated instructional materials. Such support of distribution provides an incentive to commercial distributors. An alternative type of subsidy may be provided to the purchaser: If a specific product is on an approved list, the funding agency may pay part of the purchase price.

Many commercial publishers are frightened away from the special education market because of our morbid interest in describing the differences between handicapped learners and their "normal" peers. This suggests that the materials developed for use by learners with one handicapping condition are useless for any other type of learner. However, it has been shown time and again that effective instructional materials possess great generalizability. For example, the Project LIFE materials, originally designed for use by deaf children, have been found to be excellent sources of language instruction for mentally handicapped children and their normal peers. The special education market is not as "thin" as the narrow categorical statements used by some special educators may suggest. The possibility of expanded markets should be emphasized to attract more commercial producers. The "thin" illusion may be removed by reference to cross-disciplinary use of materials and the use of such broader terms as "children of low developmental ages." However, it should be made clear that we are not recommending a shotgun approach to instructional materials development, but an application of basic principles of individualized instruction. Commercial producers who are competent in this area will find that "secondary" markets significantly increase the volume of potential sales.

Another way to encourage the entry of commercial producers into the market for the handicapped is to suggest adaptations of effective existing materials rather than development from scratch. Such adaptation can be accomplished through the use of specialists in specific handicapping conditions and through repeated learner verification and revision. An excellent example of this kind of instructional adaptation is provided by the Biological Sciences Curriculum Study. ME NOW and ME AND MY ENVIRONMENT are adaptations of the parent packages for mentally handicapped learners.

Alternative Approaches to the Instructional Development Process

A frequent complaint from commercial producers is that most funding agencies emphasize an approach to instructional development which is extremely different from the one used by commercial producers. Grants and contracts de-emphasize creative media production and emphasize research-like activities and insist on specific procedures for analysis and evaluation. RFPs imply that there is one validated way to produce instructional materials. However, even the most ardent instructional developer would concede that there is still a long way to go before a praxiology of instructional development can provide guaranteed prescriptions. At this time, it is unnecessary to insist on the exact nature and sequence of steps in the process of producing instructional materials. Such insistence is shortsighted because it keeps out anyone except members of the inbred clique and hastens a premature hardening of the instructional development arteries.

While the specific process is left to the choice of the producer, it is essential to establish some criteria for instructional products before public monies are awarded for the development.

There is some agreement among funding agencies, instructional developers, and consumers that instructional materials for the handicapped should contain the following three elements:

1. *A set of instructional objectives* which specify the outcomes which the instructional material is capable of producing. Such specifications enable the teacher to match the needs of the local learners with the potential effects of the instructional material.

2. *Availability in a complete package.* This includes not only the mediated materials, but also specifications for using them.

3. *Validation data* on the actual effects of the materials. These data indicate to what extent the objectives of the instructional material are actually achieved. While field testing delays bringing the material to the market, it helps the consumer check congruence between objectives and actual effects of the material.

All three elements listed above are essential for judging the worthwhileness of instructional materials, and the degree of congruence among them is a measure of professional production. By insisting on these elements, but giving producers the freedom to use whatever process they want to, we can encourage more commercial participation in this area of instructional development.

Some instructional developers (e.g., Baker, 1973) have strongly recommended the need to explore alternative approaches in order to evolve more flexible and effective procedures. There is much to gain by encouraging commercial producers to utilize their own approaches to instructional materials development for the handicapped learner.

An Intermediate Instructional Technology

The thin-market illusion for instructional materials for the handicapped makes it unlikely to attract major media producers. A potential breakthrough in instructional development for the handicapped will occur from newer outfits which involve small teams of competent specialists and work on moderate budgets to achieve an optimal level of slickness and effectiveness in their products. These organizations can afford to operate on low overheads and achieve fairly high media quality within limited budgets by hiring free-lance writers and artists and by subcontracting technical processing.

In conjunction with the advent of these medium-sized organizations, a new technology of instructional development is also emerging. The process used in this technology resembles the systems approach model but with optional sequences to optimize available time and talent. Relinquishing the affluence of funded projects, this modified process requires cost-effective justification of various activities. Refinement of this intermediate technology will enable more commercial producers to adapt the rigor of the systems approach to the restrictions and realities of the market place for instructional materials. Most commercial publishers have an edge with their expertise in the area of media design. What they need is an acceptable adaptation of analytic and evaluative activities so that they do not end up as academic exercises. The following discussion provides guidelines for reducing the affluent, advanced technology to an innovative, intermediate level.

An Analysis of Instructional Analyses

The types of analyses recommended in the instructional-development process are listed and briefly described in Table 12.1.

The outcomes column in this table needs to be highlighted: It stresses the fact that all analyses have to be justified in terms of prescriptions for instructional development. If developers are seduced into making ends out of any of these activities, they may justifiably be accused of indulging in futile exercises. The commercial producer can recognize diminishing returns when additional investments of resources turn up no useful guidelines for instructional development. In addition to this general caveat about pre-

TABLE 12.1

ANALYTIC ACTIVITIES IN THE
INSTRUCTIONAL DEVELOPMENT PROCESS

Type of Analysis	Input	Process	Outcome
1. Needs analysis	Specification of a priority area.	Collection of information from relevant people on the ideal and actual state of affairs in the specified area.	Identification of basic discrepancies in the specified area which lend themselves to an instructional solution.
2. Context analysis	Situations in which the instructional material is to be used.	Direct and indirect collection of information on the resources and constraints in the instructional situation.	Specifications of such requirements for the instructional materials as length, price limit, modularization, teacher role, and adjunct materials.
3. Learner analysis	Definition of the target population for whom the instructional material is to be developed.	Direct and indirect collection of information about those characteristics of the target population which are relevant to the development of the instructional material.	Prescription of starting point, sequence, number, and types of examples, level and style of language, and other such instructional variables.
4. Task analysis	Major topic or instructional task.	Various procedures for systematically identifying necessary and sufficient subtasks required to attain the main goal of instruction.	A sequenced set of specific behavioral objectives.

venting superfluous steps, here are some specific guidelines for achieving optimal returns from various analyses:

Needs analysis.

1. A basic rule in needs analysis is to involve as many divergent groups as possible. For example, in conducting a needs analysis for the mentally handicapped, special educators, administrators, resource and regular teachers, representatives of community groups and concerned organizations, parents of handicapped and normal children, and psychologists may all be involved. A related rule is never to expect total consensus among these constituencies but to keep the conflicts at a creative level.

2. Larger numbers are less important during needs analysis than broader representation. Similarly, sophisticated test construction provides very little additional information. Simple questions about what people would like to happen in their field and what is actually happening provide relevant information.

3. Background information on potential need areas can be obtained from professional literature and special interest groups. Many national organizations concerned with different handicapping conditions have information on their basic needs available on a continually updated basis. Unnecessary rediscoveries can be avoided through systematic retrieval of free and available information.

4. The term "needs analysis" means different things to different people. The intermediate technologist may avoid unnecessarily sophisticated varieties and stay with direct, parsimonious approaches. Of special utility to instructional developers are a group of needs analysis techniques called front-end analysis (Harless, 1971), or performance analysis (Gilbert, 1967). These techniques assess the importance of different needs in terms of their economic impact. They also help analysts sort out those needs which cannot (and should not) be tackled with the development of instructional materials.

Context analysis.

1. This type of analysis can be conducted as a market survey to find out the most acceptable media format for the teacher-consumer. Information should be collected about budget and schedule restrictions before elaborate instructional packages are developed.

2. There is a big difference between teachers' verbal behaviors and their actual classroom performances with regard to the use of media. Context analysis should focus on direct and unobtrusive observations on what is happening in the classrooms.

3. An important piece of information to be collected during this analysis is the price the consumer is willing to pay for convenience. This determines the degree of finish in the instructional material and helps the producer decide which elements can be entrusted to local "production."

4. Educational contexts seldom change drastically. Information collected during the development of one instructional material is useful for future development activities.

Learner analysis.

1. This type of analysis is of critical importance with handicapped learners. Much of the information is already available in the professional literature. A useful technique for sorting out relevant information from the irrelevant kind is to ask the question, "How does this fact influence the design of the instructional material?"

2. The factor which most heavily influences the learner's level of mastery upon completion of instruction is *entry level* in the beginning. This information can be obtained by making an estimate based upon teachers' opinions and constructing a diagnostic test to measure a suitable range of competencies below and above this estimate.

3. The level and preferred style of language by the target population is another important characteristic influencing design of instructional material. The learner's level of language is critical even when the proposed instructional material does not use any printed

language; the learner's level of reception of spoken language has to be determined. With a completely nonverbal instructional package, the learner's level of visual literacy plays an important role.

4. Attitudes of learners toward the instructional topic and the media format constitute another major learner characteristic relevant to instructional development. These attitudes can be directly measured to suggest strategies for using positive components to motivate the learner into attending to negative ones.

Task analysis.

1. The real secret in conducting a task analysis is knowing when to stop. Any instructional task, especially those for handicapped learners, can be analyzed *ad infinitum* to result in extremely atomized "enabling" objectives. Preparing a volume with hundreds of explicitly stated *trivial* objectives serves no instructional development or public relations function. The task analyst should objectively terminate the analysis when the subtasks lose their relevance to the main objective.

2. Basic task analysis can be conducted simply by beginning with the main objective and repeatedly asking the question, "What should the learner be able to do at the next level of simplicity in order to accomplish this?" This successive reduction process comes to a conclusion when the learner's entry level is reached. Sometimes this seemingly logical procedure becomes blocked; a suitable unblocking strategy is to drop down a couple of simpler levels and attempt to build up to the more complex ones.

3. Different types of instructional content lend themselves to different types of instructional analysis. A procedural task is best analyzed by an information process approach (Merrill, 1976). This type of analysis results in an algorithmic description of the steps. For content requiring generalizations and discriminations, the concept analysis procedure (Markle and Tiemann, 1969) is recommended. This procedure enables the analyst to identify the critical and variable attributes of the concepts and prescribes elegant examples for teaching and testing the concept.

An Evaluation of Evaluative Activities

A spate of literature in recent years has created controversies in the area of evaluation of instructional materials. The proliferation of technical jargon has created confusion rather than clarification, especially when new terms are coined to represent the same concept. Commercial producers are concerned about legislation mandating learner verification and revision. Some producers question the validity of LVR, pointing out that continued consumer demand for an instructional material constitutes sufficient evidence of its instructional worth, as noted by Komoski earlier in this volume. Most commercial producers are frightened by suggested LVR procedures with sophisticated test instruments, large populations of handicapped learners and complex data analysis, all of which require large investments of time, talent, and other resources. Actually, however, beneath the myth and mystique surrounding learner verification and revision lie a few little known "secrets" supportive of a low-budget, intermediate technology approach:

1. *The number of students involved in tryout of instructional materials can be kept very small* and yet achieve significant improvement in the instructional materials. Many evaluators suggest that informal individual tryouts with five to ten learners produce optimal improvements in the material. There is empirical evidence to support this suggestion (e.g., Kandaswamy, Stolovitch, and Thiagarajan, 1976).

2. *Critical to the improvement of instructional materials is not the quantity, but the validity and relevance of data.* The most useful data are obtained from test items that directly measure the attainment of the instructional objectives for the material. Since these test items usually constitute an integral part of the total instructional package, no additional costs are involved in their construction. In addition to the terminal test data, built-in test items within the material provide progress checks and identify instructional breakdowns at their earliest point of occurrence.

3. *Not data collection but revision* makes the difference in

LVR. Time and money spent in making appropriate revisions on the basis of limited data have a greater payoff than accumulation of additional data. Techniques for converting learner-verification feedback into suitable revisions have not yet been clearly identified, except for a few notable exceptions (e.g., Gropper, 1975). However, any effective instructional designer appears to be capable of becoming an effective modifier of materials.

4. *Doubts about the feasibility of using LVR with mediated packages appear to be unjustified.* Commercial producers concede the utility of LVR for print materials, but the spectre of extensive, expensive revisions frightens them off from trying out nonprint materials with learners. But some techniques suggest various shortcut procedures which do not involve slick productions. Mockups, scripts, storyboards, and cheaper pilot versions can be tried out with handicapped learners to identify all major problems (Zuckerman, 1954). Systematic, successive verification and revision ensures that only minor revisions are needed during final rounds. Final revisions can be economically carried out through the addition of adjunct print materials and suggested activities in the teacher's guide.

Commercial Production Can Be Improved

The role of commercial producers of mediated instructional materials for handicapped learners is increasing in its importance. There are many ways in which the Bureau of Education for the Handicapped can encourage and reinforce systematic development of effective instructional materials by these producers. This chapter has suggested a number of guidelines, including the following:

- BEH should encourage collaborative efforts between commercial producers and academic institutions. This will enable the academics to conduct thorough analysis and systematic evaluation and the entrepreneurs to undertake creative design and production.

- BEH should stress the expanding volume of the market for

individualized instructional materials by de-emphasizing narrow categorical definitions of handicapped learners.

• BEH should strongly urge academic instructional developers to collaboratively work with commercial producers from the early planning stages of their instructional development projects in order to use the creative design and competent marketing talents of the latter.

• BEH should educate consumers about the importance of validation data on commercial instructional products and subsidize the purchase of validated materials.

• BEH should insist and subsidize summative field testing of instructional materials, and provide sufficient time and funds and support for these activities.

• BEH should provide more freedom for commercial producers by permitting them to select specific processes and media and to experiment with alternative approaches to instructional development as long as they result in effective, useable materials.

• BEH should reward those areas in which commercial producers currently excel—cost cutting, creative design, and effective marketing.

• BEH should support and encourage commercial distribution of instructional materials developed by academic organizations. Administrative and legal obstacles against efficient distribution and profit making should be eliminated.

• BEH should welcome and support the growth of medium sized instructional development organizations by treating them on equal terms with large commercial producers and university-based R & D centers.

References

Baker, E. L. The technology of instructional development. In R. M. W. Travers (Ed.), *Second handbook of research on teaching.* Chicago: Rand McNally College Publishing Company, 1973.

Gilbert, T. F. Praxionomy: A scientific method for the determination of instructional needs. *Management of Personnel Quarterly*, 1967, *6*(3).

Gropper, G. L. *Diagnosis and revision in the development of instructional materials.* Englewood Cliffs, N.J.: Educational Technology Publications, 1975.

Harless, J. H. *An ounce of analysis.* Falls Church, Virginia: Harless Educational Technologists, 1971.

Hofmeister, A.M. *Testing and treatment validity.* Logan, Utah: Special Education Department, Utah State University, 1976.

Kandaswamy, S., Stolovitch, H. E., and Thiagarajan, S. Learner verification and revision: An experimental comparison of two methods. *AV Communication Review*, 1976, *24*(3).

Markle, S. M., and Tiemann, P. W. *Really understanding concepts: Or, in frumious pursuit of the Jabberwock.* Chicago: Tiemann Associates, 1969.

Merrill, P. F. Task analysis—an information processing approach. *NSPI Journal*, 1976, *15*(2).

Zuckerman, J.V. Predicting film learning by pre-release testing. *AV Communication Review*, 1954, *2*(1).

Author's Note

The author wishes to express his appreciation to the following for their helpful comments on an earlier draft of this chapter: Alan M. Hofmeister, Director, Outreach and Development Division, Exceptional Child Center, Utah State University, Logan, Utah; Philip Lewis, President, Instructional Dynamics Incorporated, Chicago, Illinois; and Harold Stolovitch, Professeur Adjoint, Universite de Montreal, Montreal, Quebec.

13.

Designing Instructional Media for Educable Mentally Retarded Learners

William H. Allen and Kay E. Goldberg

It is the major purpose of this chapter to present guidelines for the design and production of instructional media to be used in the teaching of mentally retarded learners. The learning characteristics of this group will be identified and described and prescriptions made for media design based upon these learning attributes. Recommendations will be presented for profitable lines of inquiry, research, and developmental projects that might be implemented in the near future in order to determine optimum models of media design for mentally retarded learners.

The far-reaching effects of the passage of the Education for All Handicapped Children Act of 1975 cannot be calculated with any great certainty at this moment, but certain outcomes are predictable: (1) the public schools will have to accommodate a greater number and wider variety of mentally retarded learners than ever before, and (2) mildly retarded children will be spending an increasing proportion of their time in the regular classroom with the support of ancillary personnel and resource materials. The potential benefits of specially designed instructional media under these circumstances cannot be overestimated. As Lance (1976) has pointed out, the proper prescription and utilization of specialized media cannot only facilitate the success of the handicapped learner within the regular classroom, but can likewise serve effectively those learners who, although not designated "handicapped" in the legal sense, still require specialized adaptations of programs and materials to benefit fully from instruction.

Given the learning problems of mentally retarded learners in such areas as abstraction, retention, comprehension, and attention, it would be difficult to imagine media of instruction with more potential effectiveness than audiovisuals (Aserlind, 1966). The special capacities of mediated instruction to hold and manipulate attention and to present information in concrete, novel, and highly organized form would appear to be well-suited to the educational needs of mentally retarded learners.

Only within the last few years, however, have investigators looked seriously at the efficacy of instructional media for teaching the retarded. It has been suggested recently, for example, that television might be used successfully with the mentally retarded as a technique to model social behavior (Baran, 1973; Fechter, 1971) and language behavior (Striefel, 1972), as well as to facilitate attention and to intensify stimulus values for improved information reception (McVey, 1973). The research in this direction has been limited by at least two considerations. First, there has been a scarcity of mediated instruction designed especially for mentally retarded learners. Educators, when they have elected to teach mentally retarded populations by means of audiovisuals, have traditionally used (with varying degrees of adaptation) materials designed for normal children. Second, much of the literature in this area of research has tended to be speculative rather than supported by hard empirical evidence.

The premises of this chapter are (1) that the time is appropriate

Designing Instructional Media   265

to evaluate empirically the effectiveness of instructional media with retarded learners; (2) that research along these lines ought to employ instructional materials designed specifically for retarded learners; and (3) that a necessary first step is to derive systematic principles of media design from current knowledge of the learning characteristics of the target population. Mahoney and Buckhalt (1976) recently made a commendable initial effort to generate guidelines for matching the cognitive skills of mentally retarded children with the content and structure of instructional media. This chapter will attempt to elaborate some of their well-reasoned proposals and add other specific media design prescriptions for the production of mediated instruction.

Certain limitations must be stated at the outset with regard to the intended audience for the instructional media proposed in this chapter. The most widely accepted general definition of mental retardation at present is that of the American Association on Mental Deficiency (1973): "Mental retardation refers to significantly subaverage general intellectual functioning existing concurrently with deficits in adaptive behavior, and manifested during the developmental period." Within the parameters of this broad definition, educators and scientists have distinguished traditionally between cultural-familial and brain-injured etiologies, between educable and trainable populations, and along numerous other dimensions of classifications. While the terms "educable" and "trainable" are becoming increasingly less useful, and while the target population for instructional media need not be circumscribed by rigid boundaries of IQ scores, it is still necessary to identify the intended audience for the media described in these pages as those mentally retarded individuals who are capable of profiting from instruction of an academic nature. Members of this group would generally be classified as "educable" or "mildly" retarded, with IQ scores falling roughly between 50-80. Even within this more limited audience there is a variety of retarded learners, including those children classified as EMR because they fall toward the lower end of the intellectual scale, and those so classified because of language differences associated with lower socio-economic status and cultural disadvantage (Sitko and Semmel, 1973; Bereiter and Englemann, 1966). It remains possible that within the target population of the mildly retarded such variables as lower socio-economic status and cultural disadvantage may interact with the mediated presentations in such a way as to make them more or less effective for various groups of learners. But there is also the likelihood that the media prescriptions generated here for instruction of an academic nature will prove to be applicable as well to media design (in such areas as social, occupational, and self-help skills) appropriate to more severely retarded children.

In making the analysis of learning characteristics of the mentally retarded, the authors examined a number of comprehensive reviews which described a broad range of learning characteristics of the mentally retarded (Baumeister, 1967; Denny, 1964; Estes, 1970; Goulet, 1968; and Lipman, 1963) and a number of individual studies. This analysis revealed a vast and unwieldy body of literature comparing normal and retardate learning performance and a body of comparative research, much of which was seriously compromised by methodological and design problems. Yet it has been necessary to use this body of literature and research to describe the learning characteristics upon which the media design prescriptions are based.

As a final prefatory note, it seems prudent to mention that while the media prescriptions proposed in the second half of this chapter are derived from cognitive and related learner characteristics described in the following sections, the effective use of instructional media for the mildly retarded should be guided by still other exigencies. Mahoney and Buckhalt (1976) have argued that the information from a cognitive profile of the mentally retarded be integrated with such specialized program information as (1) the prerequisite knowledge or skills, (2) the nature of the instructional objective, (3) the sequence of instruction, and (4) the criterion behavior.

Learning Characteristics of the Mentally Retarded

This section is not a review of learning research in the formal or comprehensive sense, but rather a description of a few learning characteristics which appear to have specific and important implications for the design of instructional media for educable mentally retarded learners. These characteristics have been selected for discussion on the basis of two criteria: (1) in most cases they reveal deficits in learning capacities and processing abilities on the part of retarded learners, and (2) they suggest a means by which media might be designed to perform a compensatory function. The identification of characteristics in this section is intended to be a preliminary effort, and does not preclude the possibility that other cognitive and perceptual characteristics may have significant implications for media design for the mentally retarded.

Attention

Attention is one of the few areas in the literature where mentally retarded learners have demonstrated fairly consistent deficits in relation to normal subjects. Alabiso (1972) reported evidence of deficiencies of retarded children in their attention span, focus, and selective attention. It has also been found that retarded subjects scan visual material less efficiently and less methodically than normals of the same chronological age (Spitz, 1969; Winters and Gerjuoy, 1969).

Research in discrimination learning (Zeaman and House, 1963) has suggested that the learning of a discrimination problem involves two stages: (1) attention to the relevant cues of the problem, and (2) making a response to the problem. Zeaman and House (1967) hypothesized that once mentally retarded subjects learned to selectively attend to the relevant cues of the task, they learned visual discriminations at a rate comparable to normal subjects. These findings concerning selective attention have generated a number of implications for teaching retarded learners. First, it follows that directing the learner's attention by pretraining on the task-relevant dimensions will facilitate learning. Second, it follows that if the retarded learner is characterized by a low initial probability of attending to the relevant cues, his likelihood of success will increase as the number of task-relevant cues increases in proportion to the number of irrelevant or distracting cues.

Abstraction

Jensen (1970) has described mental abilities as a hierarchy, the levels of which are distinguished by the degree of information processing required between input and output. He distinguished further between Level I abilities (involving rote processes) and Level II abilities (involving abstract or conceptual processes). Jensen argued that although children in a typical EMR classroom will demonstrate a wide range in performance on rote tasks, they are all considered by researchers to be deficient on tests involving abstract and conceptual abilities. Studies of paired-associate learning have also revealed an increasing disadvantage of mentally retarded subjects relative to normals as the task becomes more abstract and verbal (Lipman, 1963).

Language

Language deficits are central to the description of mental retardation; indeed, the most common standardized intelligence tests used to classify individuals as mentally retarded are largely tests of language abilities. Research in language behavior reviewed by Sitko and Semmel (1973) found the mentally retarded to be deficient in such language areas as syntactical complexity, sentence length, vocabulary, abstraction, and articulation. In addition, retarded children manifest a discrepancy between receptive and expressive language which is greater than for normals (Walker, Roodin, and Lamb, 1975). The literature has suggested certain educational strategies to compensate for language deficits in mentally retarded learners by reducing the verbal demands of the task. These include (1) simplifying the language of the instructional message (Mahoney and Buckhalt, 1976), (2) selecting a response mode not requiring verbal output from the learner (Walker, Roodin, and Lamb, 1975), and (3) repeating the task instructions frequently (Denny, 1966).

Memory

Many studies have compared the memory performance of normals and retardates. Reviewing the research in long-term memory, Belmont (1966) determined that so many of the studies suffered from methodological flaws that there is almost no solid evidence either to support or contradict the classic hypothesis of retardate memory loss. Although some evidence of a short-term memory deficit has been reported (Ellis, 1970; Scott and Scott, 1968), it has been suggested by Brown (1975) that the short-term memory deficiency be interpreted as one example of the retarded individual's deficiency in the intentional use of strategies to reduce information load by such means as organizing, transforming, or elaborating the presented material.

The memory performance of retarded learners appears to be facilitated by a number of factors, including (1) the presentation of information in a highly organized form (Spitz, 1973), (2) distributed practice in the learning of materials (Madsen, 1963), (3) the provision of strategy training so that the learner may reduce the information load spontaneously (Brown, 1975), and (4) a high level of meaningfulness of items to be remembered (Cobb and Barnard, 1971).

Generalization

The ability to generalize or transfer has been found to be related to mental age (Smith, 1968). Mentally retarded subjects do demonstrate transfer of learning, although there appears to be little assurance that retarded children will generalize information to noninstructional settings unless explicitly told to do so (Mahoney and Buckhalt, 1976). Denny (1966) made a number of recommendations for promoting positive transfer with retarded learners, including (1) distributed repetition during original learning (well-spaced within and across sessions), (2) a wide variety of different versions of the same stimulus quality, (3) training the meaning of each concept in a wide variety of contexts, and (4) the establishment, in later training, of verbal mediators such as training the subject to verbalize the concept.

Implications for the Design of Media

From the learning characteristics discussed in the preceding section, it is possible to extract a few general principles which may be used to guide the design of instructional media for educable mentally retarded learners.

1. Instructional media may be designed to compensate for deficient attention processes of EMRs by directing their attention to the salient aspects of the task and the stimulus content to be learned.

2. The relatively inefficient learning processes of the retarded may be facilitated by reducing the amount of information in the instructional presentation.

3. Even with reduced information load, it is recommended that the instructional message be highly structured and redundant to facilitate learning and recall.

4. The retarded should be encouraged to participate actively in the learning process and be given explicit instructions in generalizing learning to new situations.

Prescriptions for the Design of Instructional Media

Given the learning characteristics of EMRs, how does one go about translating such knowledge into effective instructional materials? In this section an attempt will be made to apply these and other EMR learning characteristics to the generation of prescriptions for the design of effective instructional materials.

A number of specific media design principles may be derived from established psychological principles of learning. It is believed that these principles may be directly applicable to the design of media for teaching EMRs. In the pages to follow, these design principles will be described and specific applications made to the design of media for educable mentally retarded learners. Suggestions will also be given for using the design principles with different types of instructional media.

A. Preparing and Motivating the Learner

Two psychological factors would appear to operate in the preparation of the learner to learn from particular stimuli: motivation and attentional set. Motivation may be defined as that internal state of the learner that leads to a desire to learn and may be produced by arousal, expectancy, or incentives. Attentional set may be defined as that internal state of the learner that controls which stimuli are to be processed and to what degree.

There is documented evidence (Anderson, 1967; Gagné and Rohwer, 1969) that the prior preparation of the learner for the instruction to follow has a facilitative effect upon learning for all types of learners, but that this effect may be particularly true for those of lower mental ability. Athough there is no direct research evidence that EMRs profit from such preparatory procedures, Ausubel and Fitzgerald (1962) did find that the use of a written "advance organizer" designed to provide a framework for the instruction to follow did benefit lower verbal ability learners. And analyses of the learning characteristics of EMRs reveal deficiencies in their attentional processes. Therefore, appropriate design of instructional media compensates for EMR learners' inabilities to direct attention for extended periods of time or to selectively attend to relevant stimuli. The critical factor involved in these techniques is the gaining of the attention of the learner. In actual practice, most motivational and learner preparatory activities will be conducted by the classroom teacher rather than "built into" the instructional media. At the same time, the developer of such media might consider how the teaching effectiveness of the material may be enhanced by actually incorporating motivational and attention-setting techniques into the material itself, both as an introduction to the lesson or through the stimulus presentation. What are some of the design procedures that may be "built into" the instructional media to prepare the EMR learner for the instruction to follow? The following procedures are suggestive of design and production approaches. Depending upon the conditions and the judgment of the designer, one or more approaches may be used in a single presentation or none used at all. The following techniques may be used *prior to* the presentation of the content to be learned as means of motivating the EMR learner or gaining his attention.

1. *Present the specific objective, goal, or competency to be achieved* by the learner from the material. This should be only a single task, presented in an uncomplicated way. Depending upon the nature of the task (i.e., simple or more difficult), a particular discrete stimulus presentation may contain one or more goal statements.

2. *Present an introductory overview or summary* of the material. This might be a simple statement of the nature of the lesson, a table of contents, or a simple outline. One must avoid presenting too much information, however, and this technique should be used with discretion.

3. *Point out the importance of learning* the material to follow by relating it to the personal needs of the individual learner. This may be accomplished by arousing a desire to achieve a particular goal, to satisfy a particular need for personal satisfaction or success, or to point out where that information learned will be used.

Designing Instructional Media *273*

4. *Arouse curiosity about the message to follow.* This may be done by providing novelty in the opening displays to capture attention. Or an expectation of particular knowledge to be gained may be developed.

5. *Give an expectation of pleasure or reward to be gained* from the material.

6. *Convince learners they can learn.* This technique motivates them toward successful performance and establishes a prior set to succeed.

7. *Relate the material to previous learnings or real-life experiences* of the learner. The introductory sequence may serve as a bridge between these past experiences and the new material to be learned.

8. *Use with different media.* Although these techniques appear to be more widely used in printed verbal material, they may be built into audiovisual materials as well. There is a tendency for the media producer or author to expect the classroom teacher to provide the necessary motivational incentives to the student. But by building appropriate introductory sequences into the actual films, filmstrips, television programs, and audiotapes, the incentives or attention-setting stimuli will appear contiguously with the material to be learned. The interest-provoking qualities of many audiovisual materials will be particularly appropriate for such goals.

B. Directing Attention to Crucial Learning Cues

The poor attentional abilities of EMRs also puts demands on the internal organization of the instructional media. Whereas the previous section presented techniques for arousing attentional processes *prior to* the actual exposure to the content to be learned, this section will give techniques for directing attention *at the same time as* the content is presented. Such techniques will serve as cues, directives, or guides to crucial aspects of the stimulus material. Again, we are concerned here with the need to compensate for

EMRs' deficient selective attention, and the suggested instructional design techniques are meant to provide instruction that will overcome such deficiencies.

There is enough supporting research evidence to draw the conclusion that learners of low mental ability can profit from presentational procedures that direct attention to crucial content to be inspected or learned. Zeaman and House's (1963) research with retardate discrimination learning supported the conclusion that lower ability learners need stimuli that assist them to focus and direct their attention. In research with low mental ability Air Force trainees, Lumsdaine, Sulzer, and Kopstein (1961) found that animated films using such attention-directing devices as arrows and pop-in labels assisted their learning. Allen, Cooney, and Weintraub (1968) found similar results with motion picture film sound track narration that directed attention to or pointed out relevant cues in the pictorial stimuli. Spitz and Webreck (1972) reported improvement in retardate learning when the redundant patterns of digit spans were highlighted by spacing or underlining; retarded learners appear to benefit from redundancy when provided with external help.

The following kinds of attention-directing devices may be built into instructional media in order to focus the attention of EMR learners upon the relevant instructional content and to maintain their attention.

1. *Provide verbal directions to attend to crucial learning cues.* These may be printed or spoken. They may be: (a) directions to attend to or look at or remember particular content that will follow, (b) descriptions or summaries of certain events to come, (c) directions as to kinds of activities the learner is to engage in when exposed to the stimulus material, or (d) verbal labels of relevant content to be learned.

2. *Present only critical cues to learning in the early parts of presentations.* Such cues should call for only single responses or associations directly relevant to learning. Irrelevant cues may be

added later in order to provide some discrimination training if appropriate.

3. *Use of visual emphasizers.* In the case of printed material, this may be accomplished by underlining essential content or use of italics, bold type, or color. With motion picture presentations, visual pointers such as moving arrows or "pop-in" labels of words or numbers are helpful. With still picture presentations, such as filmstrips and slides, visual pointers may also be used to call attention to pictorial features demanding learner attention.

4. *Use of spoken directions in audio narration.* Directing attention verbally is most often done in the sound tracks of motion pictures and sound filmstrips or slide presentations. The learner may be directed to "look at," "find," "look for," or "see" certain features in the pictorial content. There is abundant evidence that such directives will control the visual inspection behavior of the learner and point out the relevant material, thus reducing the likelihood that the EMR learner's attention will be distracted by the irrelevant material in the stimulus presentation.

5. *Use of motion.* Where it is feasible (instructionally and economically), motion pictures may be used, thus utilizing their superior capabilities to capture and maintain EMR learner attention. Changes within the visual field act as cues and capture attention immediately. However, some caution may be needed in the use of motion pictures to teach EMRs, and it is important that such films emphasize the relevant content and not distract the learner by nonessential movement in other parts of the visual field.

6. *Use with different media.* Attention-directing and maintaining techniques may be built into all media types, although to different degrees of effectiveness. Printed media, of course, may use typographic emphasizers, whereas pictorial media may be more easily adapted to visual pointers. All audiovisual media may incorporate verbal attention-directing to features in the visuals, and motion pictures and television are the only media types that can profit from the use of motion as an attention-gainer.

C. Obtaining Active Learner Participation and Response

The efficacy of active response-evoking procedures in enhancing learning has been adequately demonstrated (Anderson, 1967; Gagné and Rohwer, 1969; Tobias, 1973), and there is at least theoretical support for the notion that low mental ability learners will profit from such activity. For example, Stolurow (1963) concluded from his review of research on programmed instruction, a method based on learner response and feedback, that the use of programmed instruction is an effective way to teach EMRs. The attention-directing and personal involving qualities inherent in the participation process would seem to compensate for deficient attentional skills of the EMRs. The following media design prescriptions would appear to take into account these factors and lead to more effective learning. It should be noted that these student responses should be followed, where possible, by confirmation or corrective feedback.

1. *Making overt active responses*. These include the building into the stimuli demands for "speaking out" or written responses by the learner to requests for response in the audio, pictorial, or printed presentations. In the case of motor skill training, opportunities for actual practice of the skill may be provided.

2. *Making covert responses*. These include the built-in requests for "thinking the answer" responses to audio, pictorial, or printed presentations. This means that the EMR learner will be told to think the answer or "say it to yourself." Control over the actual responding mechanism is less certain with EMRs than if an overt response were required; so the technique might be used largely when overt responding is not possible.

3. *Use with different media*. The feasibility of using response-elicitation (and associated correcting or confirming feedback to be discussed below) will vary with different instructional media. Although learner response may be called forth by any medium, it may be more easily accomplished with printed materials, which are normally used by the learner at a pace to conform to his

Designing Instructional Media 277

unique learning requirements. On the other hand, pictorial and audio materials such as motion pictures, sound filmstrips, and audio recordings usually require student or teacher intervention into the stimulus transmission process (to stop and start the display equipment) and sometimes the use of more than one piece of equipment. The student manipulation of audiovisual equipment may, however, be sufficiently interesting and involving for the EMR learner to override some of the problems of using response-demand techniques with audiovisual materials.

D. Providing Correcting or Confirming Feedback to Student Response

Associated with active student response is the principle of correcting or confirming feedback and knowledge of results of the response. The effectiveness of this procedure has been verified for learners in general (Lumsdaine, 1963; Anderson, 1967; Gagné and Rohwer, 1969; Tobias, 1973), but there have been few direct studies of its use with EMRs. The following applications to media design are suggested.

1. *Furnishing feedback to learner responses.* Feedback may be given to elicited responses by printed, spoken, or pictorially depicted answers. These answers may confirm the responses given by the learner, correct errors made by him, clarify misconceptions that may exist, provide practice of the correct response, or serve as reinforcing rewards for the correct response. Care must be taken with EMR learners to make the feedback immediately and in a way that will lead to the correct answer rather than a sense of failure.

2. *Use with different media.* As was the case with the learner participation and response techniques, different media and presentational devices will have varying capabilities for furnishing corrective feedback. All media except computer-mediated instruction are limited in their abilities to correct or confirm the correctness of the learner's response. They cannot show in what ways responses

conform to the correct answers. They can merely display the correct answer and depend upon the learner to determine whether or not the answer agrees with, or to what degree and in what ways it may differ from, the correct answer. Only computer-mediated instruction may be designed to be adaptive to the actual response made by the learner and to determine the next appropriate steps for the learner to take. This limitation of conventional media to provide adaptive feedback places an added responsibility on the media designer to build the feedback into the stimulus material in ways that will assist the EMR learner to use the corrective material.

E. Repeating Instructions for Overlearning

The repetition of information or the content to be learned, in an identical or varied form, greatly facilitates learning (Ausubel, 1968; Gagné, 1970; and Lumsdaine, 1963). This necessity for repetitive presentation of the content is particularly apparent for EMR learners. Zeaman and House (1963) have pointed out the importance of repeating the stimuli frequently in order to assure overlearning. The following applications to media design are presented.

1. *Providing identical repetition.* Most repetition of content that occurs consists of the repeated presentation of the *same* material. This may take the form of drill on words, numbers, and associations. Or, with audiovisual material, the same film or filmstrip itself may be repeated two or more times, either in succession or spaced over a period of time. Within a single presentation the same word or phrase or idea may occur a number of times. The intent of this kind of repetition is to give the EMR learner repeated opportunities to learn the material and will often be associated with opportunity for learner response and subsequent feedback or correction.

2. *Providing varied repetition.* Less easy to accomplish is the task of varying the content in such a way as to present the target material from an altered point of view or in a different setting.

This will assist the EMR learner to generalize the learning to new situations. An interesting example of such repetition is found in *Sesame Street* wherein the letters of the alphabet are presented to preschoolers in many different and varied formats, repeated and repeated.

3. *Use with different media.* All instructional media seem to be adaptable to application of repetitive techniques. The designer of media for the EMR learner may find that the so-called audiovisual media (films, filmstrips, audiotapes, computer-mediated instruction) are more flexible than printed textual materials as channels for presenting more interesting and varied repetitions. They permit a mixture of verbal and pictorial stimuli or permit a more game-like setting (as with the use of computerized instruction). Such media may have a further advantage in that they may be repeated a number of times without losing patience or tiring. Those learning tasks that require repetitive drill may be more efficiently put into some mediated form and made readily accessible to the EMR learner.

F. Reducing the Information Load

The deficient information-processing capabilities of low mental ability learners place certain requirements upon the design of the materials used in instruction: namely, the reduction of the information load by (a) pacing the presentation at a slow rate of development, (b) limiting the amount of information presented, and (c) simplifying the materials and tasks. Studies by Gropper and Lumsdaine (1961) and Gropper and Kress (1965) verified the inability of low ability students to learn from rapidly paced instructional media. Eckhardt (1970) reported studies that pointed out the decrements in learning by low ability learners from materials that were "compressed" or shortened so as to include more information per unit of time. The following applications of these findings to media design may be considered.

1. *Decreasing the rate of presentation.* The handicap that EMRs

encounter when presented with rapidly paced stimulus material calls forth the need for a more deliberate and gradual presentation of the content. The rate of speech in audio recorded materials and in the narration of pictorial presentations should probably be delivered at no more (and probably less) than 100 words per minute for that material containing content that must be learned. Similarly, the content (concepts, facts, discriminations, associations, etc.) to be learned should be distributed over time rather than massed in a short period. This means that the concepts and ideas to be learned should be presented at an easily comprehensible rate of speed, with the stimulus sequences of sufficient length to permit adequate time for mental processing.

2. *Limiting the amount of information.* Another factor contributing to the reduction of information processing requirements of low ability learners is the decreasing of the amount of information impinging upon the learner's sensory receptors at any particular time. For example, visual displays requiring attendance and assimilation of the content should be simple, uncluttered, and specific to the requirements of the learning task. Irrelevant material that may distract the learner from attending to the particular content to be learned should be eliminated if possible. The low ability learner's attention is easily distracted; so instructional material should be designed to decrease this probability. EMRs have difficulty in distributing their attention among communication channels and in switching their attention from one sensory reception channel to another. Therefore, care must be taken to avoid simultaneous presentation in two channels (usually visual and audio) unless adequate time is allowed for mental processing. This means that sound motion picture, slide-tape, televised, or sound supplemented printed materials must be so designed that the stimuli in the two sensory channels do not conflict for attention but are mutually supporting and redundant. But even when the content of the two channels is related, adequate cues or directives for the switching of attention should be included.

3. *Simplifying the materials and tasks.* The information-processing requirements placed on the learner may be further reduced by presenting the material in a simple and direct way, by requiring the performance of uncomplicated and simple tasks, and by dealing with concrete rather than abstract content. Mahoney and Buckhalt (1976) have pointed out the importance of presenting information in a concrete manner, illustrating abstractions with concrete examples, and reducing the complexity of the material by very simple direct language and relationships between the language and its referents. This means that the tasks to be performed should be simple ones and of short enough duration to permit the EMR learner to follow the sequence of the task. Thus, tasks should be presented in small steps, each step developing logically from the preceding one and building up to the terminal knowledge or performance to be acquired.

4. *Use with different media.* These design techniques appear to be equally applicable to all types of instructional media. It is particularly important to design them into such fixed-pace media as motion picture films and televised presentations, the delivery rates of which are not easily controlled by learners—that is, they cannot stop, start, and repeat the sequence. Audiotape and sound filmstrip presentations may be more easily controlled by learners, but even these media place a requirement on them to perform manipulatory tasks and make decisions about the appropriateness of repeating sequences that may be beyond their mental capabilities to perform; thus the need for the media developer to design any kind of instructional medium placing minimal information-processing demands on the learner.

G. Organizational Outlining or Structuring of the Content

Because of the EMR's deficient skills in organizing and categorizing incoming information or stimuli, procedures should be employed to organize the material for easier mental processing. The more complex the material, the more frequently such techniques should be used. The following applications of this finding are suggested.

1. *Use headings.* The use of printed or spoken headings or subheadings of major divisions of the content will assist the EMR learner to group and organize related units of information into a relevant context. Such headings may include the insertion of topical statements of the stimuli to follow and should be used frequently to break up large bodies of expository material. With printed materials, normal headings and subheadings may be used. With films and televised presentations, this may take the form of inserted printed subtitles or spoken introductions (e.g., "The next part will tell you about ... ").

2. *Presenting the material in a sequential order.* The sequencing of the material from more simple to more difficult has already been discussed. In order to assist the learner in following this sequence, enumeration of the points to be presented (e.g., "first," "second," etc.) or other visual or audio cues to the sequential order should be employed where appropriate.

3. *Use with different media.* This design procedure may be used with any instructional medium. The building in of organizational features of the content material may be applied to printed, audiovisual, or audio media. It may be particularly necessary to do so with audiovisual and audio media types because their fixed-pace presentational characteristics may place some information-processing demands on EMR learners. They are not as easily repeatable as are the printed media and may demand a more sequentially structured organizational form. In any event, all instructional media are adaptable to the application of these organizing techniques.

H. Presenting Models for Imitation

There is a prevailing reason to believe that the furnishing of models to be imitated may be a quite effective technique for teaching EMR learners certain kinds of skills or tasks. Mahoney and Buckhalt (1976) have pointed this out and have shown that these learners may require models that they may emulate. Koran, Snow, and McDonald (1971) found that video-modeling techniques which portrayed skills to be learned by means of videotapes benefited low rather than high ability learners. The following applications to instructional media design may be made.

1. *Furnishing a model for imitation.* The most obvious design technique is that of presenting the actual skill to be learned or task to be performed. This type of presentation would be most prevalent in perceptual-motor learning tasks wherein the learner must learn to perform a specific motor skill, usually in a fixed order. The skill to be learned should be graphically displayed, devoid of irrelevant and distracting material, presented (at least in the beginning) at a deliberately slow pace, with opportunities given for learner participation and practice, with correcting feedback if possible, and repeated with varied examples. It may be seen that the best use of models for imitation is in combination with many other design techniques.

2. *Use with different media.* Audiovisual media would appear to be more effective than printed verbal materials in presenting models for imitation or for supplantation of mental processes. The motion picture film may be the best medium for presenting such stimuli because it can show the continuous step-by-step progress of operations and transformations in a realistic way.

I. Use of Memory Strategies

Retarded learners characteristically fail to systematically use memory strategies such as clustering or mnemonic elaboration to reduce the information load of incoming material (Brown, 1975). There is evidence to suggest that when retarded subjects are provided with prior instructions to "cluster" list items according to categories (i.e., "Tell me all the animals you remember from the list"), the recall of items is significantly greater than in the control condition (Gerjuoy and Spitz, 1966). Similarly, studies of paired-associate learning with retardates have demonstrated that when retarded subjects are provided with mnemonic elaborations to relate word pairs (such as sentences associating the words), learning is improved (Jensen and Rohwer, 1963; Turnure and Walsh, 1971). Although the information presented by instructional media is usually more sophisticated than lists and word pairs, the literature does imply that when retarded learners are provided with explicit strategies for remembering information, performance will be facilitated. Although research in the use of media-generated strategies is lacking, the designers of instructional media for retarded learners might build strategy training into presentations and include opportunities within the presentations for retarded learners to practice on their own.

J. Using Memory Strategies

Although the information presented by mediated instruction is usually more sophisticated than lists and word pairs, and although research in the area of media-generated strategies is lacking, the designers of instructional media might use the following techniques to build strategy training into presentations based on the above comments.

1. *Using clustering strategies.* The learner may be encouraged to cluster incoming material by explicit instructions (i.e., "At the end of the lesson you will be asked to name all of the animals in the story."). The mediated presentation might offer visual or verbal examples of how to organize the information, and also provide periodic opportunities for the retarded learner to try out individual strategies.

2. *Using mnemonic strategies.* If the information in the presentation lends itself to mnemonic codes or elaborations (such as simple sentences containing key words or ideas) the learners should be provided with these aids and encouraged to practice them and to develop their own.

3. *Use with different media.* Strategy training might be used

with any medium, although it seems to be especially suitable for use with printed materials. When using printed media retarded learners may refer to the suggested strategy at their own pace.

Recommendations for Further Research and Development

Research on Instructional Media Design

This chapter has reported research and indicated the theory that might apply to the design of media for the instruction of the mentally retarded. The research conclusions, however, were based largely on comparisons of learning between high ability or normal learners and lower ability learners that were not classifiable as mentally retarded. The assumption was made, in using these findings, that differences in learning between high and low mental ability individuals would be even more pronounced for the mentally retarded. There is sound theoretical justification for this projection. Nevertheless, there is a crucial need for empirical research that would confirm the conclusions and further indicate the precise nature of the characteristics of the instructional media.

It is suggested, therefore, that a program of research support be undertaken for the determination of optimum models for the design of instructional materials for the mentally retarded.

Evaluation of Existing Instructional Media

An evaluation of the teaching values of existing instructional media would appear to be useful to educators of the mentally retarded. This activity could be conducted in two phases. The first phase could entail the development of criteria by which such learning materials may be evaluated. The second phase would then provide for an extensive survey of existing materials and their evaluation by means of the criteria set up. Such a project would also provide a widescale inventory and description of existing instructional materials.

References

Alabiso, F. Inhibitory functions of attention in reducing hyperactive behavior. *American Journal of Mental Deficiency*, 1972, 77, 259-282.

Allen, W. H., Cooney, S. M., and Weintraub, R. *Audio implementation of still and motion pictures.* USOE Final Report, Project No. 5-0741. Los Angeles: University of Southern California, Research Division, Department of Cinema, 1968.

American Association on Mental Deficiency. *Manual on terminology and classification in mental retardation.* Washington, D.C.: American Association on Mental Deficiency, 1973.

Anderson, R. C. Educational psychology. *Annual Review of Psychology*, 1967, 18, 103-164.

Aserlind, L. Audiovisual instruction for the mentally retarded. *Audiovisual Instruction*, 1966, 11, 727-730.

Ausubel, D. P. *Educational psychology: A cognitive view.* New York: Holt, Rinehart, and Winston, 1968.

Ausubel, D. P., and Fitzgerald, D. Organizer, general background, and antecedent learning in sequential verbal learning. *Journal of Educational Psychology*, 1962, 53, 243-259.

Baran, S. J. TV and social learning in the institutionalized MR. *Mental Retardation*, 1973, 11, 36-38.

Baumeister, A. A. Problems in comparative studies of mental retardates and normals. *American Journal of Mental Deficiency*, 1967, 71, 869-875.

Belmont, J. M. Long term memory in mental retardation. In N. R. Ellis (Ed.), *International review of research in mental retardation* (Vol. 1). New York: Academic Press, 1966.

Bereiter, C., and Englemann, S. *Teaching disadvantaged children in the preschool.* Englewood Cliffs, N.J.: Prentice-Hall, 1966.

Brown, A. L. The role of strategic behavior in retardate memory. In N. R. Ellis (Ed.), *International review of research in mental retardation* (Vol. 7). New York: Academic Press, 1975.

Cobb, J. H., and Barnard, J. W. Differential effects of implicit associative values on short-term recall of retarded and nonretarded children. *American Journal of Mental Deficiency*, 1971, *76*, 130-135.

Denny, M. R. Research in learning performance. In H. Stevens and R. Heber (Eds.), *Mental retardation: A review of research.* Chicago: University of Chicago Press, 1964.

Denny, M. R. A theoretical analysis and its application to training the mentally retarded. In N. R. Ellis (Ed.), *International review of research in mental retardation* (Vol. 2). New York: Academic Press, 1966.

Eckhardt, W. W., Jr. *Learning in multi-media programmed instruction as a function of aptitude and instruction rate controlled by compressed speech.* Unpublished doctoral dissertation, University of Southern California, 1970.

Ellis, N. R. Memory processes in retardates and normals. In N. R. Ellis (Ed.), *International review of research in mental retardation* (Vol. 4). New York: Academic Press, 1970.

Estes, W. K. *Learning theory and mental development.* New York: Academic Press, 1970.

Fechter, J.V. Modeling and environmental generalization by mentally retarded subjects of televised aggressive or friendly behavior. *American Journal of Mental Deficiency*, 1971, *76*, 266-267.

Gagné, R.M. *The conditions of learning.* New York: Holt, Rinehart, and Winston, 1970.

Gagné, R.M., and Rohwer, W.D., Jr. Instructional psychology. *Annual Review of Psychology*, 1969, *20,* 381-418.

Gerjuoy, I. R., and Spitz, H. Associative clustering in free recall: Intellectual and developmental variables. *American Journal of Mental Deficiency*, 1966, *70*, 918-927.

Goulet, L. R. Verbal learning and memory research with retardates. In N. R. Ellis (Ed.), *International review of research in mental retardation* (Vol. 3). New York: Academic Press, 1968.

Gropper, G. L., and Kress, G. C., Jr. Individualizing instruction through pacing procedures. *AV Communication Review*, 1965, *13*, 165-182.

Gropper, G. L., and Lumsdaine, A. A. *An experimental comparison of a conventional TV lesson with a programmed TV lesson requiring active student response.* Studies in Televised Instruction Report No. 2. Pittsburgh, Pa.: Metropolitan Pittsburgh Educational Television Stations WQED-WQEX and American Institutes for Research, 1961.

Jensen, A.R. A theory of primary and secondary familial mental retardation. In N. R. Ellis (Ed.), *International review of research in mental retardation* (Vol. 4). New York: Academic Press, 1970.

Jensen, A. R., and Rohwer, W. D. The effect of verbal mediation on the learning and retention of paired-associates by retarded adults. *American Journal of Mental Deficiency*, 1963, *68*, 80-84.

Koran, M. L., Snow, R. E., and McDonald, F. J. Teacher aptitude and observational learning of a teacher skill. *Journal of Educational Psychology*, 1971, *62*, 219-228.

Lance, W. D. What you should know about P.L. 94-142. *Audiovisual Instruction*, 1976, *21*, 14-15.

Lipman, R. S. Learning: Verbal, perceptual-motor, and classical conditioning. In N. R. Ellis (Ed.), *Handbook of mental deficiency*. New York: McGraw-Hill, 1963.

Lumsdaine, A. A. Instruments and media of instruction. In N. L. Gage (Ed.), *Handbook of research on teaching*. Chicago: Rand McNally, 1963.

Lumsdaine, A. A., Sulzer, R. L., and Kopstein, F. F. The effects of animation cues and repetition of examples on learning from an instructional film. In A. A. Lumsdaine (Ed.), *Stu-*

dent response in programmed instruction. Washington, D.C.: National Academy of Sciences-National Research Council, 1961.

Madsen, M. C. Distribution of practice and level of intelligence. *Psychological Reports,* 1963, *13*, 39-42.

Mahoney, G., and Buckhalt, J. Instructional media for mentally retarded children. In F. B. Withrow and C. J. Nygren (Eds.), *Language, materials, and curriculum management for the handicapped learner.* Columbus, Ohio: Charles E. Merrill, 1976.

McVey, G. F. Learning experiences via educational technology for the EMR. *Mental Retardation,* 1973, *11*, 49-53.

Scott, K. G., and Scott, M. S. Research and theory in short-term memory. In N. R. Ellis (Ed.), *International review of research in mental retardation* (Vol. 3). New York: Academic Press, 1968.

Sitko, M.C., and Semmel, M.I. Language and language behavior of the mentally retarded. In L. Mann and D.A. Sabatino (Eds.), *The first review of special education* (Vol. 1). Philadelphia: JSE Press, 1973.

Smith, R.M. *Clinical teaching: Methods of instruction for the retarded.* New York: McGraw-Hill, 1968.

Spitz, H.H. Effects of stimulus information reduction on search time of retarded adolescents and normal children. *Journal of Experimental Psychology,* 1969, *82*, 482-487.

Spitz, H. H. Consolidating facts into the schematized learning and memory system of educable retardates. In N. R. Ellis (Ed.), *International review of research in mental retardation* (Vol. 6). New York: Academic Press, 1973.

Spitz, H. H., and Webreck, C. A. Effects of spontaneous vs. externally-cued learning on the permanent storage of a schema by retardates. *American Journal of Mental Deficiency,* 1972, *77*, 163-168.

Stolurow, L. M. Programmed instruction for the mentally retarded. *Review of Educational Research,* 1963, *33*, 126-136.

Striefel, S. Television as a language training medium with retarded children. *Mental Retardation*, 1972, *10*, 27-29.

Tobias, S. Review of the response mode issue. *Review of Educational Research*, 1973, *43*, 193-204.

Turnure, J. E., and Walsh, M. K. Effects of varied levels of verbal mediation on the learning and reversal of paired associates by educable retarded children. *American Journal of Mental Deficiency*, 1971, *76*, 60-67.

Walker, H. J., Roodin, P. A., and Lamb, M. J. Relationship between linguistic performance and memory deficits in retarded children. *American Journal of Mental Deficiency*, 1975, *79*, 545-552.

Winters, J. J., Jr., and Gerjuoy, I. R. Recognition of tachistoscopically exposed letters by normals and retardates. *Perception & Psychophysics*, 1969, *5*, 21-24.

Zeaman, D., and House, B. J. The role of attention in retardate discrimination learning. In N. R. Ellis (Ed.), *Handbook of mental deficiency*. New York: McGraw-Hill, 1963.

Zeaman, D., and House, B. J. The relation of IQ and learning. In R.M. Gagné (Ed.), *Learning and individual differences.* Columbus, Ohio: Merrill Books, 1967.

Authors' Note

The authors wish to express their appreciation to the following for their helpful comments on an earlier draft of this paper: Gerald Hasterok, Associate Professor of Education, Department of Special Education, University of Southern California, Los Angeles, California; and W. Howard Levie, Associate Professor of Education, Audio-Visual Center, Indiana University, Bloomington, Indiana.

14.

Mainstreaming the Mildly Handicapped: Some Research Suggestions

Thomas C. Lovitt

Need for a Definition of Mainstreaming

Mainstreaming is not an illusive construct like Learning Disabilities. Therefore, it can and should be defined. It is my belief that if an agreeable definition of mainstreaming can be written, it will serve to guide and systematize the research on that topic.

Toward this end, I recommend that a generic definition be adopted, one that includes the important components of mainstreaming. Those components should establish the parameters for research. Although each mainstreaming situation is unique, they might differ only to the extent that they feature one component or another.

During the early stages of mainstreaming research, investigators could focus on the few broad components of mainstreaming. In so doing, the probability would be increased that several investigations would pertain to a common theme. Later, as the process of mainstreaming developed, researchers could branch out and concentrate on more subtle elements.

If mainstreaming proceeds in the absence of an authorized definition, the research which follows will be disconnected and repetitive. To corroborate such a gloomy forecast we need only to reflect on the desultory and repetitious approach taken by the few researchers in learning disabilities, a group without an agreeable definition.

As for an adequate definition, the one by Kaufman, Gottlieb, Agard, and Kukic (1975), seems to be appropriate:

> Mainstreaming refers to the temporal, instructional, and social integration of eligible exceptional children with normal peers, based on an ongoing, individually determined, educational planning and programming process and requires clarification of responsibility among regular and special education administrative, instructional, and supportive personnel (p. 4).

This definition has three major components: (1) integration, (2) educational planning and programming process, and (3) clarification of responsibility. Each of these components might next be divided into subcomponents; for example, integration includes the aspects of temporal and instructional involvement. Educational planning and programming has to do with the instructional objectives and procedures. The third component, clarification of responsibility, embraces the importance of making specific educators accountable for implementing and actualizing certain educational objectives. Obviously, these sub-components could be refined still further. But, to reiterate, if those involved with mainstreaming can agree on a generic definition, then researchers can focus on the components of that definition. By so doing, a collection of studies might emerge which shared a common concern. Once those studies were synthesized, it is possible that some general principles would become obvious which might then be disseminated to the field.

Need for Alternative Research Methodologies and Assessment Systems

If mainstreaming, or for that matter any other aspect of education, is to develop because of research, a sound methodological base must be formed. There is a definite need either to improve our current research methodologies or to seek new ones. It is just as critical to improve the manner in which practitioners monitor the performances of children.

Research Methodologies

In reference to research, it is imperative that we do not repeat the methodological mistakes of investigators who conducted the series of efficacy studies in the 50's and 60's. When those researchers studied the relative merits of regular versus special class placement, they identified a group of MR children in a special classroom and another group of MR youngsters in a regular class. Next, they administered achievement tests and social adjustment scales once or twice a year. Finally, they subjected their data to various statistical treatments and announced the winners.

The inclination is great to study the merits of mainstreaming in much the same way, but we must resist the temptation. The reasons for not using the methodology of our forebears to study the current situation are several, and many of them were pointed out by Kirk (1964), in his disgust with the original efficacy studies. He said:

> ... There has not been a clear-cut definition of a special class, the curriculum, or the qualification of special teachers. Special classes vary widely in organization and in curriculum and teaching methods. Qualifications of teachers vary from well-trained teachers to those subjected to short-term summer courses taught largely by instructors who have had little training or experience with special classes. The administrative labeling of a group of retarded children as a special class for the purpose of receiving state subsidy does not assure it being a special class for experimental purposes (pp. 62-63).

Kaufman *et al.* (1975) were just as opposed to the use of traditional research methodologies to study features of mainstreaming when they said:

> Given the complexity of mainstreaming constructs, a between-groups research paradigm provides information of very limited utility for decision-making purposes ... The information obtained from a between-groups paradigm provides little insight regarding specific aspects of either the segregated or the mainstreaming treatments which differentially affect pupil outcomes. The conceptualization of mainstreaming as a multidimensional treatment involving numerous administrative and instructional options requires the use of a research paradigm which does not concentrate only on between-group variance. ... The extensive variability possible within the suggested definitional framework requires research paradigms which will permit results to be attributed to the effects of specific *within-treatment* variations (pp. 10-11).

The need for different educational research methodologies has been expressed by educators who are not necessarily identified with mainstreaming. Recently, the editors of *Reading Research Quarterly* (1974-1975) complained that much of the past reading research had not been addressed "... To the most important issues and concerns related to understanding the reading process—the teaching of reading and the field of reading in general." They were critical of reading researchers because they lacked "... The tools, techniques, methodologies, and approaches ... which could help them study important matters of reading."

Finally, they stressed the "... Need for research designs and new approaches that allow variables to emerge from the situation being studied ... and suggested that teachers and researchers interact ... in order for the latter to draw upon the insights, understanding, and wisdom of the former for new thoughts and hypotheses, for unanswered questions, and even for possible new approaches to studying the learning process" (pp. 49-52).

The editors of that journal did not recommend that researchers take a carefree approach toward the investigation of reading matters. Similarly, Kaufman and his colleagues were not suggesting that researchers use unsound paradigms to investigate the components of mainstreaming. Both sets of critics realize that research must be conducted in order to solve complex issues, and both pointed out that traditional research methodologies may be too constraining.

Recently, some of our funding agencies have taken a more tolerant position in reference to research methodologies. According to the research guidelines offered by the *Joint Effectiveness Review Panel*, an organization authorized to endorse projects sponsored by the Commissioner of Education and the Director of NIE, control methods other than between subjects comparison are permissible. Although experimental controls are firmly endorsed, they suggest that within-group designs are allowable. They acknowledge the technique of obtaining baseline data before the treatment and comparing that information with data taken throughout the treatment (Department of HEW, Memorandum, 1976).

The National Institute of Education has also liberalized their research criteria for some investigations. A recent request for proposals from that organization encouraged research "... aimed at providing better solutions to methodological problems arising from non-experimental designs; i.e., non-laboratory field studies which do not provide for random assignment" (Basic Skills Research Grants Announcements, National Institute of Education, 1976).

Assessment Systems

Just as we need better research methodologies in order to study more effectively the variables which influence the practice of mainstreaming, we need better assessment systems to monitor the performances of youngsters in mainstreaming situations. Just as educational researchers have been locked into methodologies which relied exclusively on randomization and statistical analysis, educational practitioners have persistently used indirect and infrequent measures in the form of achievement tests to monitor the performances of children.

In spite of the many criticisms that have been directed toward achievement tests since their inception, several new ones are published each year and they are used more often. Today, during these periods of universal scepticism and distrust, achievement tests have been widely used in efforts to verify the effects of educational programs.

Achievement tests should be censured because they often measure behaviors which are not taught; they assess performance indirectly. Whether or not a particular educational program is successful, according to an achievement test, is often dependent on the degree of congruence between that program and a particular test. This degree of correspondence between a program and a test can influence the scores of children more than other variables, such as the qualities of the teacher, the types of children in the class, or the character of the instruction. In support of this argument, Pany and Jenkins (1976) demonstrated how the conformity between certain reading series and particular achievement tests might influence the test scores of youngsters.

Just as achievement tests are often indirectly related to what is taught, they generally provide infrequent measures of performance; a second reason these tests should be censured. They are commonly given only once a year. Occasionally, they are administered twice—before and after a treatment. Such infrequent measures fail to take into account any one of a dozen variables which could influence performance one way or the other on specific days.

A third criticism of achievement tests is that the data derived from them do not reflect development. At best, they indicate a static reflection of performance. Because only one or at most two impressions of an individual's performance are available, it is impossible to determine whether he is able to change in respect to that behavior during a brief period of time.

An Alternative Research and Assessment Method

In my opinion, Applied Behavior Analysis is a method which should be considered seriously by researchers and practitioners concerned about the matters of mainstreaming. This method is eminently suitable for practitioners because it offers a replacement for the ubiquitous but inappropriate achievement test. When the Applied Behavior Analysis method is used to monitor pupil performances, teachers can measure performances directly and frequently and, because of the latter, can obtain an indication of development. To illustrate, if a teacher wanted to measure a pupil's ability to read orally from a *Ginn* text, she or he would have the pupil read from that book and measure behavior directly. Furthermore, the teacher would require him or her to read under identical circumstances for several days. Any extreme score would be perceived within the context of several scores. Finally, all those scores would be graphed, and would, therefore, provide a dynamic indication of performance. The teacher by inspecting those data would know whether the pupil improved gradually, didn't improve at all, or if performance steadily worsened. In summary, because behavior is measured over a period of days, a teacher can explain a pupil's performance for any single day and learning rate or development throughout a series of days.

The Applied Behavior Analysis method could also accommodate researchers' needs for more realistic investigative techniques. When this method is used several measures of a behavior are obtained *before* and *during* the treatment. Oftentimes, a series of measures are gathered *after* a treatment has terminated. When these before, during, and after data are used, each subject serves as his own control (within-subjects design). An individual's data across experimental conditions are examined. Performance is not compared with other subjects whose characteristics are assuredly different.

Within-subjects designs are *realistic*. Since they do not require that subjects be randomized, they can be accommodated by schools. By contrast, investigators who ask public school people to randomize their subjects are not often welcome in those settings. Within-subjects designs are *powerful*; the ultimate findings are individually relevant. Educational decisions can be made in response to each subject's performance. When other designs are used, however, placement or treatment decisions can be made for only groups of individuals.

To continue, the Applied Behavior Analysis methodology should be considered because its ingredients and the skills required to use them are the same for researchers and practitioners alike. Researchers do not use a set of tools or a language different from that employed by teachers. Both groups define behaviors in the same way; they count and graph them in the same way. The teaching patterns used by practitioners are similar to the research designs used by investigators. Since the two groups use a common language and nearly identical procedures, it is easy for them to communicate with one another. To my knowledge, there is no other methodology which offers such a rapprochement.

Need for Multiple and Longitudinal Measures

Mainstreaming is an extremely complex process; many people, in several situations, are involved. When a youngster is shifted from one educational environment to another, numerous individuals could be influenced by the move.

Educational research has characteristically, and irrespective of the methodology, focused on one variable for each subject in a study. If, for example, the effects of a reading program on the abilities of fourth graders were to be assessed, a reading test might be administered before and after a treatment and gain scores of the youngsters were determined. If their reading scores improved significantly, the program was judged as successful. The researcher of such a study would ordinarily imply that only reading was modified as a result of the treatment.

In a study like that, such direct simplicity may result, but it is quite likely that some behaviors not measured during the study were modified as much as the target behavior. Since mainstreaming is a more complex process than reading (indeed, it encompasses reading in many instances), multiple behaviors must be assessed when it is investigated. If, for example, pupils are being sent from a self-contained classroom for learning disabled youngsters, several of their behaviors should be monitored before they enter the regular classroom. Data pertaining to many academic behaviors should be obtained: oral reading, comprehension, writing, addition, to name a few. Furthermore, several behaviors should be monitored which might describe their attitudes, self-confidence, and levels of independence. There are certainly other behaviors which might be recorded.

Not only should data be obtained to describe youngsters who will be mainstreamed, but data should be gathered which describe other important individuals in this drama. For instance, data should be gathered, before a child is transferred, from the children in the special class and from the youngsters in the new class. Information about the receiving and sending teachers should be gathered. Data should also be obtained which describe critical behaviors of the mainstreamed child's parents and siblings. Naturally, these data should continue to be kept, after the child was shifted to a regular class.

Furthermore, those data should be obtained for a long period of time. Currently, most educational research studies are of very short duration. It is the rare investigation which runs an entire school year. Such brief studies on the effects of mainstreaming could be flagrantly misleading. It is possible that within the first three months learning disabled children are enrolled in a regular class, the majority of their behaviors—academic, social, attitudinal —decelerate. It might be revealed, however, that during the fourth and fifth month of mainstreaming some of their academic performances begin to improve. If data were kept throughout the second year, they might indicate that social skills and attitudes about school began to improve. If information were obtained for a few more years they might reveal that most behaviors steadily improved throughout the tenure of such children in regular classes, although several slumps and periods of maintenance were noted along the way. We could as easily speculate about the other characters in the cast: receiving and sending teachers, pupils from special and regular classes, and their respective families.

If such an accumulation of data were analyzed before and during mainstreaming, a very sophisticated computer and extremely knowledgeable analyst would be required to digest the information. Those data would probably reveal that some individuals were positively affected by the move, others, negatively, and some were not influenced. Only after all the data were processed, however, could a determination be made as to whether a good move had been made.

Research on Mainstreaming

The remainder of this chapter will be devoted to a presentation of suggestions for future research on mainstreaming mildly handicapped youngsters.

The approach I have taken to investigate mainstreaming is to specify some components of that process. Certainly others could conceptualize different categories. If, however, some of the components of mainstreaming appear to be reasonable, at least initially, research might proceed in one of two ways to study mainstreaming. One strategy would be to investigate thoroughly one component at a time, then eventually put together a package of empirically determined parts. The alternate strategy would be to investigate initially an entire package (much the way former researchers studied the process). Then, if positive effects were noted, the researcher could arrange a series of studies to investigate some of the components of the package.

I selected nine categories and within each offered a number of research suggestions. Although I attempted to eliminate the over-

Mainstreaming the Mildly Handicapped 301

lap across divisions, a certain amount is yet apparent. The first section pertains to "Descriptive Research." In this category, there are suggestions for studying and explaining the status quo. The second category deals with "Logistics Research." In that part, some thoughts are offered which might prompt research on shifting students from one situation to another and the allocation of responsibilities throughout those periods. In part three, some research suggestions are included about "Curriculum Research." They have to do with the specification of the behaviors which should be taught the mildly handicapped and how they should be taught.

The fourth category focuses on "Research on Management Tactics." Some comments are included about studying various strategies for managing troublesome behaviors. Section five pertains to "Research on Modeling." Included there are suggestions for arranging modeling investigations within the context of mainstreaming. In the next section, "Research on Children Tutoring," comments are included about the influential characteristics of tutoring situations. This category is a particularly fruitful area for research.

Section seven pertains to "Research on Pupil Management." Suggestions are furnished on how to study the involvement of students in various instructional matters. In the next section, "Research with Parents," some research ideas are offered which might ultimately aid parents to relate to their youngsters and their teachers. The last section pertains to "Research with Mainstreaming Teachers." Comments are offered about research which is exclusively pertinent to those regular teachers who receive handicapped youngsters.

1. Descriptive Research

Before too many modifications of the mainstreaming process are attempted, some educators should describe a few existing situations. Researchers should describe situations of at least three types within the mainstreaming system. They should select and explain several exemplary regular classes without special children, mainstreaming classes with special children, and special classes with only special children. Still other researchers should describe in detail a number of mainstreaming systems. In these latter accounts they would describe the total process: types of classes, how pupils are transferred from one situation to another, which personnel are responsible at particular times, among other features.

These descriptive investigations would serve several purposes, one of which would be to explain generally the current state of the art. Such descriptions would serve as historical accounts. As aspects of the process were modified, those changes would be related to the initial circumstances.

A second benefit to be derived from these descriptions is that once they were explained it is likely that a number of problems would emerge. A description would reveal, probably, that certain aspects of the system are irrational and others are vaguely developed. Once they are exposed, researchers could attempt to resolve them. The probability is great that the results of such investigations would be implemented readily since they were prompted by disclosures of the system currently in use.

A third reason for describing current mainstreaming practices, particularly specific situations, is that those data would serve as baseline information. For example, if a district obtained data from several of their regular classes before handicapped children were sent to those situations, and during the time they were enrolled, administrators and others would be able to evaluate certain aspects of the mainstreaming process. Depending on which data were kept, they could learn whether the regular students improved, maintained, or deteriorated as a function of the mainstreamed children. They might also learn how the situation affected the new child, his old classmates, his new teacher, his old teachers, and his family.

The possibilities are virtually limitless when it comes to selecting which features of the three situations to describe. Certainly, the important academic behaviors of the youngsters should be detailed. The choice of these would be dependent on their ages and capabilities. Furthermore, information about the materials and instructional techniques should be presented. In addition, the children's attitudes should be explained as should the manner in which they relate to one another. Information about the teacher's interactions and attitudes should certainly be provided. Data should be offered about the supportive personnel: how many there are, of what type, and how they function.

As for the teachers, some studies pertinent to their attitudes and concerns should be undertaken. Data, for example, about the anxieties of regular teachers who will receive handicapped youngsters might be gathered. Zawadki's (1973) dissertation was an initial attempt to list some of the worries of regular teachers.

Those studies of a current set of attitudes could stimulate subsequent research. If, for example, some teachers held attitudes believed false or harmful, investigations could be arranged which sought to modify or replace them. If the attitudes were altered, other studies might be arranged to monitor the lasting impact of the attitude treatment or the extent to which it generalized to other situations. Research could also be conducted to determine the effects of teacher attitudes on pupil performance. It would be useful to know the extent to which those variables were related.

Although it is complex to explain adequately regular or special classes, it is even more complex to describe an entire mainstreaming system. In order to do so, researchers must not only explain the types of classes and pupils, but they must detail the logistics of the system: how the pupils are assessed and transferred from one situation to another. They must explain how parents and ancillary persons are involved in the process. They must present the steps used for attaining compliance. Birch (1974) has provided a model that might be considered by researchers who set out to describe exemplary mainsteaming systems.

2. Logistics Research

Considerable research needs to be done on the movement of youngsters from one setting to another and the ensuing responsibilities of personnel. To begin with, a general description of ideal situations should be detailed. Such a description could be derived from the previous explanations of noteworthy mainstreaming situations. Perhaps several such guidelines should be published, one for large urban systems, one for suburban areas, and one for rural areas.

These guidelines would contain outlines for establishing exemplary special classes, resource and regular classes, and for arranging model delivery systems. In those guidelines would be recommendations about which personnel to engage, and what their competencies and responsibilities should be. Recommendations would be extended on how to assess children's academic performances and other behaviors, and, perhaps, on how to categorize children for instructional purposes. Furthermore, recommendations would be furnished on how best to route children from one setting to another, e.g., from regular to special or special to regular situations.

These accounts of ideal or validated programs could then be considered by specific school districts. If several schools adopted those guidelines there would be some uniformity across mainstreaming situations, following after which (if a number of districts adhered to the same standards) some research on many aspects of mainstreaming could take place.

One of the initial tasks would be to explain in detail what occurs during every step of the routing process. The procedures used to transfer a child from a regular class to a special situation should be explained. Included in this explanation would be a listing of the tests or other data which were used. Also included would be an account of who obtained the data, and who interpreted them. Furthermore, a justification should be detailed on how it was decided which programs were offered to a pupil sent to a special location. Information should be included as to who administered the programs, and very importantly, how it was decided the pupil was eligible for re-entry.

Obviously, such a detailing of steps and responsibilities would be more complex the more options that were available in a district. Nevertheless, each step along the way should be noted.

Once the status quo of a district was detailed and if pupil performance data and other information were routinely kept, research might begin. At that time, any one of a hundred variables might be manipulated which pertained to the movement process. If data were kept prior to the manipulation and during that period the process for routing children was consistently followed, and if later, data continued to be gathered after some variable of the system was changed and if those new conditions were likewise consistently practiced, any change in the data might be attributed to the altered variable.

A district could, for example, decide to study the manner in which children were reintegrated from special, self-contained rooms to regular classes.

3. Curriculum Research

An extremely important, if not the most important, feature of any educational program, whether mainstreaming is involved or not, is the identification of the curriculum. Although the definition of those behaviors which should be taught is as much a philosophical or sociological matter as it is a concern for educational researchers, a determination of what will be taught must be made before any research can take place.

Most people would agree that the basic skills should form a large part of the curriculum for the mildly handicapped. They would assert that these youngsters should be instructed to read, write, spell, and cipher. In this regard, considerable research of the task analysis type should be arranged. Researchers and program developers must refine those subject matter areas into manageable units. Many of the steps which comprise reading, for example, have been specified by researchers and program developers. There is some agreement among those individuals that children should learn initially the sounds of letters, certain CVC words, and blends. Others believe that different units should be learned. Although the specification of those elements may be tentative, they must nevertheless be specified and catalogued in all the subject matter areas.

Once those elements are defined, they should be arranged in a sequence or sequences. Once again, some of these initial arrangements may be somewhat arbitrary. When the tasks have been specified and placed in a logical sequence, considerable research might begin. At that time, researchers could test the efficacy of any sequence. They might determine that some elements of a sequence could be eliminated, others should be added, or still others should be rearranged.

It is possible to conduct more sophisticated research in respect to the arrangement of skills because the competency level for any component of the sequence can be adjusted.

The results of these researches on the steps of a program, their arrangement, the extent to which any element should be developed, would be significant indeed. Those descriptions could be relayed to practitioners and developers of curricular materials. Conceivably, they would use that information to redesign their materials and to instruct regular or handicapped youngsters more effectively.

Curricular matters apart from the basic skills should also be identified for the mildly handicapped. Many educators insist that these youngsters are as deficit in respect to certain social skills as they are in the basic skill areas. Others contend that these youngsters have little confidence and weak self-concepts. Some have pointed out that the mildly handicapped have difficulty making and maintaining friends. Still others have stressed the fact that, generally, the mildly handicapped lack the social skills of their more normal peers. Certainly, a great deal of research should be conducted on these topics.

Another set of behaviors which perhaps separates some of the mildly handicapped youngsters from normal children relates to independence. I have been told by some regular teachers that the handicapped children in their classes are often well behaved and perform adequately when it comes to reading and other academic subjects, but they are more dependent on them than are the other youngsters. They say that many handicapped children can't move from one work station to another unless they are told when and where to go, have difficulty continuing with a task if they come to a difficult problem or word, and can't select a free-time activity after they finish a task.

A great deal of research should concentrate on developing independence skills and the behaviors required to live in groups. In order to determine these skills, researchers should identify the extent to which children are expected to be independent and to behave as group members in regular classes. Next, some programs or other arrangements must be established in order to teach those skills. Then research studies might be conducted to determine the best techniques for instructing those behaviors.

Some educators argue that the curriculum for the mildly handicapped in respect to group living should be expanded. They say that although it is necessary for those children to develop skills which enable them to be accommodated by groups, it is equally important that they develop other behaviors so they might interact with groups as vital members. Those educators encourage teachers to arrange situations whereby cooperative situations are established, fostered, and maintained. They stress the importance of teaching about developing respect and responsibility for other people, indeed for *all* organisms. Many teachers and parents are deeply concerned that children fail to develop attitudes and behavioral patterns which support those beliefs.

Apart from the work which should be done to define the broad and specific elements of the curriculum for the mildly handicapped, considerable energy should be expended in efforts to identify effective yet simple techniques for instructing these behaviors and skills. In the field of special education there has been a tendency to advocate the use of elaborate and expensive techniques. The rationale has been, perhaps, that since the common techniques which were used with normal children were not effective with these special children, those techniques must be changed drastically. This use of highly sophisticated techniques has been particularly true in regard to certain of the mildly handicapped: learning disabled, dyslexic, neurologically impaired.

It is imperative that effective, simple techniques be developed for use with the mildly handicapped. For if regular teachers are asked to manage a few mainstreamed handicapped children in addition to their current flock, they must have a repertory of extremely effective techniques which can be easily administered.

In the past few years some research with learning disabled youngsters has demonstrated that when specific behaviors are identified for instruction, simple techniques serve the purpose. For example, Lovitt and J. Smith (1972) demonstrated that verbal instructions modified positively a boy's verbalizations. D. Smith and Lovitt (1975) showed that verbal instructions, simple demonstrations, and basic reinforcement contingencies influenced mathematics performances of several youngsters. J. Smith and Lovitt (1973) reported that a boy's ability to solve arithmetic problems improved when he was given a rule to follow. Lovitt and D. Smith (1974) illustrated that a pupil's accuracy on arithmetic problems improved when a withdrawal contingency was arranged. Lovitt and Hansen (1976) showed that oral reading rate and comprehension improved when pupils could skip some of their stories contingent on performance. None of the interventions in those studies are costly or complex.

More research of this type could dispell the current beliefs of many teachers and educators, that the only way to teach certain mildly handicapped youngsters is to deluge them with a flood of esoteric and expensive techniques. Research should continue to assess the extent to which basic techniques such as modeling, verbal instructions, feedback, and reinforcement contingencies can effectively and consistently alter academic performances.

In reference to curriculum research, some investigations should be arranged to determine the best location for instructing certain behaviors. Currently, some children are sent from regular to special classes because a few of their academic and social behaviors are not up to par. It is sometimes believed that if they are taught those skills in self-contained or resource situations, they will be able to return and function appropriately in the mainstream. For some children or for certain behaviors such an assumption may be unreasonable. Research should, therefore, be encouraged which seeks to determine the most effective location for the instruction of certain behaviors.

Furthermore, some investigations should be directed toward situational generalization. Procedures must be developed which disclose how best to maintain behaviors in one setting when they were taught in another. Jenkins, Barksdale, and Clinton (1974) conducted some intriguing studies of this type. One of their investigations was concerned with the instruction and generalization of oral reading and comprehension across settings.

4. Research on Management Tactics

Many of the mildly handicapped youngsters who will return to regular classes in the first wave of mainstreaming were evicted initially because they were disruptive, hyperactive, or inattentive. Some of their behaviors were perhaps altered in a positive direction when they were sent to smaller, special classes. The likelihood is great that these changes occurred because the special teachers consistently modified the conditions which created or maintained those deviant behaviors in the regular class. It is also likely that although certain of those behaviors were changed in the special setting, where certain conditions prevailed, they will revert back to their original form when the first conditions are reestablished. All this is to say that regular teachers must acquire new and better skills for managing disruptive, hyperactive, or inattentive children. It is unreasonable to expect special teachers to change certain behaviors of youngsters to the extent those behaviors are permanently altered.

It is vitally important for some regular teachers to acquire better management skills, because there are already a few children in their classes who behave in many respects like the handicapped pupils they will soon receive. Those youngsters already consume great amounts of their time and energy. In situations of that type it would be disastrous if groups of troublemakers were enrolled before the teachers could manage the obstreperous youngsters they are currently assigned.

Thanks to the behavior modifiers, considerable research has been conducted in special and regular classes in regard to the management of unruly behaviors. This research should be continued in mainstreaming classes.

One aspect of this research should concentrate on identifying, categorizing, arranging, and evaluating potential reinforcers in mainstreaming classes. Although behavior modifiers have identified dozens of potential reinforcers (e.g. Walker and Buckley, 1974, pp. 32-34) from comic books and crayons to watching television and playing baseball, thousands more could be labeled. Once those events are noted they should then be categorized. They should, for one thing, be listed as to expense, from most to least.

Researchers should also investigate different ways for arranging these potential reinforcers. Although a vast literature exists on various response-to-point ratios and exchange systems, researchers should attempt to conceptualize other systems for granting events for specified performances. There is a great need for systems which can be used in large classes and managed by few instructors. Finally, researchers should evaluate the potential reinforcers which have been identified and continue this practice with future motivators. A lexicon of "reinforcers" should be developed which lists the events, describes the circumstances during which they were used, and summarizes the results of each situation.

Behavior modification researchers have published many reports which focused on managerial concerns such as out-of-seats, talkouts, and other disruptive behaviors (e.g., Hall, Fox, Willard, Goldsmith, Emerson, Owen, Davis, and Porcia, 1971; O'Leary and Becker, 1967; Madsen, Becker, Thomas, Koser, and Plager, 1968). Most of these studies dealt with a single or with a few individuals in either tutorial or classroom settings.

A substantial technology has developed from those studies which provides several useful techniques for curtailing the behaviors of individuals. Some of the specific techniques which have emerged are punishment, extinction, time-out, differential reinforcement of other behavior (DRO), differential reinforcement for a low-rate of responding (DRL), and response cost. Several articles have been published which illustrate the effectiveness of these techniques. A comprehensive review of those tactics and how they might be implemented in school situations was assembled by Sulzer and Mayer (1972). Extensive as this literature appears to be, however, more research should be conducted to discover other tactics useful for controlling the behaviors of individuals.

In the past few years, behavior modifiers have conducted considerable work with groups of children in regular and special classes. They have investigated the effects of various group contingencies on the behaviors of several members of a group. Wilcox and Pany (1976) compiled an excellent review of those studies.

In another review of group-oriented contingencies, Litow and Pumroy (1975) described three such contingencies, the first set was referred to as *dependent group-oriented contingency systems*. An example of this type of contingency system would be to grant free-time to the entire class contingent on the on-task behavior of *one disruptive member* of that class. An example study of this type was presented by Wolf, Hanley, King, Lachowicz, and Giles (1970). They modified the off-task behavior of a girl in a remedial classroom.

Their second category of group-oriented contingencies was called *interdependent group-oriented contingency systems*. An example would be if free time for all the students were contingent on *all* students remaining in their seats for a specified time. Barrish, Saunders, and Wolf (1969) used this contingency to modify the talk-outs and out-of-seats of pupils in a fourth grade class.

The third system was referred to as *independent group-oriented contingency systems*. An example of this approach would be if free time for *each* class member was contingent on *his or her* being able to stay seated. McAllister, Stachowiak, Baer, and Conderman (1969) used this system to reduce inappropriate talking and turning around in a high school English class.

Considerable research related to group management systems should continue, for teachers will be expected to deal with several troublesome youngsters at a time. Research might be guided by the conceptual framework of Litow and Pumroy, or other schema could be developed. There would be some merit, however, if the same conceptual system was followed by several investigators, because the research within and across various categories could be compared as to relative effectiveness. If this collaborative approach were followed, future researchers might learn, for example, that one of the contingencies presented here was more effective with certain behaviors but another system was better suited for the management of other behaviors.

5. Research on Modeling

One of the primary reasons for mainstreaming is that handicapped youngsters will be able to associate with normal pupils. Ostensibly, the reason for advocating these relationships is that the

Mainstreaming the Mildly Handicapped 313

normal children will serve as models. The assumption is that handicapped children will be able to imitate the more acceptable social behaviors of the normal students. This assumption is extended by those who believe the handicapped may even imitate some of the higher level cognitive responses of the normal children. In this regard Kaufman *et al.* (1975), said:

> ... The more time mentally retarded children are integrated into regular classes, the greater should be the opportunity for them to model appropriate behavior exhibited by nonhandicapped peers. Finally, the more time mentally retarded children spend in regular classes, the more they will be exposed to the cognitive stimulation generated by the regular class (p. 5).

This quote implies that mere presence will enhance the modeling process. Admittedly, the potential model and imitator must be in the same arena before imitation can take place, but it may be unreasonable to infer that the handicapped child will imitate certain behaviors of the nonhandicapped youngsters simply because they are together. Moreover, it is doubtful that educators would *want* the handicapped youngster to imitate indiscriminately *all* the behaviors of nonhandicapped peers. Although some behaviors of the handicapped would be highly appropriate, socially and educationally, other behaviors would be exceedingly inappropriate. Some behaviors of normal children would, in fact, be far more deviant and unacceptable than the inappropriate behaviors of the handicapped youngster.

The first task of researchers concerned with modeling and mainstreaming is to identify which behaviors of the handicapped should be improved, and of those, which ones might be modified by imitation. The next task should be to select a class of youngsters, presumably nonhandicapped, who display the target behaviors. Once such a location is identified, the handicapped youngsters should be placed in that situation. It appears to me, and this is a research question, that the handicapped should be admitted to situations where they have a chance of imitating the behaviors adjudged appropriate by others. I would hypothesize that, other conditions being equal, handicapped pupils will imitate from nonhandicapped youngsters to the extent they have the prerequisite behaviors in their repertoires for acquiring more advanced skills.

Another task for researchers on the topic of modeling would be to identify those conditions, beyond proximity, which promote and maintain modeling. Some of those factors have been detailed by Sarason and Sarason (1973). Their conceptualization of the modeling process was greatly influenced by Bandura's research (Bandura, 1965; Bandura, 1967). The Sarasons claimed, for one thing, that it is important whether the model is reinforced or punished. If the model is reinforced, imitation is more likely to occur; if the model is punished, imitation is less likely to occur. According to them, another factor related to modeling is whether the observer is reinforced or punished. They contend that the probability was increased that the observer would imitate the behavior of a model if the observer was reinforced and less likely if punished. Another factor which could influence modeling is the status of the model. The Sarasons argued that an admired and respected model is more likely to be imitated. Media, of course, are an excellent way of presenting controlled examples of behavior to be imitated.

Although there have been a fair number of modeling studies with children, few have been conducted in regular classrooms. One of those rare studies was conducted a few years ago by Csapo (1972). In her investigation, which took place in a regular classroom, several emotionally disturbed youngsters were seated next to normal pupils. The disturbed children were told to imitate certain appropriate behaviors of their normal peers and the latter were told to reinforce them for doing so. She concluded that the models helped to extinguish several inappropriate behaviors of the disturbed children.

Investigations should be conducted in regular classrooms where factors other than rewarding the observers are studied. Researchers should concentrate on other components believed to be related to modeling. Research should also be encouraged which sets out to discover factors which influence modeling other than those presented by the Sarasons and Bandura.

In mainstreaming situations it is generally assumed that the handicapped will model certain behaviors of the nonhandicapped pupils. It would seem just as reasonable for the nonhandicapped to imitate certain behaviors of the handicapped youngsters. Peterson, Peterson, and Scriven (1977) presented a methodology which would allow researchers to study handicapped and nonhandicapped children as both modelers and imitators.

It has been my experience that some handicapped youngsters are more sympathetic and understanding of human frailities than their normal peers. Some of the handicapped youngsters are able to tolerate wider ranges of human behaviors than are their normal chums. Bryan, Wheeler, Felcan, and Henak (1976) reported that a group of learning disabled pupils were more generous than their nonhandicapped peers. If these observations are true, it would be profitable to arrange modeling studies whereby the handicapped served as models and the nonhandicapped pupils as observers in order to determine whether the latter would become more tolerant, understanding, and generous.

6. Research on Children Tutoring

The mainstreaming effort would be accelerated greatly if children were trained to teach. If regular teachers are expected to design and implement individualized educational programs for an increasingly diverse population, they must have assistance. The most available resource for providing that help is the children in their classes. Considerable research, therefore, should be encouraged on this topic.

Other benefits could accrue from using children as teachers. It may be discovered that some students acquire certain behaviors more effectively when they are instructed by children than by adults. Another benefit which would be derived from using children as teachers is that they will learn a worthwhile, possibly marketable skill. If they are instructed to be teachers, it is conceivable that they will be better able to help others after they leave school, not the least of whom might be their own children. Another benefit which might be derived from using children as tutors is that the tutors and tutees would learn that anyone can serve as a teacher or student; those roles are not necessarily dependent on age.

Recently, an extremely well organized review on the topic of children tutoring was written by Devin-Sheehan, Feldman, and Allen (1976). They reviewed 82 studies in their manuscript, many of which pertained to handicapped or underachieving youngsters.

According to them, the two major variables which affect the outcomes of tutoring are the characteristics of the tutor and tutee, and the characteristics of the tutoring situation. As to the first factor, the authors offered several conclusions which could relate to mainstreaming. One was that low-achieving tutors can be effective teachers of reading for younger children. Another was that the reading abilities of low achievers generally improved when they tutored younger children in reading. A third conclusion was that the relative level of competence between the tutor and tutee may be a crucial factor in tutoring situations. They suggested that this question was deserving of future research. Pertinent to this point, several matchups might be arranged: older handicapped could teach younger handicapped or nonhandicapped children, younger nonhandicapped might teach older handicapped children.

They also suggested that research should be conducted in respect to sex pairings. Interestingly, the few available studies they located yielded results which were contrary to the same-sex dictum we have customarily assumed. Furthermore, they recommended that research be arranged to investigate the effects of race and socio-economic status, since this topic was of great importance and few investigations have focused on those matters.

As to the second factor which could affect the tutoring process

—the characteristics of the tutoring situation—the authors complained that investigations of these variables have not been satisfying. They criticized the researchers in this area because they had operated in a haphazard and unsystematic manner. Constructively, however, the reviewers defined several areas which should be investigated.

According to them, some research should concentrate on temporal factors, since the literature contained no studies which compared differing amounts of time spent in tutoring. Another area which they believed should be investigated relates to the number of tutees per tutor. The authors claimed that no evidence was available pertaining to the relative effects on the tutor of tutoring one or many tutees.

They maintained that a third area of research should focus on the training of tutors, since the research which compared the effects of one training program with another or compared a training program with no training was inconclusive. A fourth area for research should be to investigate the effects of teaching approaches, either inductive or deductive, since, according to them, the data regarding those methods are sparse but provocative.

7. Research on Pupil Management

This is a particularly important area of research to consider. One purpose for assisting children to manage aspects of their academic programs is for the same reason that children should be trained as tutors. They can provide assistance to their teachers. As I indicated earlier, if teachers are expected to manage several children, many of whom require unique programs, they will need help. Furthermore, as I mentioned, the largest and most available resource from which to draw is a classroom of children. Not only can they be trained to tutor one another, but they can be instructed to manage many of their own affairs.

We have conducted a few pupil management studies with elementary age, learning disabled children at the University of Washington (Lovitt, 1973). Some of these youngsters were taught to manage many instructional components: to time their performances, to check their answers, to count the number of correct and incorrect responses, to analyze their error patterns, to chart their correct and incorrect rates, to determine when an instructional intervention should be scheduled, to select an appropriate intervention, and to monitor their performances until the desired rates were reached. Considerable research of this type should continue in order to identify more precisely other instructional components. Once those components have been pinpointed, research should be stimulated to determine the best ways to teach them.

Beyond the fact that pupils should be taught to manage many of their affairs in order to assist teachers, they should be taught self-management skills so they might become more independent as students, and later, as adults. It is my belief that pupil management instruction should be considered as part of the curriculum. I contend that it is just as important to teach children to manage their own lives as it is to teach them to read, write, or to relate to other individuals. Some fascinating research with this purpose in mind might be conducted.

It would be of great interest, for example, to teach some children at a young age certain self-management behaviors, then to continue teaching them more and more elements of self-instruction throughout their careers, then to monitor their lives for several years after their release from school. I would hypothesize that they would behave quite differently than individuals whose curricula did not include an emphasis on self-management. I would expect the former citizens to be better able to adjust to change and certainly less dependent on others for guidance, instruction, and entertainment.

A third reason for emphasizing pupil management research is that children (as well as adults) are often highly motivated when they are allowed to manage certain features of their lives. We have conducted a few projects which indicated that when self-management components were contingently arranged for a certain level of academic performance, their behaviors were affected positively. In one project we arranged self-scheduling contingent on a specified level of saying the sounds of letters (Lovitt, 1973). Those data indicated that when pupils could earn the privilege of scheduling, their performances were better than during conditions when this contingency was not available. Subsequent research might arrange other elements of instruction in order to determine whether they too were motivating for certain pupils. If teachers are expected to manage large groups of heterogeneous youngsters, they must have a huge repertory of potential reinforcers.

8. Research with Parents

Parents are another resource which must be more seriously considered. The help of parents should be enlisted for the same reason that the energies of pupils are involved, to help teachers instruct their youngsters.

Parents can and indeed have in the past been called upon to help teachers. Perhaps the most fundamental way they have and could continue to provide assistance is to handle certain clerical chores. They could run off dittos, collect lunch money, pass out and grade papers, and perform dozens of other duties.

Most of the time when parents assist with these chores, they are supervised rather casually. The parents show up at school and teachers tell them what to do and sometimes how it should be done. If the parent is capable and independent, a positive interaction develops between the teacher and parent. If the parent is incompetent, however, the relationship deteriorates. Some field based research on how best to train parents to help with these duties would increase the likelihood that they would be used more efficiently.

At another level, some research could be conducted on how best to communicate with parents. This matter is becoming more crucial all the time. According to one of the regulations of P.L. 94-

142, parents of handicapped children are required to sign several documents at various times before important educational decisions for their children can be made.

Teachers need to know how to assess, first of all, the level at which they can initially communicate with parents. Some parents can be told a great deal about their youngsters' progress, whereas others can assimilate a lesser amount of information. Once the level of understanding has been determined, research might attempt to discover how best to increase the amount of information which can be presented to parents, and how best to increase the frequency with which these communications take place. I would hypothesize that many of the suspicions and concerns that parents and teachers now have toward one another could be alleviated if the quality and frequency of interactions between the two were increased.

Research with parents might focus at yet another level, that of maintaining some of the programs begun in the schools. Many times teachers establish programs with children which are effective, but they are convinced those procedures would be even more impressive if they were managed at home as well as at school.

In many instances it would be a simple task to enlarge these programs. Depending on the youngster's target behavior, the parent might be asked only to reinforce certain behaviors when they happened or to deny privileges when other behaviors occurred. Some interesting research which established guidelines for setting up cooperative programs between the school and home would be useful, particularly for those children who are difficult to teach.

Research should be arranged with parents at another level. Many of them could be taught to manage, on their own, certain of their children's behaviors. They could be instructed on how to eliminate and how to develop certain behaviors.

The research on several behavior modifiers has, in fact, demonstrated rather convincingly that parents can be taught to decelerate a wide range of behaviors, from bed wetting and displaying tics, to destroying toys and having tantrums. The work of Patterson and his colleagues has been particularly impressive in demonstrating that when a planned program is arranged for parents, they can effectively deal with many behaviors (Patterson, 1971; Patterson and Gullion, 1968). Other programs have been designed to assist parents to manage unruly behaviors (Dinkmeyer and McKay, 1976; McDowell, 1974; Kroth, 1972). Research should be extended which seeks to determine how best to train parents to deal with the irritating behaviors of their children.

Research which attempts to teach parents to assist their children to *develop* behaviors should receive a high priority. To date, there has been little research on this topic. Many times, parents are informed of their many responsibilities for instructing their children. At other times, they are warned never to teach their youngsters; they are constantly admonished for teaching their children to read. Some exciting research could be arranged to determine how best to teach parents to help their children learn to read, write, and cipher. This is a particularly important area of research for parents of mildly handicapped youngsters.

9. Research with Mainstreaming Teachers

Many of the research areas mentioned earlier would involve teachers who received mainstreamed youngsters. They would be the primary characters in some of the descriptive research and certainly, they would be involved in research on logistics. In many instances they would assist with the research on various curriculum matters. Mainstreaming teachers would definitely be involved with the research on management tactics, and would play an important role during some of the research on modeling. Furthermore, these teachers would be involved, at least indirectly, when some of the research on tutoring and pupil management is conducted. In addition, some of them would be very active during many of the investigations with parents. There are nevertheless, four research themes which should be supported which pertain specifically to teachers.

One research topic should concentrate on the interactions between mainstreaming teachers and other professionals. Since some of the youngsters who will be sent to regular classes will arrive with dossiers full of commentary from many professionals, receiving teachers must know how to interpret this mass of information. Furthermore, many of these mainstreamed children will receive special services from professionals such as ophthalmologists, psychiatrists, and social workers while they attend regular classes. The mainstreaming teacher must know how to process the information from those professionals in order to best program for the children.

Another reason these teachers must be knowledgeable about the the practices of other professionals is that they must intepret and evaluate them for parents of exceptional children. Teachers of exceptional children receive several calls each week from the parents of children in their classes or from others asking about the validity of certain clinics, books, schools, medicines, or treatments. These parents are concerned about their children and want to help them. They are, therefore, vulnerable to any new or different scheme which purports to aid their youngsters. Therefore, when teachers are asked about these practices, they must be able to provide accurate advice that is readily understandable. Some research on this topic could suggest ways that teachers can best provide this information to parents.

Another research theme could focus on communicating with "special" parents. It has been my experience that many parents of mildly handicapped youngsters, particularly parents of learning disabled or dyslexic youngsters, are extremely knowledgeable. Many of them are professional people and have spent a great deal of time and money attempting to determine why their child is having problems with school. Several of those parents have visited dozens of clinics and specialists. As a result of those experiences, they have accumulated a formidable vocabulary. When they converse with a mainstreaming teacher and use words or phrases such as "strephosymbolia," "dyscalculia," "multi-sensory," "cross modality," "ITPA," and "lateral dominance," the teacher is often intimidated. The consequences of such a response could be that the teacher avoids other contacts with those parents and treats the child somewhat negatively. Research should attempt to discover ways to assist mainstreaming teachers to interact confidently with these parents.

A fourth research topic concerning the receiving teachers would be to determine how best to reinforce them for being capable teachers. Commonly, the reward for a teacher who accepts a handicapped child and does a creditable job, is another handicapped child who is difficult to teach. Although this is a natural progression of events, those accepting teachers could be driven quickly to their limits.

There must be more imaginative ways to reinforce the teachers who adjust to a wide range of pupil behaviors. One way to determine how to maintain their illustrious behaviors would be to ask them what they wanted. Some of them might opt for more inservice sessions, more ancillary support, more and different materials. These are approaches that others have recommended as rewards for mainstreaming teachers. If the teachers were asked, however, what events or circumstances they prefer, they might suggest other reinforcers.

Epilogue

When we consider mainstreaming within the context of other educational practices, some paradoxes emerge. For one thing, many school systems are in dire straits financially. As a result, class sizes are fairly large. Under these conditions it would seem unlikely that teachers would welcome still more pupils in their classes and, beyond that, children who require special or different techniques.

The hard times I referred to earlier, however, could promote mainstreaming. It might be that school administrators envision the money they will receive from P.L. 94-142 as an opportunity to repair or remodel their schools or even construct new ones. They may realize that since the citizens of their districts won't pass levies to finance these endeavors, they can obtain the needed monies by mainstreaming handicapped youngsters.

Meanwhile, as educators, unions, and private citizens attempt to work out the details of mainstreaming, the private schools may stand to win. It might be that the mainstreaming movement, like busing, will stimulate an exodus of children from public to private schools. It could be that as the regular classes in the public schools educate more and more handicapped youngsters they become schools for the less able and the poor, and the private systems attract more of the brightest and the wealthy (not that this isn't true today). On the other hand, the law permits money to follow the handicapped child into private schools, potentially encouraging establishment of private schools for handicapped children.

Permit me to change course momentarily so that I might comment on the great amounts of data which teachers must keep, whether or not they intend to use them for research purposes. In the state of Washington, and I'm sure this is true elsewhere, teachers in resource and self-contained situations are *now* required to maintain an incredible record system. Although some teachers are able to gather a fair amount of reliable data, they are becoming overburdened as more agencies demand accountability. As regular teachers become associated with mainstreaming, they too will be pressured to keep records.

Currently, in some classrooms, teachers spend more time keeping records than they do instructing children. Often, the paraprofessionals—aides, parents, university students—spend more time with the children than do the credentialed teachers! If we expect teachers in self-contained, resource rooms, or regular classes to keep a significant amount of data, we may reduce even more the time they relate with youngsters. So ... why not reverse the roles, train the paraprofessionals to keep data and allow teachers to teach. Legions of data keepers could be trained to gather the data which are currently required. They could also monitor many features of mainstreaming programs advocated here and thus facilitate several research efforts. These data keepers could be turned out by the dozens in community colleges. Even universities could train them. See Conant (1973) for an excellent study of the work productivity of professional and paraprofessional personnel.

One last word about mainstreaming, and this applies to the inauguration of other special programs in the schools. When will the instigators of programs such as this learn to consider initially the people who must implement the programs?

Mainstreaming was begun by philosophers, albeit socially sensitive folks. Later, the movement was advanced by legislators, lawyers, and groups of citizens. Still later, some professors in higher education endorsed the plan. Then, some school boards and superintendents jumped on the wagon. They were followed by a few building principals and other middle management people. And so it went. All the way from the philosophers to the principals, the social and educational advantages of mainstreaming were proclaimed.

Rarely, however, were the teachers asked about mainstreaming. Many of them, in fact, do not look forward to receiving handicapped youngsters in their classes. They know their teaching assignments will be more difficult. They know too that their only rewards will be a series of inservice meetings and more visitations from their "helpful" resident school psychologists.

References

Bandura, A. Influence of model's reinforcement contingencies on the acquisition of imitative responses. *Journal of Personality and Social Psychology,* 1965, *1,* 589-595.

Bandura, A. Behavioral modification through modeling procedures. In L. Krasner and L.L. Ullman (Eds.), *Research in behavior modification: New developments and implications.* New York: Holt, Rinehart, and Winston, 1967, 310-340.

Barrish, H.H., Saunders, M., and Wolf, M.M. Good behavior game: Effects of individual contingencies for group consequences on disruptive behavior in a classroom. *Journal of Applied Behavior Analysis*, 1969, *2*, 119-124.

Basic skills research grants announcements. The National Institute of Education, Spring, 1976.

Birch, J. W. *Mainstreaming: Educable mentally retarded children in regular classes.* Reston, Virginia: The Council for Exceptional Children, 1974.

Bryan, T., Wheeler, R., Felcan, J., and Henak, T. "Come on dummy." An observational study of children's communications. *Journal of Learning Disabilities*, 1976, *9*, 661-669.

Commoner, B. If I were the science adviser: Some luminaries have their say. *Science*, 1976, *6*, 464-467.

Conant, E.H. *Teacher and paraprofessional work productivity.* Lexington, Mass.: D.C. Heath, 1973.

Csapo, M. Peer models reverse the "one bad apple spoils the barrel" theory. *Teaching Exceptional Children*, 1972, *5*, 20-24.

Devin-Sheehan, L., Feldman, R. S., and Allen, V. L. Research on children tutoring children: A critical review. *Review of Educational Research*, 1976, *46*, 355-385.

Dinkmeyer, D., and McKay, G. D. *Systematic training for effective parenting.* Circle Pines, Minn.: American Guidance Service, 1976.

Dunn, L. M. Special education for the mildly retarded—is much of it justifiable? *Exceptional Children*, 1968, *35*, 5-22.

Hall, R. V., Fox, R., Willard, D., Goldsmith, L., Emerson, M., Owen, M., Davis, F., and Porcia, E. The teacher as observer and experimenter in the modification of disrupting and talking-out behaviors. *Journal of Applied Behavior Analysis*, 1971, *4*, 141-149.

Jenkins, J. R., Barksdale, A., and Clinton, L. Improving reading comprehension and oral reading: Generalization across behaviors, settings, and time. Unpublished manuscript, College of Education, University of Illinois, 1974.

Kaufman, M. J., Gottlieb, J., Agard, J. A., and Kukic, M. B. Mainstreaming: Toward an explication of the construct. *Focus on Exceptional Children*, 1975, 7, 1-12.

Kirk, S. Research in education. In H. H. Stevens and R. Heber (Eds.), *Mental retardation: A review of research.* Chicago: University of Chicago Press, 1964, 62-63.

Kroth, R. *Target behavior.* Bellevue, Wash.: Edmark Associates, 1972.

Litow, L., and Pumroy, D. K. A brief review of classroom group-oriented contingencies. *Journal of Applied Behavior Analysis*, 1975, 8, 341-347.

Lovitt, T. C. Self-management projects with children with behavioral disabilities. *Journal of Learning Disabilities*, 1973, 6, 138-150.

Lovitt, T. C., and Hansen, C. L. The use of contingent skipping and drilling to improve oral reading and comprehension. *Journal of Learning Disabilities*, 1976, 9, 481-487.

Lovitt, T. C., and Smith, D. D. Using withdrawal of positive reinforcement to alter subtraction performance. *Exceptional Children*, 1974, 40, 357-358.

Lovitt, T. C., and Smith, J. O. Effects of instruction on an individual's verbal behavior. *Exceptional Children*, 1972, 38, 685-693.

Madsen, C. H., Becker, W. C., Thomas, D. R., Koser, L., and Plager, E. An analysis of the reinforcing function of "sit down" commands. In R. K. Parker (Ed.), *Readings in educational psychology.* Boston: Allyn & Bacon, 1968, 265-278.

McAllister, L. W., Stachowiak, J. G., Baer, D. M., and Conderman, L. The application of operant conditioning techniques in a secondary school classroom. *Journal of Applied Behavior Analysis*, 1969, 2, 277-285.

McDowell, R. L. *Managing behavior: A parent involvement program*. Torrance, Calif.: B. L. Winch and Associates, 1974.

Memorandum written by Lois-ellin Datta, Education Division, Dept. of Health, Education, and Welfare, August 11, 1976.

Methodological incarceration. *Reading Research Quarterly*, 1974-1975, *10*, 49-52.

O'Leary, K. D., and Becker, W. C. Behavior modification of an adjustment class: A token reinforcement program. *Exceptional Children*, 1967, *33*, 637-642.

Pany, D., and Jenkins, J. R. Curriculum biases in reading achievement tests. Unpublished manuscript, College of Education, University of Illinois, 1976.

Patterson, G. R. *Families: Application of social learning to family life*. Champaign, Ill.: Research Press, 1971.

Patterson, G. R., and Gullion, M. E. *Living with children: New methods for parents and teachers*. Champaign, Ill.: Research Press, 1968.

Peterson, D., Peterson, J., and Scriven, G. Peer imitation by nonhandicapped and handicapped preschoolers. *Exceptional Children*, 1977, *43*, 223-224.

Sarason, I. G., and Sarason, B. R. *Modeling and role-playing in the schools*. Human Interaction Research Institute, 10889 Wilshire Blvd., Los Angeles, California, #RO-20388, 1973.

Smith, D. D., and Lovitt, T. C. The use of modeling techniques to influence the acquisition of computational arithmetic skills in learning disabled children. In E. Ramp and G. Semb (Eds.), *Behavior analysis: Areas of research and application*. Englewood Cliffs, New Jersey: Prentice-Hall, 1975, 283-308.

Smith, J. O., and Lovitt, T. C. Pinpointing a learning problem leads to remediation. *Teaching Exceptional Children*, 1973, *5*, 181-182.

Sulzer, B., and Mayer, G. R. *Behavior modification procedures for school personnel*. Hinsdale, Illinois: The Dryden Press, 1972.

Walker, H. W., and Buckley, N. K. *Token reinforcement techniques*. Eugene, Oregon: E-B Press, 1974.

Wilcox, B., and Pany, D. Use of group contingencies in classroom management: A review and evaluation of research. Unpublished manuscript, College of Education, University of Illinois, 1976.

Wolf, M. M., Hanley, E. L., King, L., Lachowicz, J., and Giles, D. K. The timer-game: A variable interval contingency for the management of out-of-seat behavior. *Exceptional Children*, 1970, *37*, 113-117.

Zawadki, R. Stratified sample of 158 regular classroom teachers, kindergarten through senior high school, from low, medium, and high wealth school districts in Pennsylvania. Unpublished research report, Victoria Center, University of Houston, 1973.

Author's Note

The author wishes to express his appreciation to the following for their helpful comments on an earlier draft of this chapter: Dr. James O. Smith, Professor, Special Education, George Peabody College for Teachers, Nashville, Tennessee; and Dr. Joseph R. Jenkins, Associate Professor, Special Education, University of Illinois, Champaign-Urbana, Illinois.

15.
What Directions Should Research Take in Developing Educational Programs for the Severely Handicapped?

Alan M. Hofmeister

This chapter will focus on possible roles and directions for research in the development of instructional programs for the severely handicapped. In the past, research has not been particularly helpful in directing the efforts of practitioners. We have received very few specific directions from the researchers. The documenting of the debilitating impact of some institutional programs has provided direction to program administrators. Unfortunately, this direction results from identifying inappropriate practices, rather than developing appropriate educational treatment alternatives. Guskin and Spicker (1968), in a review of educational research in mental retardation conducted between 1960 and 1967, concluded:

> There are undoubtedly many more promising approaches to educational research in mental retardation. It is to be hoped that a review of this field in 1980 would find many investigations which go far beyond the current style of research which, as yet, has contributed pitifully little that is of value for the educational practitioner (pp. 272-273).

Most practitioners are concerned with the day-to-day instructional decision making, and their questions often focus on specific techniques and materials suited for individual children in specific environments. Many of the early research studies did not document educational treatment procedures in a manner that would facilitate replication of the treatment. The concerns were usually generalized and stressed such issues as schooling versus no schooling, or institutional placement versus community placement. These studies did serve some purpose; when their rather meager data were combined with the weight of moral and legal arguments provided by parent organizations, the right to educational services was won for the severely handicapped.

Now that there is a recognition of the rights of the severely handicapped to education, researchers should reduce emphasis on broad comparative research designs. Research should not be concerned with the problems of developing the most effective treatment programs. In summary, the present challenge is the development of a technology for teaching the severely handicapped.

Who Are the Severely Handicapped?

The Bureau of Education for the Handicapped (BEH) has described severely handicapped children as:

> Those who, because of the intensity of their physical, mental, or emotional problems or a combination of such problems, need educational, social, psychological, and medical services beyond those which are traditionally offered by regular or special education programs, in order to maximize their full potential for useful and meaningful participation in society and for self-fulfillment (P.L. 94-142, Section 121.2).

For purposes of program planning, the above description is somewhat helpful in that an interdisciplinary thrust is emphasized. However, designating "traditionally offered" special education programs as points of reference is not very helpful, in that some states have already established a tradition of serving the severely handicapped, and hopefully, educational services for the severely handicapped will soon be a national tradition.

The Office of Human Development uses another definition that overlaps the B.E.H. definition. It is the definition of "developmentally disabled" and reads as follows:

> The term "developmental disability" means a disability of a person which—(A)(1) is attributable to mental retardation, cerebral palsy, epilepsy, or autism; (2) is attributable to any other condition of a person found to be closely related to mental retardation because such condition results in similar impairment of general intellectual functioning or adaptive behavior to that of mentally retarded persons or requires treatment and services similar to those required for such persons; or (3) is attributable to dyslexia resulting from a disability described in clause (1) or (2) of this subparagraph; (B) originates before such person attains age eighteen; (C) has continued or can be expected to continue indefinitely; and (D) constitutes a substantial handicap to such person's ability to function normally in society (P.L. 94-103, Section 102.7).

If we were to consider only those most severely affected in the population described as "developmentally disabled," we would be describing a population very similar to the B.E.H.'s "severely handicapped" population.

From a program-planning point of view, both the previously mentioned definitions represent an improvement over earlier and more categorical definitions of such terms as "severe mental retardation." Programs for the severely mentally retarded rarely contain just mentally retarded persons. They are essentially programs for individuals with a variety of mental, physical, and emotional handicaps.

In *Assessment of Selected Resources for Severely Handicapped Children and Youth*, Abt Associates (1974) offered the following definition, which describes in more detail the types of problems a treatment program will focus on.

- Severely handicapped children and youth were functionally defined as those persons age 21 and under who are either mentally retarded, emotionally disturbed, deaf-blind, or multiply handicapped and who exhibit *two or more* of the following behaviors with a degree of regularity:
- Self-mutilation behaviors such as head banging, body scratching, hair pulling, etc., which may result in danger to oneself;
- Ritualistic behaviors such as rocking, pacing, autistic-like behavior, etc., which do not involve danger to oneself;
- Self-stimulation behaviors such as masturbation, stroking, patting, etc., for a total of more than one hour of a waking day;
- Failure to attend to even the most pronounced social stimuli, including failure to respond to invitations from peers or adults, or loss of contact with reality;
- Lack of self-care skills such as toilet training, self-feeding, self-dressing, and grooming, etc.;
- Lack of physical mobility including confinement to bed, inability to find one's way around the institution or facility, etc.

The above definitions suggest, but do not specify, the characteristics of educational programs for the severely handicapped. In comparison to programs for normal and mildly handicapped persons, programs for the severely handicapped will include:

(1) curriculum content which is often very different;
(2) parent involvement as a requirement, not as an option;
(3) involvement at an earlier age, usually infancy;
(4) a continuation through adulthood in many cases;
(5) a level of structure and planning unparalleled in education;
(6) the extensive involvement of several disciplines; and
(7) operation in many environments, the classroom being only one.

The needs in educational program development for the severely handicapped are massive, and time is critical. We have to face the fact that legislation has outpaced our ability to deliver (i.e., programs for the severely handicapped have been mandated, but we do not as yet have a comprehensive range of validated programs

What Directions Should Research Take? 335

and associated implementation procedures available to meet this mandate).

Research and Educational Practice

We rarely discuss the problem of research with the handicapped without confronting the problem of why research findings take so long to affect practices. Commonly, the dissemination system is held accountable, but some authorities charge that the problem lies in the nature of the research being conducted. Wattenburg (1963) asks:

> Do lawyers wait twenty years to digest the latest Supreme Court ruling? Do dentists dawdle decades in adopting new techniques? Or, let us ask, what would his colleagues do to a doctor who continued to use high concentrations of oxygen with premature babies even six months after studies had appeared relating this practice to blindness (p. 375)?

In the examples cited by Wattenburg, we can understand why the findings involved were adopted immediately into mainstream practice in their respective disciplines. It was not just the result of a dissemination process; it was because of the nature of the research. When research gives clear direction to the practitioner in important problems, rapid dissemination will usually follow. In special education, the practical implications of research are not always obvious, and often with good reason.

"Impractical" is a descriptor "applied" researchers sometimes use in referring to "basic" research. The basic researcher has something to commend him, in that he is often very frank about the immediate practical implications of his research. Of more concern is the "applied" researcher, who each year spends millions of dollars to develop "innovative" programs which promptly cease to exist the day after the last federal dollar is spent. There are two major reasons for the lack of implementation of many research project products.

(1) *Failure to consider the cost effectiveness of the program.* A treatment program that is beyond the budgets of the prospective consumers is clearly of limited immediate value, regardless of perceived worth.
(2) *Failure to stress program improvement.* This often happens when the data related to effectiveness are collected so late in the project that they cannot be used to upgrade the treatment procedures.

Regarding the relative importance of research in education, Lamke (1955) made the following comment more than twenty years ago, and perhaps the scene has changed little since then:

> If the research in the previous three years in medicine, agriculture, physics, and chemistry were to be wiped out, our life would be changed materially, but if the research in the area of teacher personnel in the same three years were to vanish, educators and education would continue much as usual (p. 192).

Instead of looking for a scapegoat, such as the dissemination process, it might be more profitable for the researcher to evaluate his research. It is quite possible that dissemination of applicable research based on important problems will follow more quickly as a function of the relevance and quality of the research.

Research Methods and Field Problems

A typical reaction to the efforts of doctoral students to research certain field treatment problems is, "That area is too sloppy and too ill-defined for good research." A more accurate reply in some cases, might be, "Yes, this is an important area of research, but we do not have the training resources to equip you with the skills necessary to undertake that research."

If we do not scare off the prospective field-problem-oriented researchers with our initial reaction, we very often redesign the problem so that our resources are equipped to handle it. In so doing, we change the research direction so that the original problem is ignored. One of the best examples of redesigning problems lies in our emphasis on comparative evaluations of instructional programs. Typical questions revolve around the problems, "How can I develop an effective educational treatment for this problem?" However, when the question has been processed for research, it is often rephrased, "Which is superior, Method A or Method B?" The fact that neither Method A nor Method B is fully developed, and that this premature evaluation may condemn one or the other to obscurity, is often overlooked.

In researching instructional programs, there are two major directions. One emphasizes developmental procedures, and the other emphasizes the formal final evaluation. Scriven (1967) used the terms "formative" and "summative" to describe these two processes. While our present tools are reasonably effective for handling some aspects of summative evaluation, they are often useless for facilitating formative evaluation. Programs for the severely handicapped are far too underdeveloped to be able to afford the emphasis on comparative evaluation that we have been forced into by lack of research resources to undertake formative research. Cronbach (1963) makes this point quite forcefully when he points out that, "evaluation used to improve the course while it is still fluid contributes more to improvement of education than evaluation used to appraise a product already on the market" (p. 675).

A Research Technology: What Characteristics?

Are our research efforts leading to the development of effective educational programs for the severely handicapped? Perhaps the most appropriate response to this question is "Yes, but slowly, very slowly." Tjossem (1976), commenting on the role of research in the development of intervention strategies for high risk infants and young children, made the following observation:

> Although they have a common goal, the distance that separates researchers from different disciplines diminishes their collective efforts. Similar gaps extend their diminishing effects along the

continuum from research to service. They exist between: (1) researchers and providers of professional services; (2) service providers from different professions as medicine and education; (3) service providers and parent consumers; and (4) parent consumers and the community. Collectively, these gaps detract from the expression of a more effective and unified program effort (pp. 28-29).

A similar concern has been expressed regarding programs for the adolescent and adult severely handicapped. Gold (1973), in reviewing research related to the vocational habilitation of the retarded, recommended the use of "middle-road researchers" with comprehensive responsibilities, including "the development and implementation of an applied technology through direct involvement with service agencies, and professional and governmental organizations" (p. 125).

Both Tjossem's and Gold's comments reflect the need for a more comprehensive and coordinated research strategy. This is understandable when one examines the service environments of the severely handicapped. The complexity and number of disciplines and agencies is almost overpowering. To assist in the development of educational programs for the severely handicapped, the research technology must reflect this concern for a comprehensive and coordinated approach.

Research and development (R & D) procedures, with their emphasis on a highly systematized approach to program development, represent a promising technology for the researcher interested in the development of educational programs for the severely handicapped. In the following section, three R & D models will be reviewed and compared.

R & D: A Research Technology for Program Development

With regard to the development of educational programs for the severely handicapped, there can be little doubt that many of our present research practices are not enhancing progress, and the identification and use of research practices that will facilitate pro-

What Directions Should Research Take? 339

gram development is a high priority. With few exceptions, descriptions of R & D have yet to appear in standard research textbooks, and training in R & D is still not a stressed component in many doctoral programs. Borg and Gall (1971) note that R & D "appears to be the most promising strategy we now have to improving education" (p. 413). Educational research and development refers to a systematic process for developing and validating an educational product. A product, used in this sense, is not limited to materials, manuals, or films, but also includes replicable methods of instruction or administrative procedures. In comparing the respective contributions of other types of research to R & D, Borg and Gall stated the following.

> Although they have many important contributions to make to education, basic and applied research are generally poor methodologies for developing new products that can be used in the schools. In applied research particularly, the researcher often finds himself comparing poorly designed, unproven, or incomplete products to determine which is less adequate. This methodology generally produces negative or inconclusive results, and at best brings about improvement in education at a slow rate. ... We should emphasize ... that educational R & D increases the potential impact of basic and applied research findings upon school practice by translating them into usable educational products (p. 414).

The following three variations of R & D models are presented to exemplify the nature of R & D.

The Borg Model

This model (Borg, Kelly, Langer, and Gall, 1970) is summarized in Table 15.1, and refers to the R & D procedures which Borg used to develop methods of inservice instruction. The data from the evaluation of these products (minicourses) showed evidence of significant long-term changes in the behavior of teachers. In one study, a minicourse for training teachers in tutoring skills, was shown to effect changes in teacher behavior, and also effect signifi-

TABLE 15.1

THE MAJOR STEPS IN THE
BORG MODEL DEVELOPMENT CYCLE

1. Research and Data Gathering	Includes review of literature, classroom observations, and preparation of reports on the state of the art.
2. Planning	Includes definition of skills, statement of objectives, determination of course sequence, and small scale feasibility testing.
3. Developing Preliminary Form of Product	Includes preparation of instructional and model lessons, handbooks, and evaluation devices.
4. Preliminary Field Test	Conducted by R & D personnel in one, two, or three schools, using between six and twelve teachers. Includes collection and analysis of interview, observational, and questionnaire data.
5. Main Product Revision	Revision of product as suggested by preliminary field test results.
6. Main Field Test	Conducted by R & D personnel in between five and fifteen schools using between thirty and one hundred teachers. Includes collection of quantitative data on teachers' pre- and postcourse performances, usually in the form of videotapes. Results are compared with course objectives.
7. Operational Product Revision	Revision of product as suggested by the main field test results.
8. Operational Field Test	Conducted by regular school personnel in between ten and thirty schools, using between forty and two hundred teachers. Includes collection and analysis of interview, observation, and questionnaire data.
9. Final Product Revision	Revision of product as suggested by operational field test results.
10. Dissemination and Distribution	Reports at professional meetings, in journals, etc. Includes work with publisher who assumes commercial distribution, and monitoring of distribution to provide quality control.

cant improvements in the achievement of their mentally retarded pupils (Stowitschek and Hofmeister, 1974).

The Hood Model

The second model is that described by Hood (1973). This model is similar to Borg's, but there are differences. Borg placed a heavy emphasis on existing research data and literature reviewing as the first stage. Hood does not, and stresses problem analysis instead. The seven stages of the Hood Model are as follows:

Stage 1. Concept. The major purpose of this stage is to conduct analysis of the need, and determine whether or not a potentially feasible solution exists. This purpose is achieved by preparing and reviewing a rough plan containing the following components:

(a) statement and justification of the need,
(b) discussion of alternative approaches, together with an evaluation of each,
(c) statement of the recommended concepts of functions, together with proposed configuration, and
(d) an initial plan roughly outlining the required activities, including their sequence, dates for accomplishment, and estimated cost.

Stage 2. Mock-Up (Preliminary Product Development). In the mock-up stage, the researchers attempt to determine, through the use of a tangible representation of the selected concepts, whether the proposed model of the product appears to meet needs. For example, if the final product was a parent training program, rough drafts of sample materials and outlines of treatment schedules and the curriculum content might be prepared. This would provide something tangible for project staff or outside consultants to evaluate.

Stage 3. Prototype (Preliminary Field Test). At this stage, the product would be field tested and evaluated with a small representative group of users. Representative components of the final product would be developed and used in this field test.

Stage 4. Performance Test. The purpose of this stage is to determine if the complete product meets specifications and to determine how it may be improved. At this stage, evaluation is more formal, including a complete plan for testing and interpretation, plus a complete set of instruments and test instructions. Ideally, the sample should be a stratified, representative sample. The criteria and standards should be pre-stratified.

Stage 5. Operational Readiness. This stage is designed to determine the product's readiness, and to make needed improvements prior to release. Operational readiness tests consist of both formal and informal elements. The formal instruments should focus on critical aspects of readiness. Informal procedures, including *ex post facto* analysis of failures, should be planned for. The criteria are primarily judgmental, and usually involve a variety of dimensions. A single composite index of acceptability may be entertained, but generally a set of minimal requirements should be pre-specified.

Stage 6. Dissemination Plan. At this stage, the product dissemination process is evaluated. The extent to which the product is reaching the target population should be a prime concern at this stage.

Stage 7. Quality Control. The purpose of this stage is the monitoring of the product to collect data for revising the product and improving the design of new and related products. The evaluation procedures used at this stage are usually longitudinal, and many will be of an informal or *ex post facto* variety.

Four-D Model

This model (Thiagarajan, Semmel, and Semmel, 1974) has characteristics in common with the first two models. A dominant emphasis in this model is that of analysis. The term "Four-D" is derived from the four major stages: define, design, develop, and disseminate. The following is a description of the four stages abstracted from the excellent sourcebook, *Instructional Develop-*

ment for Training Teachers of Exceptional Children (Thiagarajan, Semmel, and Semmel, 1974). The examples used in the description apply to the development of special education teacher training materials. The underlying constructs, however, have considerable generalizability to other special education problems.

Stage 1. Define. In this first stage, the problems are analyzed and instructional objectives identified as a result of the analysis procedures. A variety of analysis procedures are recommended at this stage, including learner analysis, task analysis, content analysis, and front-end analysis. The authors describe front-end analysis as:

> The study of the basic problem facing the teacher trainer: to raise the performance levels of special education teachers. During this analysis, the possibilities of more elegant and efficient alternatives to instruction are considered. Failing them, a search for relevant instructional materials already in circulation is conducted. If neither pertinent instructional alternatives nor materials are available, then the development of instructional material is called for (p. 6).

This front-end analysis has much in common with Hood's Concept Stage, in that both are concerned with analyzing different alternatives to determine if a potentially feasible solution exists. The following is an example of front-end analysis in special education program development.

> I have calculated the impossibility of widespread application of three models currently in use in limited special education programs. These strategies are special classes for the emotionally disturbed, resource teachers for gifted children, and resource teachers for children with special learning disabilities. ... If these models are projected on the state or federal level, along with the support services needed to train the necessary professionals, they are beyond any reasonable attainment.
> For example, to provide services to gifted students in the resource teacher model, 50 universities must each turn out 15 master teachers (M.S. +) per year for 10 years. Not one univer-

sity is producing anything like that now (Gallagher, 1976, p. 173).

Stage 2. Design. The purpose of this stage is the design of prototype instructional materials, including the selection of media and formats for the material, and the production of an initial version.

Stage 3. Develop. In Stage 3, the prototype instructional materials are modified through expert appraisal and developmental testing with actual trainers. In this stage, the cycle of testing, revising, and retesting is repeated until the material works consistently and effectively.

Stage 4. Disseminate. Before disseminating the materials, a summative evaluation in which the material is used under replicable conditions is undertaken. Following the summative evaluation, the terminal stage of final packaging and diffusion occurs.

From the overview of the three R & D models, it should be evident that the R & D process includes many of the research procedures in use in basic and applied research. The R & D process stresses the comprehensive and systematic use of existing knowledge and research skills to provide the field with a validated product ready for use.

One early reference to an R & D procedure in developing an educational program for the severely handicapped is reported by Bricker (1970). In this report, Bricker described the steps involved in developing a program for teaching language. Three stages were specified as follows.

> *Stage 1.* The first stage would involve small numbers of subjects over long periods of time. ... When such efforts are successful, we may assign the term "valid" to the program. Any program that has demonstrated empirical success in attaining the terminal goal can be considered to be valid, regardless of the materials or methods used.
>
> *Stage 2.* This stage involves the specification of the sequence of training in an explicit program that defines approximations as well as the performance level necessary to move from one step to

What Directions Should Research Take? 345

> the next in the program. This program was then given to a relatively untrained person who used it according to instructions with a large sample of children. The sample was drawn at random from a specified population of children (e.g., ambulatory, language deficient, severely retarded). The empirical results of the application indexed the replicability of the program.
> *Stage 3.* The third stage in program development concerns program efficiency. ... The problem of efficiency is dependent on whether we, or others, can find an easier or quicker path to the same destination (p. 18).

We can see in Bricker's stages a concern for many of the same things later R & D model builders stressed. For example, in Stage 1, Bricker was very concerned with formative evaluation. In Stage 3, we see an emphasis on searching for more effective alternatives —an aspect Hood (1973) stressed in his concept stage.

Any consideration of research priorities must give serious consideration to R & D if research efforts are to have an impact on the whole field. For too long, research activities have been directed by such forces as the restrictions of existing doctoral programs, and the personal interests and skills of researchers. The time has come to look objectively at the needs, and design the resources and activities to fit such needs. A change in the training of prospective researchers is clearly needed. Edwin Martin (1976), in commenting on the skills of present college staff to train personnel to work with the severely and profoundly handicapped, stated, "as professionals, we must pay the price, even if it is somewhat embarrassing, of learning new skills and attitudes before we teach others" (p. 125).

Research and Program Replication

Reference has already been made to the issue of disseminating research findings. Unfortunately, this issue is often presented as though there are two separate processes: research and dissemination of research findings. Dissemination problems are just as much the responsibility of the researcher as other educational problems.

Dissemination in many research projects is often little more than a commitment to publish the findings, or present at a conference, an act essentially out of the research process (particularly since so few presenters have had the courage to assess the impact of their convention presentations).

It is possible to design research to increase the dissemination potential. A review of Borg's R & D Model will reveal two major field test stages—a "main field test" conducted by R & D personnel, and an "operational field test" conducted by school district personnel. Greater involvement of prospective consumers should add more validity to the evaluations of programs under development.

The use of replications, particularly replications under normal budget restraints, represents an effective way to assess the exportability of a research product. Another procedure is the use of instructional "packaging." A research finding in the form of research reports is one important step removed from the practitioner. The finding, translated into validated instructor manuals and pupil materials, the tools of the practitioner, will greatly increase the potential for use. When we assemble all the components in a form that is relatively self-contained and ready to use with a minimum of outside help or training, we have an instructional package.

The concept of an instructional package is an important one for the researcher, because it facilitates both dissemination and further research—it is observable and replicable; it can be validated as a unit; it can be analyzed; it can be transported to other sites and other researchers; and, perhaps of most importance, it increases the chance that program developers will be able to build on past efforts, rather than repeat past mistakes.

The instructional package represents an important concept given the present problems facing those implementing educational programs for the severely handicapped. For most fields in education, the basic training is acquired through preservice programs. The field of the severely handicapped is faced with the fact that few training institutions supply specialized in-depth preservice training in the education of the severely handicapped. And, should such preservice facilities develop soon, it would still be many years before the preservice training would be felt in the field. Immediate personnel needs will have to be met by inservice training. This inservice training will have to be highly exportable to reach the thousands of personnel in need of the technical assistance. The instructional package is an ideal vehicle for exporting such technical assistance.

Evaluation Efforts

One reason for the community concern that has resulted in legislation to increase services for the severely handicapped has been the nature of existing services. The programs in many residential institutions were found to be debilitating. With regard to institutional programs, the concern was not so often the lack of a program, but the quality of the existing program. Techniques to ensure the ongoing monitoring of the quality of programs is a pressing need. We need low cost systems which will provide data on the services being received by the severely handicapped.

In a reference to general educational practices, Worthen (1972) made the following observation:

> Despite ... trends toward accountability, it is safe to say that only a tiny fraction of the educational programs operating at any level have been evaluated in any but the most cursory fashion, if indeed at all. Verbal statements about evaluation and accountability are abundant, but genuine evaluation of educational programs is pathetically rare (p. 1).

Worthen's observations could easily be applied to present-day educational programs for the severely handicapped. In many areas, we are behind our counterparts in related disciplines. Glass (1976) observed:

> Evaluation in law enforcement and criminal corrections has the best record of findings with clear payoff. Studies of police work

and criminal rehabilitation have uncovered potentially huge savings. One feature after another has been altered experimentally, and crime and recidivism rates have remained unchanged. These "no difference" findings, the bane of the experimentalist scientist, are grist for the evaluator's mill. If cutting reformatory sentences in half does not produce increased recidivism, then shorter sentences are 100% more cost-effective, *ceteris parilus*. Doing as as well as in the past, but doing it more cheaply is a gain in value as surely as is doing better at a greater cost. A growing body of evaluation research in legal studies exemplifies meticulous scholarship and imaginative data analysis (p. 11).

In special education, we are experiencing an increase in the frequency of references to evaluation. Federal training and service grants often go so far as to recommend the general evaluation model to be used. While this may seem a strong move to stress evaluation, it often means more frustration to the practitioner. Telling a practitioner to use a general evaluation model is about as helpful as telling a pilot to use a plane when he flies. When the jargon of most evaluation models is deciphered, it usually reveals the same basic process: (1) the identification of appropriate objectives; (2) the implementation and monitoring of procedures to reach the objectives; and (3) the collection of data to determine if the objectives have been achieved. While this process is not unimportant, the practitioner still needs instruments and procedures field tested and validated for his population and environment. This we lack.

The publication *Standards for Residential Facilities for the Mentally Retarded* (Joint Commission on Accreditation of Hospitals, 1971), was an early effort to facilitate the evaluation of residential programs. This publication was followed by *Standards for Community Agencies* (Joint Commission on Accreditation of Hospitals, 1973). These publications are important, in that they represent serious efforts to develop evaluation tools for programs in specific environments.

Programmatic evaluations are still in a developing stage. There is

What Directions Should Research Take? 349

at present an all encompassing interest in evaluating programs in terms of resources and facilities. This taxonomic approach has been criticized by Muma and Baumeister (1975), who concluded:

> We anticipate that alternative process-oriented approaches will eventually replace taxonomic approaches, for the latter cannot bring about the imperative change in the present primitive system of delivering services to the retarded population (p. 344).

In 1971, the Phi Delta Kappa (PDK) Commission on Education listed a number of deficiencies responsible for holding back the development of evaluation in education. The deficiencies were:
(1) lack of adequate evaluation theory;
(2) lack of specification of the types of evaluation information which are most needed;
(3) lack of appropriate instruments and designs;
(4) lack of good systems for organizing, processing, and reporting evaluative information; and
(5) lack of sufficient number of well-trained evaluation personnel (Stufflebeam *et al.*, 1971).

Advances have been made with regard to the first concern, the lack of adequate evaluation theory. The early theoretical efforts (Provus, 1969; Scriven, 1967; Stake, 1967; and Stufflebeam, 1968) have been developed and enhanced, and we now have a considerable theoretical base for the development of specific evaluation techniques. The second concern, specification of the types of evaluative information most needed, is a major problem retarding the development of evaluation techniques for programs for the severely handicapped. The constructs we use as benchmarks for evaluating the mildly handicapped are not always universally accepted for the severely handicapped. For example, Bank-Mikkelsen (DDO Newsletter, 1977) made the following comments regarding two of these constructs, "integration" and "normalization."

> Normalization has been equated with integration. It is a mistake ... to adapt any particular strategy for all persons. Each service plan should be evaluated in terms of how it will further the goal of normalization (realization of the individual's full potential to live in society) for that individual. In some cases, segregated, intensive programs might be best suited to meet the goal (p. 3).

Constructs such as "normalization" have to be translated into more specific constructs before evaluation researchers can develop the instruments and procedures necessary to evaluate programs for the severely handicapped. Unless we have clarification of our value system regarding goals for the severely handicapped, our evaluation efforts will continue to focus on easily collected and often trivial descriptive data.

While researchers are often quick to point out that data gathered in connection with new programs may be suspect because of atypical funding bases or novelty effects, the most reliable types of data (those gathered from established programs) often go uncollected for want of practical, valid, program evaluation procedures.

The need for more specific and effective evaluation tools is with us already, and this need will become more acute. Schipper and Kenowitz (1976) have predicted an increasing need for sophisticated program evaluations of private, as well as public, school programs by state agencies.

Research and Program Costs

The issue of program costs has been stressed, and it is important, but the reader should not automatically conclude that there is a direct relationship between budget size and the quality of educational services presently provided the severely retarded. In a cross-institutional, cross-cultural study of resident-care practices for retarded persons, McCormick, Balla, and Zigler (1975) found very little relationship between program costs and the quality of care. The implication is clear—we are not yet effectively using the resources presently allocated to the severely handicapped. Parent organizations and other advocate groups are presently pressing federal and state governments for more fiscal resources for the provision of services to the severely handicapped. This effort and the credibility of the field of special education have much to lose if researchers do not concern themselves with data on the cost-effectiveness of programs and program components.

Collecting data on cost-effectiveness does not always appeal to researchers. Making a breakthrough in a theoretical area may carry considerably more potential for recognition among other researchers. Cost-effectiveness and related programmatic issues are important if theoretical constructs are to reach implementation. As Muma and Baumeister (1975) have observed:

> The politics and realities of establishing and funding programs quickly converts theoretical issues into operational problems that have, again and again, proven difficult to manage. Because of these problems, typical programs for the retarded have often been severely limited in range of services and quality of opportunities for individual growth (p. 337).

Interdisciplinary Effort

Educational research should not be restricted to the activities of educators. Other disciplines have important educational roles in providing services to the severely retarded. The local public health nurse working with the parent of an infant Downs Syndrome child has important educational responsibilities in training the parent in appropriate child care practices.

In training of the severely retarded, the boundaries between disciplines often fade. For example, for several years, the Utah State University Affiliated Exceptional Child Center has been developing materials to teach self-care skills to the severely handicapped (Hofmeister, Gallery, Hofmeister, Atkinson, and Henderson, 1977). To date, the same materials have been used by classroom teachers, parents, occupational therapists, physical therapists, mobility and orientation specialists, nurses, and psychologists. Interdisciplinary involvement is inescapable in treating the severely handicapped. Such involvement has to be reflected in educational research efforts. In relation to this issue, Edwin Martin (1976) commented:

> More than many areas of human service delivery, education of the profoundly and severely handicapped calls for interdisciplinary efforts. I believe that while examples of successful efforts do exist, in general we are still caught up in parochialism. Each discipline values itself more highly than it honors others. Each knows a little more about the real truths (p. 125).

In considering interdisciplinary effort, the educational researcher needs to be aware that other professionals have much to contribute to curriculum content and methodology, and that an extensive amount of education is done outside the classroom by professionals and paraprofessionals from other disciplines. The design and validation of programs must reflect this interdisciplinary involvement.

An excellent example of interdisciplinary effort in the development of a treatment approach tailored to the needs of the severely handicapped in the public schools is the "Integrated Therapy Model" used in the Madison Public Schools. A basic assumption underlying the model was reported as follows.

> The Integrated Therapy Model assumes that assessment of motor abilities can be conducted most efficaciously in natural environments (e.g., classrooms, homes, buses). If the therapist observes the students' motoric functioning in natural environments, he/she will be able to assess motor performance across many different natural settings, materials, cues and persons. This allows the therapist to secure a more valid representation of general motoric functioning. The integrated model also assumes that if the teacher, the therapist and parents *jointly* devise the program it can be incorporated into daily living and educational activities and will have direct relevance to immediate, as well as long term develop-

mental needs. Thus, most "significant others" will be included in the therapy program. Educational activities can be arranged so that performance of target skills can be encouraged (or required) across a variety of natural settings, materials, cues, and persons (Sternat, Nietupski, Lyon, Messina, and Brown, 1976, p. 6).

Service Delivery Models

One of the major problems in developing educational programs for the severely handicapped is that traditional educational service delivery models built around the classroom are often inappropriate in other situations. Of what use is the classroom for training a parent in a rural area or a working mother in an inner-city area? In treating the severely handicapped, we are faced with the problems of:

(1) a new curriculum,
(2) new teaching methods, and
(3) ways of delivering the curriculum and methods.

The added problems of travel, staffing, and time compound the usual problems of what to teach and how to teach.

The researcher will have to be concerned with a comprehensive data base in developing a service delivery model. A finding of statistical significance between achievement scores may prove meaningless when data related to travel costs, personnel training costs, treatment time, communication costs, and supervision costs are taken into consideration.

One of the best examples of comprehensive programmatic effort in the development of service delivery models is the work of the Teaching Research Staff in Monmouth, Oregon. This group has been highly successful in replicating their service model. The reasons for the extensive impact of their research and development efforts include:

(1) a rigorous data orientated approach to all aspects of management and administration (Fredericks and Baldwin, 1976);
(2) a concern for replication by the extensive documenta-

tion of all instructional procedures (Fredericks, Riggs, Furey, Grove, Moore, McDonnell, Jordan, Hanson, Baldwin, and Wadlow, 1976);

(3) an emphasis on comprehensive services, including the training of parents and volunteers (Baldwin, Fredericks, and Brodsky, 1973);
(4) the serious study of costs and the overall cost-effectiveness of the program being developed (Baldwin, 1977); and
(5) systematic and researched procedures by which interested agencies can replicate the service delivery model.

Areas for Program Development

The provision of programs for the severely handicapped requires a mobilization of resources on a scale much more extensive than we ever conducted for the mildly handicapped. There is a strong move to locate programs for the severely handicapped in the regular public school systems. This integration is commendable in that it indicates an acceptance of responsibility by public education. Such integration is far from commendable, however, if it implies that the traditional parameters of regular education are to be applied to the severely handicapped. Traditional parameters include such practices as:

(1) five hours of education, five days a week;
(2) start of formal school between five and six years of age;
(3) three parent conferences a year; and
(4) nine months of schooling a year.

These practices are not necessarily consistent with the needs of the severely handicapped child, who will require well programmed instructional experiences most of his waking hours. Such instructional experiences should start during the infant years.

The traditional administrative and classroom mangement practices of regular education are totally inappropriate for educating the severely handicapped. Educators of the severely handicapped

What Directions Should Research Take?

are faced with management and manpower problems unparalleled in educational history. If we apply usual manpower resources and management procedures to the severely handicapped, we may end up with little more than a babysitting service.

It must be recognized that early research relating to special classes for the severely and moderately retarded did not support such classes over community living without special class attendance (Cain and Levine, 1963; Hottel, 1958). Cain and Levine's (1963) observational data indicated that 56% of classroom time was non-instructional and significant portions of the remaining 44% was classified as "low adequacy" instruction. The implication from the data is clear—many of the special classes were, in reality, little more than babysitting services.

Programs that provide intensive instructional experiences have to be developed. This will usually mean large amounts of one-to-one instruction. Providing one-to-one instruction in the classroom will usually involve the training of aides or volunteers. The educational agency then has to train the important adults in the severely handicapped child's life. A group of ten severely handicapped pupils will generate training responsibilities for up to 20 parents or parent surrogates, and from 2 to 10 classroom aides or volunteers. Paraprofessional training is an area for educational program development.

Other areas for educational program development include:
(1) parent training in infant stimulation and language development;
(2) the training of group home staff to provide educational, as well as custodial services;
(3) the training of staff to provide homebound educational services for the severely handicapped;
(4) the training of school staff to effectively coordinate the school and home programs;
(5) the training of professionals to counsel the families of the severely handicapped;

(6) the training of school administrators in the non-traditional requirements involved in the provision of services to the severely handicapped; and

(7) the training of professionals in the effective coordination of the multidisciplinary treatment needs of the severely handicapped.

A total intervention program consists of two major components —treatment and prevention. Unlike the etiology of mild handicaps, which is often lost in a morass of hereditary and environmental factors, the causes of severe handicapping conditions are often more obvious. A significant number of these are preventable, and therefore, substance for educational programs. Research related to the development and validation of programs aimed at (1) the prevention of birth defects, and (2) genetic counseling, are two examples which have preventive implications for severe handicapping conditions.

Recommendations

The following efforts would facilitate program development efforts via research:

(1) an emphasis in RFP's on research techniques compatible with program development, instead of program comparison;

(2) the support of graduate training which equips future researchers with program development research skills, such as R & D techniques;

(3) the support of development and evaluation procedures and instruments specifically validated for use in the evaluation of programs for the severely handicapped; and

(4) the support of graduate training programs designed to equip future field leaders with evaluation skills capable of the valid monitoring of ongoing treatment programs for the severely handicapped.

This chapter has identified two developing technologies—educational research and development (R & D) and program evaluation. Hopefully, these two technologies, one concerned with the development of programs and the other with the quality control of existing programs, will add significantly to the quality of life of severely handicapped persons.

References

Assessment of selected resources for severely handicapped children and youth, Vol. 1. Cambridge, Mass.: Abt Associates, 1974.

Baldwin, V. L. *Group homes for developmentally disabled children.* Monmouth, Ore.: Instructional Development Corporation, 1977.

Baldwin, V. L., Fredericks, H. D., and Brodsky, G. *Isn't it time he outgrew this? or A training program for parents of retarded children.* Springville, Ill.: Charles C. Thomas Publishers, 1973.

Borg, W. R., and Gall, M. D. *Educational research: An introduction (2nd ed.).* New York: McKay, 1971.

Borg, W. R., Kelly, M. L., Langer, P., and Gall, M. *The minicourse: A microteaching approach to teacher education.* Beverly Hills: Macmillan Educational Services, Inc., 1970.

Bricker, W. A. Identifying and modifying behavioral deficits. *American Journal of Mental Deficiency*, 1970, 75(1), pp. 16-21.

Cain, L. F., and Levine, S. Effects of community and institutional school programs on trainable mentally retarded children. *CEC Research Monograph*, 1963, Series B, No. B-1.

Cronbach, L. J. Course improvement through evaluation. *Teachers College Record*, 1963, 64, pp. 672-683.

DDO Newsletter, H.E.W. Office of Human Development. Normalization idea becoming complex, Jan.-Feb. 1977, p. 3.

Fredericks, H. D., and Baldwin, V. *A data based classroom for the moderately and severely handicapped.* Monmouth, Ore.: Instructional Development Corporation, 1976.

Fredericks, H. D., Riggs, C., Furey, T., Grove, D., Moore, W., McDonnell, J., Jordan, E., Hanson, W., Baldwin, V., and Wadlow, M. *The teaching research curriculum for moderately and severely handicapped.* Springfield, Ill.: Charles C. Thomas Publishers, 1976.

Gallagher, J. J. Planning for early childhood programs for exceptional children. *The Journal of Special Education,* 1976, *10*(2), pp. 171-177.

Glass, G. V. Introduction. In G. V. Glass (Ed.), *Evaluation studies: Review annual (Vol. 1).* Beverly Hills, Calif.: SAGE Publications, 1976.

Gold, M. C. Research on the vocational habilitation of the retarded: The present, the future. In N. R. Ellis (Ed.), *International review of research in mental retardation (Vol. 6).* New York: Academic Press, 1973.

Guskin, S.L., and Spicker, H.H. Educational research in mental retardation. In N.R. Ellis (Ed.), *International review of research in mental retardation (Vol. 3).* New York: Academic Press, 1968.

Hofmeister, A. M., Gallery, M., Hofmeister, J., Atkinson, C., and Henderson, H. *Training for independence, fundamental self-care, and functional training for daily living.* Niles, Ill.: Developmental Learning Materials, 1977.

Hood, P. D. Evaluation stages for major laboratory products. In J. K. Hemphill (Ed.), *Educational development: A new discipline for self-renewal.* Eugene, Ore.: University of Oregon Printing Dept., 1973.

Hottel, J. V. *An evaluation of Tennessee's day class program for severely mentally retarded children.* Nashville: George Peabody College for Teachers, 1958.

Lamke, T. Introduction. *Review of Educational Research,* June 1955, p. 192.

Martin, E. W. On Justice Douglas and education for the severely/ profoundly handicapped. *The Journal of Special Education*, 1976, *10*(2), pp. 123-126.

McCormick, M., Balla, D., and Zigler, E. Resident-care practices in institutions for retarded persons: A cross-institutional, cross-cultural study. *American Journal of Mental Deficiency*, 1975, *80*(1), pp. 1-17.

Muma, J. R., and Baumeister, A. Programmatic evaluation in mental retardation: Alternatives to taxonomic approaches. *The Journal of Special Education*, Winter 1975, *9*(4), pp. 337-344.

Provus, M. M. Evaluation of ongoing programs in the public school system. In R. W. Tyler (Ed.), *Educational evaluation: New roles, new means. The 68th Yearbook of the National Society for the Study of Education, Part II*. Chicago: National Society for the Study of Education, 1969.

Schipper, W. V., and Kenowitz, L. A. Special education futures—a forecast of events affecting the education of exceptional children: 1976-2000. *The Journal of Special Education*, 1976, *10*(4), pp. 401-413.

Scriven, M. The methodology of evaluation. In R. E. Stake (Ed.), *Curriculum evaluation. American Educational Research Association Monograph Series on Evaluation, No. 1*. Chicago: Rand McNally, 1967.

Stake, R. E. The countenance of educational evaluation. *Teachers College Record*, 1967, *68*, pp. 523-540.

Standards for community agencies. Chicago, Ill.: Joint Commission on Accreditation of Hospitals, 1973.

Standards for residential facilities for the mentally retarded. Chicago, Ill.: Joint Commission on Accreditation of Hospitals, 1971.

Sternat, J., Nietupski, J., Lyon, S., Messina, R., and Brown, L. Integrated vs. isolated therapy models. Abstract of part I—Occupational and physical therapy services for severely handicapped students: Toward a naturalized public school service delivery model. In Brown, L., Scheuerman, N., and Crowner, T., *Madison's alternative for zero exclusion: Toward an integrated therapy model for teaching motor, tracking, and scanning skills to severely handicapped students, Vol. VI, Part 3.* Madison, Wisc.: Madison Public Schools, Dept. of Specialized Educational Services, 1976.

Stowitschek, J., and Hofmeister, A. M. Effects of minicourse instruction on teacher performance and pupil achievement. *Exceptional Children*, 1974, *40*(7), 490-495.

Stufflebeam, D. L. *Evaluation as enlightenment for decision-making.* Columbus, Ohio: Evaluation Center, Ohio State University, 1968.

Stufflebeam, D. L., Foley, W. J., Gephart, W. J., Guba, E. G., Hammond, R. L., Merriman, H. O., and Provus, M. M. *Educational evaluation and decision-making in education.* Itasca, Ill.: Peacock, 1971.

Thiagarajan, S., Semmel, D. S., and Semmel, M. I. *Instructional development for training teachers of exceptional children: A sourcebook.* Reston, Virginia: The Council for Exceptional Children, 1974.

Tjossem, T. D. Early intervention: Issues and approaches. In T. D. Tjossem (Ed.), *Intervention strategies for high risk infants and young children.* Baltimore, Md.: University Park Press, 1976.

Wattenburg, W. W. Evidence and the problems of teacher education. *Teachers College Record*, 1963, *64*, pp. 374-380.

Worthen, B. R. *Impediments to the practice of educational evaluation. Research paper no. 60.* University of Colorado: Laboratory of Educational Research, 1972.

Author's Note

Appreciation for helpful comments on an earlier draft is extended to Dr. Hugh S. McKenzie, Director, Center for Special Education, University of Vermont; and Dr. Gary Adamson, Department of Special Education, University of New Mexico at Albuquerque.